Credible

Credible

The Power of Expert Leaders

AMANDA GOODALL

PUBLICAFFAIRS

NEW YORK

PublicAffairs
Hachette Book Group
1290 Avenue of the Americas, New York, NY 10104
www.publicaffairsbooks.com
@Public_Affairs

Printed in the United States of America

Originally published in hardcover in Great Britain in 2023 by Basic Books UK,
an imprint of John Murray Press, an Hachette UK company

First US Edition: July 2023

Published by PublicAffairs, an imprint of Perseus Books, LLC, a subsidiary of
Hachette Book Group, Inc. The PublicAffairs name and logo is a trademark of the
Hachette Book Group.

The Hachette Speakers Bureau provides a wide range of authors for speaking events. To find
out more, go to www.hachettespeakersbureau.com or email HachetteSpeakers@hbgusa.com.

PublicAffairs books may be purchased in bulk for business, educational, or promotional use.
For more information, please contact your local bookseller or the Hachette Book Group
Special Markets Department at special.markets@hbgusa.com.

The publisher is not responsible for websites (or their content)
that are not owned by the publisher.

Typeset in Janson Text by Hewer Text UK Ltd, Edinburgh

Library of Congress Control Number: 2022951661

ISBNs: 9781541702509 (hardcover), 9781541702523 (ebook)

LSC-C

Printing 1, 2023

This book is dedicated to Mother Nature
and all the experts I hope will save her.

Contents

* Chapters 6 and 7 include contributions from Natasha Maw, Dr Jaason Geerts, and Patty Fahy, MD.

Preface

School ended at sixteen. They were happy for me to go, and I was happy to leave. Being 'military brats', it was the last of many schools that my brother and I attended, on both sides of the Atlantic. For the next seven years I trotted around catwalks in several countries wearing remarkable clothes, with big hair and strong make-up. I was an *un*exceptional fashion model, which didn't matter too much because the fashion industry probably wasn't for me (aside from the clothes, that is, and maybe the hair and make-up). But while I was there I saw first hand the power of exceptional leaders and their influence on organizations. Designers like Betty Jackson, Willi Smith, who sadly died prematurely in 1987, and the inimitable Vivienne Westwood, who was producing iconic clothing into her eighties.

At age twenty-two, a cheap flight brought me to Delhi via Kabul, then occupied by the Soviet Union. From the Indian capital I took a scenic thirty-hour train journey a long way south and east to Srikakulam, in the state of Andhra Pradesh. A Jeep ride completed my trip to a remote village called Kotturu, and into an expired medical centre's operating theatre, which was to be my home for the year. It was a rural development project led by an exceptional man. I was there to learn. H. R. Prakash was tall and imposing yet gentle. He could speak to anyone and did so in at least four languages, English, Hindi, Telugu, and Tamil. Prakash knew a great deal about aid and development, and how to manage delicate relationships with politicians and landowners; he was clever, had profound integrity, and heaps of emotional intelligence, long before the world even knew what it was.

After another decade, which included fundraising for various organizations campaigning for a better world, I returned to education at the London School of Economics (LSE). To the surprise of those who knew me at school, I did quite well. I also learned that changing the world needs more than youthful optimism and theories built on emotion. It requires examination through detailed data, to test hypotheses and work backwards from there.

Following my undergraduate education I worked closely with three leaders, two in the UK and one in the US. It was the observations I made about these presidents of universities that motivated my PhD research at Warwick Business School, and took me into a career in academe.

So what have I observed about leadership in my life, my work, and eventually my research?

It is that those who really motivate others, set the highest standards and ultimately make their organizations great, are people who have deeply learned their craft. They are credible core business experts. They are not rootless generalists who flit from organization to organization.

This book is the summation of fifteen years of empirical research into leaders. It uses quantitative data to examine all kinds of organizations and settings in an attempt to reach a generalizable form of 'truth'.

I start by asking what we can learn about leadership from the world's most successful organizations; who is leading our best hospitals, the highly innovative tech firms, the top basketball teams, and the most enduring banks? This matters, because the very best institutions – in any setting – have the status and wealth to choose whomever they like as their CEO and line management. If they choose experts, this tells us something important. Something really important. And, as we will see, it is predominantly expert leaders, those who are credible, those who have credibility, who are the managers and leaders of the *best* companies.

I have examined leadership across all industries and found that core business expert leaders enhance organizational performance, produce happy and productive workplaces, and create a series of other spill-over effects like improved innovation, attracting top talent, and positive 'signalling' to stakeholders. Crucially, in a world threatened by climate catastrophe as a result of short-termist profit maximizing, experts opt for a more sustainable long view.

Expertise isn't a consumer good you can buy off the shelf; nor is it something that is acquired once you hold an MBA certificate in your hand – it takes time and tenacity. People often point to robots, artificial intelligence, and other emerging technologies as the future of business. Yet, organizations also have much to gain by making one simple but profound adjustment: cultivating talented leaders with deep industry expertise and then training them with the requisite management and leadership skills. Such a trans-formation promises to make our workplaces happier and more productive, our politicians and corporate brands more respected, and our private companies and public sector more innovative, dynamic, and robust.

This book is for you if you run a company. It will convince you that the most successful firms put experts into their leadership and management, and it will help you find, keep, and develop the best experts inside your own organization.

This book is for you if you're a rising star. It will motivate you to become an expert yourself by working diligently in your selected field and adding leadership and management skills to your expert portfolio gradually, and never at the expense of core business knowledge.

And if you are already an expert thinking about becoming a leader, *this book is for you*. When you leave the expert bench and go into the boardroom, you will have to practise respect for and be open-minded towards those with qualities other than technical expertise, and you will have to learn new ways of being. You will find your former expert colleagues probably think less of you, and ask you, tiresomely, why you wanted to become a leader. But if you can be an expert *and* a leader, then you will contribute significantly more.

The pendulum has swung way too far down the generalist managerial path. Generalists have created workplaces riven with bureaucracy, metrics, management jargon, and other impediments to productivity, longevity, and innovation. And we have acquiesced to non-experts on climate change – leaving us in sight of another extinction. I believe that our world urgently needs credible expert leaders.

I

When Non-experts Fly the Plane

'What banking qualifications have you got, Mr Hornby?'

A forty-two-year-old man, in an expensive dark blue suit and a nondescript tie and pink shirt, takes a shallow breath. The questioner, Nick Ainger, a Member of the British Parliament, who began his career as a dock worker in south Wales, and has seen a side of life inconceivable to the man in the expensive suit, leans forward across the table. His eyes slightly harden. Mr Ainger waits for an answer, although he knows the answer. Mr Andrew Hornby waits to answer, although everyone in the room knows the answer.

'I do not have any formal banking qualifications.'

Mr Ainger's thoughts on receiving this reply are unknown and may have been unprintable. What he did know, however, was that the man sitting opposite him, whose previous experience had been running a grocery business, had just ruined one of the world's most important banks. As this book will go on to argue, when non-experts are put in charge of organizations, disaster often strikes.

Andrew Hornby was CEO of HBOS, one of the largest financial institutions in Europe, when interrogated by Ainger on 20 February 2009, while the world was suffering the aftermath of the worst financial crisis since the Great Depression (1929–39). The room was a grand one, and full of adrenalin and journalists. A fourteen-member cross-party Treasury Select Committee were questioning four astoundingly well-paid British bankers.[1] In addition to their interrogation of Hornby, the inquisitorial committee were interviewing Sir Fred Goodwin and Sir Tom McKillop, former chief executive and chairman of Royal Bank of Scotland (RBS) respectively, and Lord Stevenson of Coddenham, its former chairman.

Andy Hornby, without mentioning that his primary degree was in English literature, went on: 'I have an MBA from Harvard Business School where I specialized in all the finance courses, including financial services.'

The fact of the matter was that none of these four senior bankers had any formal banking qualifications.

In a £28 billion merger in 2001, Halifax and Bank of Scotland became HBOS, then the fifth largest bank in the UK. In February 2005 the *Guardian* newspaper ran a headline 'Bank Managers Getting Younger' when Andy Hornby became chief operating officer of the merged HBOS. A year later, at the age of thirty-nine, Hornby succeeded James Crosby as HBOS CEO. He embarked on a forceful campaign to increase the bank's stature relative to four other industry giants: Lloyds TSB, Royal Bank of Scotland, HSBC, and Barclays.

Hornby's expansion strategy proved catastrophic. Instead of focusing on sound, long-term business goals, Hornby pushed the bank to aggressively pursue riskier loans to maximize short-term profits. This led to a £213 billion gap between loans and deposits.[2] In 2008, with the United Kingdom's national economy at risk, taxpayers extended to Lloyds and HBOS a £20 billion bailout. The UK's National Audit Office, the watchdog of public spending, estimated that around £1.2 trillion was eventually paid out by British taxpayers after colossal mistakes were made by these and other bankers. At that time, the working population of Great Britain was approximately 30 million people. If you do the arithmetic, that comes to a cost of £40,000 ($54,400) per person. The average annual wage in Great Britain was then close to £20,000 per annum.

Citigroup Inc. is another of the world's largest banks. It too nearly collapsed in 1991. Between the late 1950s and early 1980s the bank had been led by two experienced commercial bankers: George S. Moore followed by Walter B. Wriston.[3] But in 1984, John S. Reed, a non-banking general manager, was appointed chairman and CEO. He wasn't shy about his lack of expertise; indeed he proudly declared that he was 'not a banker'.[4] Like Hornby, Reed had management degrees, but from MIT. In 1991, for the first time in its history, the bank failed to pay annual dividends and the company lost around a billion dollars.[5] To get out of the hole, thousands lost their jobs, and savage cost-cutting ensued. Reed was sacked in 2000. But rather than learn from their mistake, the board hired two similar men, one a corporate lawyer, Charles O. Prince III, and the other an economist, Robert E. Rubin. In the 2008 financial crisis the bank almost collapsed a second time. Like HBOS, Citigroup was bailed out by the government, which cost US taxpayers $517 billion. Prince was let go, but Rubin convinced them he should stay. Rubin earned $115 million in pay between 1999 and 2008.[6]

Andy Hornby had once been described as the 'whizz kid of British banking'.[7] Educated at Oxford University, and finally Harvard, his early professional life was in the cement business of Blue Circle Industries, then on to supermarket chain Asda, where he became a managing director at the age of thirty. After running grocery supermarkets, Hornby then moved to a top management job in a major bank, with virtually no core business knowledge or experience in banking.

A few years after the 2008 crisis, I struck up a conversation about Hornby with an acquaintance of his at the London School of Economics. When I mentioned Hornby's lack of banking qualifications and experience, or core business knowledge, he replied: 'Andy is a really smart guy, you know.' 'So,' I said to my friend, who was a smart guy himself, 'you wouldn't mind, then, if he performed surgery on you should you ever have the misfortune to need it?'

Another more recent example of the disastrous consequences of having non-experts in leadership positions occurred as I was completing the book.

On 6 September 2022, Elizabeth Truss won the competition to become leader of the Conservative Party after Boris Johnson was forced to step down. As a result, she became the next prime minister of the United Kingdom and immediately appointed her close political ally Akwasi Kwarteng Chancellor of the Exchequer ('Finance Minister' in other countries' terminology). Due to the peculiarities of the British political system, a tiny proportion of the British electorate had put them in charge of the United Kingdom's economy and society. It was to prove an extraordinary natural experiment vividly demonstrating what happens when leaders not only lack expertise themselves, but also ignore the deep expertise available to them.

Forty-eight hours after taking office, on 8 September, Truss and Kwarteng sacked the most senior civil servant in the Treasury (the nation's finance department). They then refused to listen to, or co-operate with, the Office of Budget Responsibility, a publicly funded body expressly created to provide independent analysis and advice on the public finances. For months before her election, Truss had derided what she called Treasury economic orthodoxy, and she and Kwarteng had hatched a radical plan to transform the nation's finances, informed not by any real knowledge of economics, but by ideology.

Truss had studied politics, philosophy, and economics (PPE) at Oxford and Kwarteng classics and history at Cambridge, eventually completing a PhD on the Great Recoinage of 1696. As one UK economics professor I spoke to, who preferred to be anonymous, said, 'If you take the most generous possible view, they have between them approximately one half of an economics undergraduate degree. It's like somebody taking a few hours of training in a prop plane and thinking they can now fly a Jumbo Jet. It's ridiculous.'

What Truss and Kwarteng did have, however, was self-belief. On 23 September 2022, Kwarteng rushed to announce a set of histori-cally extraordinary tax cuts in a mini-budget. These cuts were enor-mous and un-costed, in the sense that no indication was given as to how the cuts would ever be funded. A financial hole of more than £45 billion suddenly appeared in the UK national accounts.

Chaos ensued. It started even before Kwarteng had finished speaking in the UK Parliament. Money-market managers around the world had been listening to the speech. Almost instantly the value of sterling fell to its lowest-ever level against the US dollar. UK government bonds were heavily sold off in international markets. The financial markets were making it clear by their action that they no longer had confidence in the people in charge of the UK economy.

Kwarteng was sacked as Chancellor on 14 October after thirty-eight days, making him the second-shortest-serving post-war Chancellor, and Truss announced her resignation a few days later on 20 October, after only forty-four days in office.

In that time, lasting harm had been done to the economy, and arguably the international reputation, of the UK. In the world's money markets, a damaging premium was quickly added by investors to UK borrowing costs in the form of higher interest rates offered on government bonds to make them still attractive to international investors and pension funds, despite Truss's perceived fiscal recklessness. This premium was dubbed the 'moron premium'. It did not just affect how easily the UK government could service its national debt, it also led to significantly raised mortgage payments for millions of ordinary citizens who were already struggling with high inflation and rising energy bills.[9]

The moron premium is a good term. It gives an evocative sense of how costly it is when non-experts are in charge of something that they simply do not understand.

And this is the point of the book. Would you like the school that educates your child to be led by a former retailer or an outstanding schoolteacher who understands children and schooling? Would you rather fly in a commercial aircraft commanded by a pilot who until recently had operated only gliders, or by someone who had spent two decades flying Airbus A320s or jumbo jets? Would you want your federal court case decided by a judge with zero courtroom experience, or by someone who had clerked for a Supreme Court justice? In any area of endeavour, *intelligence is no substitute for technical expertise or experience*. To think otherwise is to leave your organization vulnerable to mediocre performance – or worse. Leaders must be credible.

Is this idea really a surprise? Imagine trying to coach a team or come up with new plays when you have never actually played the sport in question. Or imagine conducting an orchestra if you can't read or play any music. Or starting Microsoft or Apple if you had never written computer code.

In a *Financial Times* article in 2018, Wolf draws on Adam Tooze's book *Crashed* to try and understand 'What really went wrong in the 2008 financial crisis?'[10] The near collapse of global banking, Tooze argues, had long-term detrimental effects: taxpayers' money was used to bail out banks around the world; politics was turned populist and nasty; there were waves of unemployment and homelessness; European integration was destabilized; extreme austerity measures were implemented; and ultimately the gulf between the wealthy and poor deepened. Herd behaviour stampeded out of control. Trust in the state was dealt a profound blow.

Perhaps the most penetrating and worrying point raised in the Wolf article was 'The fact that the people who had been running the system had so little notion of these risks'.[11] A lack of government regulation facilitated the bundling and rebundling of assets that became impossible to untangle, with financial packages designed by physics PhDs based on mathematical formulae that few could understand.[12] People who had been in banking for years struggled to comprehend the complexities. So how were CEOs with no banking credentials and no experience going to keep up?

In this chapter I will describe the problems associated with this shift towards generalists and away from expert leaders, namely the people who hold deep accumulated knowledge about their firms. And I will provide stark evidence of why being an all-purpose manager is not enough.

The role of non-experts in corporate failure

'Home Depot Inc. Chairman and Chief Executive Robert Nardelli has abruptly left the company after a year of heavy criticism of everything from his pay package to the underperforming retailer's corporate governance,' read a Reuters lead article in 21 January 2007.[13] Robert Louis Nardelli was born in the north-eastern part of Pennsylvania. He completed a bachelor of science in business at Western Illinois University and an MBA at the University of Louisville. Nardelli has been what you might call 'a serial CEO' who led many firms, and made huge amounts of money from his various leadership roles.

Nardelli started his career at General Electric (GE) in 1971, where he was mentored by GE's legendary CEO Jack Welch. Welch was the Elon Musk of his day, a rock star who seemed to be known by everyone. When I interviewed Patrick Harker, then dean of the University of Pennsylvania's Wharton School, he joked that all MBA students longed for Jack Welch, the most influential business leader of his era,[14] to be the dean of their business school.

Robert Nardelli was reportedly known in GE as 'Little Jack' due to his promotion by Welch.[15] Nardelli rose to become president and CEO of GE Power Systems, but his ambition was to become 'Big Jack', and succeed his mentor in the top job, a race he eventually lost. Nevertheless, minutes after resigning from GE, Nardelli was invited to take over at the home-improvement retailer, The Home Depot, where he was CEO from 2000 to 2007.[16]

The Home Depot had been led by its founder Bernie Marcus, who started the business in 1978. His mission was to make all kinds of building materials and equipment accessible to the general public, selling from warehouses in a retail model now seen around the world. *Wired* magazine journalist Joe Flaherty praised the innovative culture of The Home Depot that had become, over its two decades, a household name.[17] Until Nardelli, that is; he knew nothing about retail and when he arrived he applied the same Six Sigma management strategy used at General Electric.[18] 'Nardelli, who had been one of Jack Welch's hatchet men at GE, then spent the next seven years driving down costs – at the expense of The Home Depot's reputation for innovation.'[19] Nardelli was reported to be autocratic and blunt, and it was claimed that he replaced employees who had years of experience and a deep knowledge of the business and its customers with cheaper, inexperienced part-time staff.[20] In 2007 Nardelli was fired by the person who had hired him, founder Bernie Marcus, who replaced him with a Home Depot veteran, to aid its return to its original focus on innovation.[21] Despite his unpopularity, Nardelli still parted from The Home Depot with a severance package estimated at over $200 million.[22]

Yet again, when Nardelli walked out of The Home Depot he was soon picked up for another CEO job, this time by car manufacturer Chrysler. So he moved from General Electric to a home improvement retail outlet and on to a car manufacturer. These are huge companies upon whose success thousands of people depend for jobs, the local economy, and investments. Would we countenance a dentist switching to become a gynaecologist with no training or experience? No. So why do we tolerate the hiring of CEOs from similarly different sectors? There are many more people's lives at risk with the latter.

'Who will Bob Nardelli fail next?' ran the headline on TheStreet in May 2009, after Chrysler cruised into Chapter 11 bankruptcy. It was 'his second failure in a top position that could mark the end of an era for celebrity CEOs', suggested journalist Robert Holmes optimistically.[23]

Sadly, it did not. Not for Nardelli, who continued his journey, in and then out, of various firms,[24] and not for industry in general.

Whether leaders have excelled in their own area or not, placing them in a new domain and expecting the same level of competence is at best naïve, as demonstrated by my research in the following chapters. Yet in the modern world it has become troublingly common. Putting unqualified people into top jobs is a reflection of a generalist management culture that dominates business and beyond, particularly in the US and UK. It is the result of placing an often equally unqualified mix of non-experts on to corporate boards, who then choose the CEOs. Selecting generalist candidates suits the headhunters, who can enlarge their pool of candidates to sell on to employers. Itinerant CEOs gain from changing job regularly, because research shows that those who move around most, accrue the highest pay.[25] Remarkably, even when CEOs fail, they still stroll out of their last elevator ride with golden parachutes worth millions, having secured contracts with these potential payouts when they sign up (as if they almost expect to fail). You win when you win, and you win when you lose. What kind of message does this send to young managers?

German businessman Léo Apotheker was fired by

Hewlett-Packard in 2011 after losing in excess of $30 billion in market capitalization during his short time as CEO. He was in post for just eleven months. Yet he left with a sum of $23 million.[26] Yahoo, when led by CEO Marissa Mayer, failed to disclose two major security breaches, in 2013 and 2014, yet awarded her a similar payout.[27] 'Marissa Mayer's $23-million severance from Yahoo may look obscene. But it's even worse,' read the *Los Angeles Times* headline in 2017, as it revealed the 'tens of millions of dollars in stock options' also held by Mayer.[28] Despite being blamed for taking British bank HBOS into virtual collapse, with the loss of 16,000 jobs and huge debts to the UK taxpayer, Andy Hornby went into another CEO position.[29] A few months after being questioned by UK politicians about the bank's failure, Hornby was back earning £2.1 million for his first year as CEO of pharmacy business Alliance Boots.[30]

Many seem to believe that bringing in an executive from outside can add a newness of thought and perspective. It can. If an organizational culture has become political and prone to infighting, or sluggish and inward-looking, it might require the kind of change that is made more easily by someone less invested in the status quo. But outside should not mean beyond the general core business or sector experience. Whoever takes over still needs to understand the industry, what motivates the key employees, and, importantly, how to diagnose problems. As we will see, the world's best and most profitable organizations know this.

The companies behind the tech we turn on every morning were started by experts who went on to become effective leaders. Some companies then switched away from credible bosses and learned a hard lesson. Apple was one, co-founded by Steve Jobs, possibly the most celebrated leader during an extraordinary time in which world populations moved way from desks to desktops. Jobs was clever, charismatic, and often combatively challenging. But he was, first and foremost, a techy expert.

Famously, a simple garage features large in the history of Steven Paul Jobs. It is where, in their first family home, his father shared his own passion for mechanics with his son;[31] where the young

Jobs started to dabble at a very early age in different kinds of electronics, and, notably, where the newfound Apple Computer Company relocated to, from Jobs' bedroom, in 1976.[32] Today, all this is world history. Although its business antics have been criticized (e.g. practising anti-competitive behaviour and using unethical business practices),[33] Apple became the first company to reach $3 trillion market value in early 2022.[34]

Back in 1983, the company was expanding and Steve Jobs decided he required an expert marketer. He recruited the former marketing executive John Sculley from his CEO perch at PepsiCo, where he had become well known during the so-called cola wars between Coca-Cola and Pepsi in the early eighties. Sculley was an experienced mid-forties business and marketing legend whereas Jobs was twenty-eight and still learning the ropes. He was also distracted. 'While Jobs pursued his MacMission he required a more orthodox chief executive to run the company. A respectable face who could sell to corporate America,' explained Andy Hertzfeld, a designer on the Macintosh Development Team.[35]

As CEO, Sculley is credited with boosting Apple's sales, turning it from a start-up into a major player.[36] However, he is possibly best known for having the dubious distinction of firing one of the greatest technology designers in business history. From the start of their relationship, Sculley and Jobs clashed. Sculley wanted to compete in the same space as IBM, whereas Jobs believed Apple deserved its own unique place. With Mackintosh sales underperforming, Sculley, in 1985, persuaded the Apple board of directors to get rid of Steve Jobs, who was then head of the Macintosh division.

There was innovation at Apple under Sculley. But there were also numerous failures. A PC price war pushed revenues down despite maintaining sales. In just one year Apple's profits dropped from $530 million to $86 million.[37] This resulted in significant redundancies at Apple, one of whom was John Sculley.[38]

When the board dispatched Sculley, they replaced him with Michael Spindler, who was viewed as a brilliant strategist but was another non-technologist who had been at the company only a few years. As CEO, he reorganized, cutting 15 per cent of the workforce and downgrading its keystone product development by regrouping the company into markets.[39] Spindler lasted until 1996. Apple was then at its lowest point.

Luckily for Apple, at the same time Steve Jobs reappeared, having been busy in the intervening decade with Pixar, Disney, and the new NeXT Computer that eventually helped save Apple.[40] He persuaded the Apple board that he was the only person who could 'get the ship pointed in the right direction',[41] which he duly did. He first streamlined:

> When we got to the company a year ago, there were a lot of products ... if we only get four, we could put the A-Team on every single one of them. And if we only have four, we could turn them all every nine months instead of every 18 months ... So that's what we decided to do: to focus on four great products.[42]

Central to Jobs' strategy was his decision to put technical experts back in charge.

> We went through that stage in Apple where we went out and thought, Oh, we're gonna be a big company, let's hire professional management. We went out and hired a bunch of professional management. It didn't work at all ... why do you want to work for somebody you can't learn anything from? ... You know who the best managers are? They are the great individual contributors who never, ever want to be a manager but decide they have to be ... because no one else is going to ... do as good a job.[43]

Steve Jobs recognized that Apple needed the best experts to become line managers, not the weak or failed technicians who had been pushed sideways into administration. He wanted people who had 'at the tips of their fingertips and in their passion the latest understanding of where technology was and what we could do with that technology'.[44] Our research shows that successful line managers will know about the technology and what happens deep in their department, because they have worked on it, developed it, and created successful products from it; and they understand how best to manage their expert colleagues, because they have performed the complicated tasks themselves, speak the language, and share the hard-won tacit knowledge from working on products such as the Mac computer, the iPod, iPhone, and iTunes.

Jobs also knew something fundamental: it is easier to train an expert to lead than it is to teach a general manager to become a technical expert. He encouraged experts to manage other experts in their area of specialism, a principle promulgated throughout the organization.

Calamity from 'situational incompetence'

Darryl Carlton lives in Queensland, on the north-east coast of Australia, a state with a population of 5 million. It is home to the Great Barrier Reef. Over a forty-year career he occupied many executive positions in the practice of information technology, both for the private sector and government bodies.[45]

In 2015 Carlton stepped back from his day job to research a question that had preoccupied him for some time: why do so many major projects continue to fail?

Here is an incredible fact: only 2 per cent of projects that exceed $100 million in labour costs are successful.[46]

One can remember the debacle over Samsung's $2,000 collapsing phone, that did just that, instantly collapse; catastrophic building projects such as the brand new apartment block in Shanghai that fell, almost perfectly intact, on its side; the many IT failures, such as those that afflicted British Airways, Delta Air Lines, the New York Stock Exchange, HSBC bank, among others.[47] While these are inconvenient, they tend not to reach the eye-watering losses incurred through the failure of public sector projects – sums that are always picked up by the taxpayer. According to Dr Okoro Chima Okereke, an expert in project failures in Africa, the effect of major failures is worse in poor countries, because they don't just lose money, they reduce future investment, trust in governments, and general faith in the future.[48]

Darryl Carlton believes IT projects continue to fail at a rate that has hardly changed over decades. Indeed, shockingly, he suggests that most commercial collapses probably go unreported.

One of the largest public IT failures was the UK's National Health Service civilian IT project. It was, in principle, a brave attempt to create a system that unified the digital health records of all Britons. The demise of what would have been one of the world's largest IT projects cost the taxpayer over £10 billion – £3.6 billion more than budgeted.[49] There are many reasons, long documented, why this project met with disaster.[50] Carlton emphasizes that many factors are necessary for success,[51] but he also believes that the absence of some or all of these *does not* cause project failure. 'Rather,' he suggests, 'they are consequences of a poorly run project due to the situational incompetence of project leaders who have direct oversight and accountability for the day-to-day workings of the project.'[52]

Carlton's own PhD research examined a spectacular IT failure on his doorstep: the Queensland Health payroll project. In 2007 the state government decided to create a new payroll system for the 80,000 employees of Queensland Health. The American multinational technology business IBM won the contract. IBM quoted A$6.7 million to complete the project and deliver in six months. After four years, and a cost that exceeded A$1.3 billion, a government commission of inquiry was established.[53] The commission reported that unethical tactics had been used by IBM employees to gain favour over other vendors, and that Queensland staff had failed to vet the potential contractors properly.[54]

During his extensive study, Carlton put in several rounds of freedom-of-information requests to the Queensland government over an extended period. He collected in excess of 5,000 pages of project documents, and another 3,800 pages of witness testimony from 170 participants.

What emerged from Carlton's study?

His published findings state, first and foremost, *that the senior executives placed in charge of the project tended to be technically incompetent, and unaware of their own incompetence.* Specifically, Carlton writes that the project executives were 'situationally incompetent', with minimal knowledge or skills in IT, which meant 'they could not infer appropriate actions in the face of adverse circumstances'.[55] The executives simply did not understand the information that was being presented to them, and interpreted professional concerns raised by Queensland Health team members as 'personality conflicts'. Indeed,

> On more than one occasion IBM complained that employees of Queensland Health were trying to hold IBM to its contract and make IBM meet its obligations. IBM convinced senior departmental management that these staff were interfering and senior management subsequently ordered their removal from the project.[56]

Carlton found that the longer the uninformed executives stayed in their roles, the less they deferred to the experts. Importantly, their incompetence also meant that they were unable to identify competence in others, and in fact, perhaps for reassurance, leaned heavily towards listening to other incompetent people.

Second, Carlton found that when there are many actors engaged in a project, which is inevitable in large IT endeavours, each party tends, if allowed, to operate according to its own agenda, and may choose not to disclose its true objectives. On the Queensland project, groups had competing priorities and conflicts predictably arose. These behaviours, he found, ebbed and flowed with ease because the senior executives were situationally incompetent and, therefore, did not have the necessary knowledge to establish where truth lay nor to judge the correct order of things.

Finally, in the absence of competent expert leadership and governance, and hence with little awareness of the mission's aims and the parameters for its success, there was a lack of clear authority and oversight. There was an 'inability or unwillingness to adopt appropriate governance processes' and 'a complete lack of accountability for failure, evident throughout the project'.[57] Thus, the project became a rudderless ship accruing ever more costs until it eventually sank. As early as 1995, the proceedings of the International Federation for Information Processing (IFIP) Conference on IT Project Failures had noted: 'someone implementing IT needs to know which levers to pull, in which context, and at what time.'[58]

On the question of governance, Carlton decided to look at the technical skills of those on Australian boards.[59] It is the governing boards that hire and fire CEOs, oversee strategy, and, importantly, are meant to apply effective supervision. All aspects require competence and experience. 'This means', suggests Carlton, 'that ... boards need some measure of IT knowledge if they expect to provide effective governance, risk management and strategic oversight of IT projects.'[60]

Carlton used the Australian Stock Exchange to access publicly available information on the qualifications and experience of Australian directors and, in particular, to ascertain the level of digital competence on Australian boards. He examined 35,000 director positions, with 37,500 reported qualifications. Carlton found that just 6 per cent of directors had qualifications in a STEM-related field or possessed a PhD. Most directors were qualified in finance (18%) or accounting (19%), with lawyers the next common group (9%), and then those with mining qualifications (8%). Directors with arts, business, or other qualifications accounted for 40 per cent. Carlton believes that this lack of accumulated knowledge and experience on Australian boards is not sufficient for there to be effective oversight of major IT projects.

If the unexpected happens

When experts are sacrificed for generalists, things can go badly wrong, as we saw when a new virus swept around the world. At the start of the Covid-19 pandemic (March 2020), previously unseen experts were pulled from various parts of nations' health systems and universities, and often placed centre stage. Politicians find experts difficult to manage. However, on this occasion, most senior politicians recognized their own stark lack of expertise. There were, of course, exceptions, like Brazil or the US, where leaders were in denial about the power of the pandemic to disrupt and maim.

Canada should have led the way in terms of preparedness for Covid-19, with a state-of-the-art epidemic alert system. The Global Public Health Intelligence Network (GPHIN) was relied upon by the World Health Organization. Instead, as the pandemic flowed across the Canadian border, 'We are not prepared' ran across the *Globe and Mail*'s front page.

The Canadian government had made what turned out to be a disastrous decision when it restructured its public health system. It shut down its world-renowned early warning system, and replaced experts with generalists. This was primarily to save money. A *Globe and Mail* investigation revealed that GPHIN 'ceased issuing international alerts on May 24, 2019, less than eight months before the outbreak in China became known to the world'. The newspaper reported that 'Experienced scientists were pushed aside, expertise was eroded, and internal warnings went unheeded, which hindered the department's response to COVID-19.'[61] Experts like Abla Mawudeku, an epidemiologist who helped build the Lighthouse Intelligence Network, were replaced by generalist civil servants with little understanding of public health.[622]

Canada's lesson about the detrimental effect of replacing experts with generalists has been deeply disruptive and costly. A recent study estimated that between March 2020 and April 2021 Canada spent $624.2 billion on Covid-19, which, the report points out, is more than it paid out during the entirety of the Second World War.[63]

Non-expert leaders have become disturbingly common in health care. In 2009 two physicians, Richard Gunderman and Steven Kanter, revealed, with data from the American Hospital Association, that fewer than 4 per cent (i.e. only 235) of nearly 6,500 US hospitals were headed by physicians. That was not always true. In 1935, for example, the picture was quite different. Physicians then ran 35 per cent of American hospitals.[64] In the US and the UK hospital boards themselves are also mainly populated by non-clinicians, which likely adds to the further appointment of non-physician general managers to CEO positions. People tend to select others who are like themselves, a phenomenon known as *homophily*, as will be discussed later.

But how can a CEO with no medical experience really know how to manage clinicians or understand patient care? When I make this point, others often turn to me and respond that heads of hospitals manage budgets of millions, and huge numbers of staff, and have very little involvement in the clinical side of things, and they might also chip in by asking what do physicians know about management and the business of health care? I then point out that the best hospitals in the US are led by physicians, not general managers (this is covered in the next chapter). Both of the world's top two hospital systems are not-for-profits. The Cleveland Clinic has an operating revenue of over $8.4 billion and an income of $330 million, with close to 68,000 employees worldwide.[65] The Mayo Clinic is similar in size, income, and success. Both of these impressive health care organizations have, since their inception, been led *only by physicians*.

Why would we think that physicians could *not* lead and manage their own institutions? They are among the cleverest and most highly trained people among us. Do we suppose that after learning the intricacies and complexities of the human body, and treating its ailments, our physicians would not be able to learn about organizational strategy, about how to fill out a spreadsheet or acquire an MBA?

In the UK, despite growing awareness of the benefits of physician leadership, CEOs with medical degrees are even rarer than in the US, and the number in management positions seems not to be increasing.[66] Moreover, in contrast to many European countries, such as Scandinavia and Italy,[67] the quantity of non-clinical general managers in the UK has risen substantially over the last thirty years.[68] When I spoke to child and adolescent psychiatrist Tanveer Sandhu, based in Birmingham, he remembered fondly an earlier period in his career.

I used to work in Finland where there were no general managers running hospitals. They were led by medical experts who were supported by different kinds of people including non-clinicians. Those who stepped up to take on a medical leadership role were assessed through clear consistent criteria based on clinical expertise and related competencies.

In the Cleveland Clinic's 2020 'State of the Clinic' staff engagement survey, 85 per cent of its worldwide workforce (all of whom are called caregivers) rated it highly as a place to work. As we will see in Chapter 4, employee engagement and job satisfaction have a substantial effect on individuals, on their productivity, on organizational performance, and on turnover, retention, and customer service.[69] Employees are happier and work harder when they have expert leaders.

When experts are ignored

Having the right manager in place can be a question of life and death, not only in health care settings but whenever experts are ignored, as happened at the US aerospace company, Boeing. In the recent tragic examples of Boeing's 737 Max aircraft crashes in Indonesia (2018) and Ethiopia (2019), all passengers and crew lost their lives. Who was to blame? An over-controlling autopilot, and an under-controlling US air safety regulator that yielded way too much authority to Boeing. 'Boeing knew about safety-alert problem for a year before telling FAA [Federal Aviation Authority],' ran the *Wall Street Journal* headline on 5 May 2019. Journalists Andy Pasztor, Andrew Tangel, and Alison Sider wrote that

> Boeing Co. didn't share information about a problem with a cockpit safety alert for about a year before the issue drew attention with the October crash of a 737 MAX jet in Indonesia, and then gave some airlines and pilots partial and inconsistent explanations, according to industry and government officials.[70]

Boeing pre-sold 350 of its Dreamliner aircraft in 2005. For the first time it intended to outsource most of the plane's structure and components to over forty different suppliers located in three continents.[71] In January 2013 the FAA grounded all fifty of Boeing's newly created 787 Dreamliners after battery fires in two planes. The Dreamliner was considered to be technologically advanced because it was lighter and used 20 per cent less fuel. Boeing was not only experimenting with a new technology; it also introduced a new build system, 'outsourcing', that it believed would be groundbreaking and cheaper.[72]

'The Dreamliner was supposed to become famous for its revolutionary design. Instead, it has become an object lesson in how not to build an airplane,' reported James Surowiecki in an article in *New Yorker* magazine. Surowiecki went back to 1997 to look for answers about the Dreamliner failures, to a time when Boeing had just been acquired by aerospace manufacturer and defence contractor, McDonnell Douglas.

Following the takeover, power was ceded to McDonnell Douglas executives. With them came a change in the corporate culture, one that was 'averse to risk and obsessed with cost-cutting'. Surowiecki wrote that 'the nerds may have been running the show in Silicon Valley, but at Boeing they were increasingly marginalized by the bean counters.' The real battle over the company's future, wrote industry analyst Richard Aboulafia, was 'between the engineers', the core business experts, 'and the finance and sales guys'.[73]

Surowiecki wrote that Boeing had built less than 40 per cent of the Dreamliner in-house. The design, engineering, and manufacture of whole sections of the plane went to fifty 'strategic partners'. The approach was heralded as a 'reinvention of manufacturing', but 'while the finance guys loved it – since it meant that Boeing had to put up less money – it was a huge headache for the engineers'.[74] The complicated supply chain created engineering challenges and caused delays. The project went over budget instead of costing less, as the managers and accountants had hoped. The person who picked up the ailing programme at Boeing, Jim Albaugh, said: 'We spent a lot more money in trying to recover than we ever would have spent if we'd tried to keep the key technologies closer to home.'[75]

What did Boeing and their executives learn from this episode?

Fast forward to October 2018. A Lion Air flight came down, tragically killing 189 people, which was followed by the Ethiopian Airlines crash, where 157 people died. A couple of months later a Bloomberg headline read: 'Boeing's 737 Max software outsourced to $9-an-hour engineers'.[76] Despite its experiences with Dreamliner, outsourcing continued, but this time many lives were lost.

Boeing engineers had complained about the pressure applied by managers to cut corners where extra costs might be incurred. Mark Rabin, a former senior Boeing software engineer laid off in 2015, was shocked when he was told by a manager in a company meeting that 'Boeing didn't need senior engineers because its products were mature'.[77] It was the in-house Boeing engineers on the Dreamliner project and the 737 Max disasters who warned of impending safety issues. They were ignored.

Investigations later identified that bad code in an automated flight control system – MCAS – was at fault in the Max planes. Boeing officials had concealed information and for six months avoided co-operating with investigators. The US Justice Department said the firm chose 'profit over candour'.[78] Boeing agreed to pay $2.5 billion (£1.8bn) to settle US criminal charges, and around $500 million to the families of the Max victims.[79]

Engineers are required to follow a strict code of practice that runs from their education into their workplace, regulated by their profession and the law. An experienced bus driver would not suddenly decide to take a school bus on a shortcut through a field of cows. An engineer whose expert knowledge and whole career is steeped in learning and adherence to a regulated path is also less likely to deviate. This is why professional credentials matter and are required for people such as electricians, psychiatrists, and engineers. Boeing's troubles continued with yet another fatal crash on 21 March 2022, this time in China, with all 132 people on board perishing. The Boeing 737-800 is part of a fleet of jets known as the Next-Generation planes, which have had safety issues associated with them, known by US regulators, since 2018.[80] For Boeing, the sacrificing of experts for short-term profit, through outsourcing and the downgrading of in-house expertise, has not gone well. Indeed, it has cost them the kind of reputational damage that could take decades to repair. Not to mention the people who died in the crashes mentioned above.

Outsourcing to non-experts

It would be foolish to say that all outsourcing is wrong since it is an aspect of modern business that is here to stay. A company, hospital, or university might offer better meals to staff by outsourcing its café to an external provider. Sometimes outsourcing makes it possible for real experts to produce a product or service, which can then be purchased by non-experts. Writer and strategy consultant Mitchell Osak believes that 'Outsourcing accelerates the diffusion of knowledge and talent to outsiders thereby lowering barriers to entry, and creating greater competition and a lower return on invested capital.'[81]

There are four key issues which should be addressed if you decide to outsource. First, and most important – tied to the message of this book – outsourcing may be the right move if the service or product outsourced is *not* a central part of the core business (but in Boeing's case, engineering is). Osak suggests that many managers 'do not know what makes their organizations tick'. Only when you truly know what your unique value proposition is can you safeguard it.[82] If you randomly ask an employee in an organization, What is your core business?, you may be surprised at the equally random content of their response.

Second, double down on the core, which requires continued and generous investment to ensure you future-proof 'your differentiating, core capabilities that drive your market position and return on assets', suggests Osak. Above all, ensure that core strategic activities are insourced and kept away from external providers who may become your competitors.[83]

Third, the commercial motivation of companies doing the outsourcing may differ greatly from the values that drive the purchasing organization. Approaches to quality, innovation, and research and development (R&D) investment may differ.

Fourth, if an expert is not also running the outsourced service that you are purchasing, then quality will typically be lost in the search for cheapness. Ensure that the outsource executives have adequate credentialling, expert knowledge, and the experience to deliver what they say they can. And this feeds into the final point. If cost is the *only* motivation for outsourcing, then there is a good chance it will ruin the enterprise.

An investigation by Emma Youle at HuffPost in 2020 led to many embarrassing revelations about the way £17 billion of taxpayers' money was awarded to contractors to provide personal protective equipment (PPE). Many of them had no history of supplying the products but some history of being 'friends' of the Conservative government.[84] In one case, reported in the *Financial Times*,[85] a Miami jewellery designer, Saiger, received £250 million of contracts to supply PPE to the NHS, which it won by paying another US consultant £21 million to help broker a deal.[86]

'We remain seriously concerned by the extent of PPE supply that is not fit for purpose,' reported the committee of the UK Parliament assessing the 'Initial lessons from the government's response to the COVID-19 pandemic'. It reported that '2.1 billion items of PPE were deemed unsuitable for being used in medical settings, equating to over £2 billion of taxpayers' money'.[87] One NHS pundit suggested that when PPE purchasing was done locally, the cost and quality were higher than when it was purchased by central government.[88]

When governments rely on non-experts

The UK has a history of placing non-experts in key positions of power. In October 2021, after incredible effort and some success getting the nation through the pandemic, a review (yet another one) of the National Health Service was announced. Who was selected to head this inquiry into the UK's health system? The government chose a former soldier, Sir Gordon Messenger. Indeed, the press reported that *not one* single clinician was among the health service review body.

Is it likely that the Royal Marines or the Royal Air Force would tolerate a review of their military services by a heart surgeon? In 2014, when the Secretary of State for Health, Jeremy Hunt, commissioned a different NHS review, he asked Lord Stuart Rose, former executive chairman of high-street retailer Marks & Spencer, to lead it. M&S is possibly best known for supplying umpteen Britons with their underwear. Rose's 68-page report, 'Better Leadership for Tomorrow', contained approximately 17,000 words: in it, *nurses* are mentioned only ten times and *doctors* appear even more rarely, at seven times.[89] What an extraordinary thing: to write a report on the National Health Service and barely mention its core workforce, without whom there is no NHS.

Governments are the largest employers in most countries, whether directly or indirectly. What they do matters to the economy of every nation. Later, in Chapter 4, I will argue that leaders are the standard-bearers of quality. Yet this is so often not the case in our governments. Whether it is Canada's weakened public health system, the colossal IT failure in Australia, bailing out US bank Citigroup, or a Florida jewellery company producing PPE for UK doctors and nurses, it is our governments who should demonstrate, through their own governance, the highest of standards when spending trillions of citizens' cash. Time and again our politicians squander public money and routinely it is because they select non-experts – whether through cronyism or in good faith – to deliver services those non-experts are not equipped to supply. Governments and their departments should be quality controllers who ensure that only core business experts are contracted.

It is sometimes claimed – and there is some evidence to support this – that the UK suffers from a so-called productivity puzzle that results in the country being less productive than comparable nations.[90] I believe the efficiency gap may be partly due to the practice in the UK of appointing people into leadership and governance roles in places where they have no core experience. In the next chapter I will explore why this may have become the case not only in the UK but more generally.

To understand why the value of expertise has been forgotten, and why it matters, let's start with the principles that underly the argument. A set of simple, logical points have emerged from my research that constitute practical tenets generalizable to today's organizations. These can be applied without the need for consultants or headhunters. They can be summarized thus:

The principles of expert leadership

1. *An organization's core business function should determine its leader*
   An expert leader is an industry specialist, proficient to a high standard in the core activity. The core business is the engine into which all other parts must fit. We'll look at this more in Chapter 3.

2. *The term 'expert' applies in all settings*
   The importance of expert leadership is not limited to certain industries or sectors. It applies across the board, from the brilliant teacher who having inspired her students moves on to lead and inspire a whole school, to the masseuse who after years of working for others trains to run her own business and sets up a spa, and the engineer who joins Mercedes as a trainee and eventually becomes its chairman and CEO.

3. *Expert leaders are essential throughout the organization*
   We need expert leaders at all levels, from non-executive directors on a governing board to the CEO and through to every level of management.

4. *The term* expert *is not elitist*
   Being an expert is not just about the professions, like medicine or the law, or about being a white-coated engineer-scientist boffin.

It refers to anyone who has mastered a trade to a high standard, for example, a talented chef who opens a restaurant.

5. *Expert leaders maximize the well-being of the group*
Expert leaders do not just improve the performance of their organizations; they also improve employee well-being and job satisfaction (see Chapter 4).

6. *Being an expert is not a proxy for having leadership and management skills*
Let's be clear. Just being competent in the core activity with no understanding of leading or managing is also insufficient. To succeed as a leader, both are necessary. We will look at this in more detail in Chapter 6.

7. *The argument over the difference between leaders and managers is more often than not an academic distinction without a real-world difference*
Both are required to travel the same path and engage in the plumbing as well as the poetry, in the words of renowned Stanford scholar James G. March. (And I will use the terms *supervisor, manager, boss,* and *leader* interchangeably throughout.)

8. *Teamworking still requires expert leaders*
Teamworking has become the norm but to effective teamworking requires skilled managers and leaders who can synthesize and represent the views of many. Even in the least hierarchical of settings, however, the buck still stops with those in charge – requiring them to draw upon the views of the collective, decide the right path to success, and take personal responsibility for their actions.

2

The Death of Expertise?

In a cartoon by Will McPhail in the *New Yorker* in early 2017, a man in an aeroplane is standing up in his seat facing the other passengers, his hand raised. 'These smug pilots have lost touch with regular passengers like us. Who thinks I should fly the plane?' he asks his fellow travellers. A dozen or so passengers have their hands raised enthusiastically in the air.[1]

That image was circulated and debated extensively. It depicts and somewhat conflates two different things. The first is the rise of the populist political movement expressed most dramatically by the election of Donald Trump in the US, but evident around the world.[2] Populism targets the so-called left behind,[3] those who once had stable jobs in areas such as manufacturing who now feel marginalized by social and political change and are struggling economically. It feeds on anti-elitism, the idea that those in power are out of touch with 'regular folk', and rejects the liberal way of thinking and behaving that generally predominated in the post-war years of prosperity. But blended into this message is a second, anti-expert voice, one that is helpful to big business and politicians alike. This is the voice of those who are irritated by the opinions of experts because those opinions can get in the way of their pursuit of personal – or corporate – power, fame, and wealth.

Experts are governed by other experts. Through study and practice over many years they have acquired numerous qualifications and gone through extensive certification, while observing regulations that are designed to protect both the public and the experts themselves. But, as we saw with Boeing's engineers, finance directors and managers are not bound by the same standards and regulations and may be reluctant to listen to the recommendations of technical experts if they involve extra time and costs. Denigrating and ignoring experts often produces fatal consequences.

The managerial class has grown substantially since the 1960s. With it, hand in hand, has emerged a decline in deference to expertise – a lack of respect for those who are experts. Tom Nichols, a former professor at the US Naval War College, believes there is a 'campaign against established knowledge' that partly comes from society's drive for equality, which 'has had the unintended consequence of fostering the idea that all opinions should be attributed equal merit'. This, he argues, goes against the underlying assumptions of modern society that presume 'scientific principles and rationality will yield the best answers to a question', and this equalization of the value attributed to opinions is what has, he believes, led to 'the death of expertise' – the title of his stimulating book.[4]

This democratization of information has been fostered by social media. Greatest weight is assigned to the opinions of those who shout the loudest; real knowledge seems to have become almost irrelevant. Facebook and other social media platforms present both laypersons' and experts' opinions together. That makes it difficult for a casual reader to assess their relative value. Throw into the mix those who deliberately seek to misinform and the absence of accountability, and you have a form of truth chaos.

Tom Nichols is blunt:

> To reject the advice of experts is to assert autonomy, a way for Americans (people) to insulate their increasingly fragile egos from ever being told they are wrong about anything. All things are knowable and every opinion on any subject is as good as any other.[5]

And this phenomenon is not unique to the US: the British politician Michael Gove famously proclaimed, 'I think the people in this country have had enough of experts . . . saying they know what is best.'[6]

Alongside this growing disrespect for expertise has been a move towards status equalization as seen in the rise of job title inflation.

Where once there were only two vice presidents there are now dozens inside every organization, which has led to the creation of yet more new job titles such as senior vice president and so on. Ironically, this is happening during a period when we are told that organizational structures are getting flatter. Another form of status maximization, and an illustration of the devaluation of expertise, is evident in the retitling of job roles; for example, the person who responds to your call to the energy supplier has become an 'energy consultant'. The irony is that while no one respects experts in general, everyone wants to be seen as an expert in their own field.

The devaluing of genuine expertise, combined with the idea that everyone's views are of equal validity can lead to things going badly wrong. On social media, life becomes a 'tyranny of the majority', and in business it can lead to a kind of feedback loop as generalist bureaucrats put systems in place that require yet more generalist bureaucrats to run them. I do not wish to generalize unreasonably, but few of the new processes that are introduced into our working environments appear to be designed to suit those who fulfil the core business tasks. This might seem paradoxical until one thinks about who does the designing. Recently I undertook a senior teaching fellowship created by the UK government's Higher Education Academy.[7] Obtaining a teaching fellowship is supposed to ensure that we academics are good teachers. Although completion of the fellowship required a lot of written work, culminating in around 12,000 words, ironically, no one ever actually observed my teaching or read any of my pedagogical resources. The part that took the most time was having to tick off numerous banal 'descriptors' that mostly meant nothing, and bore little relationship to the actual process of academic teaching.

So who heads the Higher Education Academy, the arbiter of our teaching quality? The CEO is a lifetime administrator who, it appears, has never taught or assessed students, nor, importantly, undertaken the academic research that is the basis of all of our teaching materials. Indeed, not a single person on their executive team has ever worked as an academic.[8]

Nevertheless, the rejection of expertise is not found every-where. Humans are not stupid. We want the best for *ourselves and our own*, supported by the latest evidence, when, for example, we bring our child to the doctor. But when dealing with issues in which we are not consciously invested, then random and even foolish answers can seem acceptable. I have found this when chatting with people about my research on expert leaders. In their own field, they will definitively explain and argue that only experts like them will do. But, if I ask the same person about a different setting, running a hospital for example, I often get told that a 'non-expert manager would do just fine', followed by a stream of arguments based on anecdote and 'common sense' rather than fact or evidence.

We want our own domain of expertise to be recognized. We believe others should respect the value of our hard-won achieve-ments. But, without seeing the inconsistency, we seem to be less concerned about recognizing other people's expertise.

An obsession with management consulting firms

A breed of politicians that include Boris Johnson and Donald Trump, often claim that they want to make government 'smaller'.[9] Yet, as these sentiments are being uttered, ever larger sums from the public purse are being tipped into the pockets of management consultan-cies. Indeed, small government could be interpreted as small involve-ment from government and big engagement by consulting firms in public policy. Politicians of all persuasions have apparently grown in their obsession with, particularly, McKinsey & Company, the Big Four of PwC, Deloitte, EY, and KPMG, and Boston Consulting. There are problems with this dependence: first, it depletes and downgrades both in-house civil service expertise and the resources that government departments receive; second, these firms cost the taxpayer eye-watering sums, yet it is often not clear that they deliver on their promise; third, there are conflicts of interest, and finally, a lack of accountability.

In his book *The World's Newest Profession* (2006), historian Christopher McKenna points to NASA in 1961, as being the first US government agency to become dependent on external contractors (spending close to $850 million of the agency's $1 billion budget). Journalist Ian MacDougall examined, in two in-depth investigations for ProPublica, the increasing influence of consulting firms. He suggests that 'Over decades, McKinsey's approach became self-reinforcing. As successive administrations chipped away at the civil service, politicians who advocate small government got the dysfunctional bureaucracy they had complained about all along, which helped them justify dismantling it further.'[10] This point was made by a British senior Conservative government minister, Lord Agnew, who said in a leaked letter during the pandemic, 'We are too reliant on consultants. Aside from providing poor value for money, this infantilises the civil service by depriving our brightest people of opportunities to work on some of the most challenging, fulfilling and crunchy issues.'[11]

Following the 2016 UK Brexit vote, spending on consultancy firms quickly grew to more than £1.5 billion in 2017–18.[12] Agnew's letter highlights the failure to develop the right skills among civil servants.

> Four years after voting to leave the European Union it is unacceptable that the civil service still has not developed the capability to deliver this . . . we seem to be ineffectual at harnessing our fast-streamers [new civil servants] to do work that is then outsourced to consultants using similar people at a vastly inflated cost. This is unacceptable.[13]

It is also relevant to the core message of this book.

A former Indian senior civil servant, who had also worked extensively with consulting firms, argued, 'if consulting firms are taking on the sovereign functions of the state, including policymaking and strategic planning, that does raise serious questions about dependency and conflicts of interest.'[14] This process of demoting civil servants, starving government departments of the necessary expertise, HR talent, and resourcing, and instead diverting public responsibilities, funds, and lots of our data into private firms is known as 'hollowing out'. The effects of this became apparent during Covid-19 when many private consultants were used, which thus reduced further the situational learning that could have been gained locally.

So how much public revenue are the consulting firms picking up?

The pandemic has shone a light on this issue. In Britain, an *FT* headline read, 'UK Public Spending on Consultants More Than Doubles'.[15] The UK's management consultant industry exceeded £11 billion in 2020, which begs the question, how many other industries are having their expertise hollowed out?

Between the start of 2016 and the end of 2021, Deloitte and McKinsey were the largest recipients of US government contracts, receiving over $13 billion.[16] Ian MacDougall looked into the detail of 'How McKinsey is making $100 million (and counting) advising on the government's bumbling coronavirus response'.[17] Partly, he suggests the high cost is because hiring McKinsey is notoriously expensive. 'A single junior consultant – typically a recent college or business school graduate – runs clients $67,500 per week, or $3.5 million annually. For $160,000 per week, you get two consultants, the second one mid-level.' One Miami-based civil servant commented, after receiving a quote from McKinsey for an advisory job, that the cost for one week's work exceeded the annual salaries of two full-time staffers. 'Apparently,' she said, 'it takes five people with staff support to do what I've been doing myself.'[18]

For the world's best-known corporate management consultants, helping tackle the pandemic has been a bonanza. UK public sector spending on consulting totalled £2.5 billion in 2020–21,[19] while the European Commission's contracts with Big Four firms rose to €156 million, Deloitte being the main beneficiary, winning contracts worth €110 million for work in 2019 and 2020. In India, consulting firms' revenues went up by nearly 11 per cent annually in the five years to 2018, totalling 4.5 trillion rupees ($64.8bn).[20] The private sector spend increased, but the public purse contributed also, encouraged by Prime Minister Narendra Modi, who awarded many of his ambitious programmes to private consulting firms.[21]

MacDougall raises the point that it is not always clear what governments get back in return.[22] This is made worse as the detail is sometimes concealed in secrecy through confidentiality clauses. Publicly owned data are often given away to these firms, who can then use the information to acquire yet more contracts.[23]

Sir Anthony Finkelstein, engineer and computer scientist, was chief scientific adviser for national security to the British government until 2021.

I saw work done for the government by Boston Consulting and they were actually very good. They came with a methodology, which was well suited to the challenge; they brought muscle where there was no muscle (everybody was very busy with their day job), and the people they brought were smart. None of the actual solutions came from Boston Consulting; the solutions came from within the organization, from people that knew and understood the problem . . .[24]

But he has also 'seen the bad model, where you have some geography graduate fresh out of university, who comes and pompously lays down what a complex organization should do, despite having no familiarity with the organization or its practices'. He believes that 'most changes should be made by those who understand how an organization works, from the inside'. And this, of course, is exactly what the consulting firms themselves do. They train their own from within.

There are many questions about the efficiency and efficacy of engaging these kinds of private firms at the very heart of government, particularly the many conflicts of interest. One day consultants can be advising on health care and public health systems, and the next day they can be selling soft drinks, tobacco, and pharmaceutical drugs. Another major concern is one of accountability, but for the purposes of this book, the key issue is the undermining not only of the expertise that exists but, perhaps even more importantly, of the ability of civil servants to acquire expertise as highlighted by Lord Agnew.[25]

So where does this devotion to generalism and disregard for expertise come from?

Managerialism and its discontents

From the 1960s both the political right and left in America and western Europe began to grow suspicious of authority premised on social class and expertise. This put experts and professionals at the centre of their critique. For the left, writes Jerry Muller, historian and author of *The Tyranny of Metrics*, 'to rely upon the judgment of experts was to surrender to the prejudices of established elites'. The political right on the other hand believed 'that public-sector institutions were being run more for the benefit of their employees than their clients and constituents'. Both positions may have been grounded in some truth. It was believed, writes Muller, that metrics would ameliorate the problem for all, including those organizations now under attack, by making 'institutions accountable and transparent, using the purportedly objective and scientific standards of measured performance'. Thus, he notes, the deification of metrics began.[26]

Philip Howard, a lawyer who has written extensively on government reform, suggests that the decline of trust in experts, and the rise in metrics and the accompanying bureaucracy, has down-graded the value of human judgement in decision-making.[27] As we will see in Chapter 5, one of the largest positive influences on employee job satisfaction is autonomy, namely, being able to make decisions. Howard believes the desire to exclude employee judgement and situational discretion in decision-making, particularly in the public sector, has become a 'theology' accompanied by entrenched practices embedded in excessive rules, over-regulation, and bureaucratization. All of these, Howard argues, are tightly wrapped up in metrics.

In *The Tyranny of Metrics* Muller explains that 'Reliance on numbers and quantitative manipulation gave the impression of scientific expertise based on "hard" evidence; it also minimized the need for specific, intimate knowledge of the institutions to whom advice was being sold.'[28] This became known, inappropriately, as 'scientific management' because of its dependence on numbers, which later became metrics and targets. Managerial 'expertise' was reduced down to a collection of skills and techniques, whereas 'expertise' had meant 'career-long accumulation of knowledge of a specific field, as one progressed from rung to rung within the same institution or business – accumulating what economists call "task-specific know-how"'.[29] This fuelled the rise and arguably the eventual dominance of managerialism, which replaced domain-specific judgement and reasoning with a flat, 'zero-barriers-to-entry' system apparently applicable in all industries, sectors, and companies.

As a result of this, respect for expertise has decreased, and in some cases disappeared completely. I cannot recall how many times I have been told that the findings from my research are 'counterintuitive' and 'not normal' because it does not chime with the dominant management culture which propagates the idea of the portability of talent and the generalizability of management practices. 'Really?' I ask, trying not to sound too Britishly sarcastic. 'It's counterintuitive to want a teacher to lead a school or a sailor to take charge of a submarine?' Unfortunately, many 'bean counters' have taken centre stage and, as Muller writes, 'corporate America morphed into the gospel of managerialism. The role of judgement grounded in experience and a deep knowledge of context was downplayed.'[30]

Yet, as we will see, successful work requires mutual satisfaction, benefit, and respect between employee and employer, and that only happens when the employer knows their business from the inside.

From bean sprouts to bean counters

Managerialism, metrics, process bureaucracy, and the rise of general managers all became prevalent in education, health care, policing, the military, business, and across government – first in the US, followed by the UK, and it has continued to spread across the globe.

In many cases what Muller describes as the 'metric monster' has taken over.

Metrics rely heavily on heuristics such as algorithms. These, mathematician Cathy O'Neil argues in her book *Weapons of Math Destruction*, can weaken democracy and reinforce discrimination and inequality, when used in the wrong way. She gives as an example the US school system's No Child Left Behind policy, where the intention was to close the 'achievement gap' between pupils but instead the misapplication of metrics led to unfortunate incentives with unintended consequences. Gaming the system to meet targets is a pattern that has been replicated across different kinds of organizations, and is something that many of us may recognize from our own workplaces, but O'Neil opens with a story about Sarah Wysocki, an outstanding schoolteacher, who fell foul of such metrics in a particularly dramatic way.[31]

Adrian Fenty became mayor of Washington DC in 2007. A key message of his campaign was the need to improve the city's constantly underperforming schools. It was assumed poor teaching was the cause of the problem, so in 2009 the mayor appointed a chancellor of Washington's schools, Michelle Rhee, whose job it was to remove failing teachers from the system. To do this, she devised a teacher assessment tool called IMPACT, and hired a consultancy, Princeton-based Mathematica Policy Research, to develop an evaluation program. Those teachers who scored in the bottom 2 per cent of the assessment would be fired. In just one year, 5 per cent, or 206 teachers, were kicked out. Sarah Wysocki taught in the fifth-grade in MacFarland Middle School. O'Neil points out that Wysocki should have had nothing to worry about. The reviews from her principal were excellent, as were those from her students' parents. 'One evaluation praised her attentiveness to the children; another called her "one of the best teachers I've ever come into contact with".' Sadly, Wysocki's IMPACT score, generated by the algorithm, was low. She was assessed to have poor maths and language skills, which represented 50 per cent of her total mark. The district duly fired her.

O'Neil notes that the Washington schools system was not seeking to penalize teachers per se. The belief was that using numbers was both objective and fair. But, she argues, a teacher's effectiveness cannot accurately be assessed through test results involving only thirty students, which, she comments, 'is statistically unsound, even laughable'. As Wysocki herself said, 'There are so many factors that go into learning and teaching that it would be very difficult to measure them all.'

The most important question, as hard-to-recruit teachers were being fired, was, what were the criteria the algorithm was based upon? Unfortunately, neither Wysocki nor the other sacked teachers were able to find anyone who understood – or would tell them – what went into the assessment criteria used in the algorithm, and why they scored so badly. But she knew, because she was told, several times, that it was very complicated and complex, inducing, as O'Neil points out, the common state of maths anxiety. The most disturbing part of Wysocki's story as told by O'Neil was that the consultants Mathematica were allowed to conceal their magic formula and maintain their secrecy. Mathematica claimed they had a right to corporate confidentiality, and if nobody knows its recipe then the assessment cannot be gamed.[32]

Despite being sacked for reasons she was never told, Sarah Wysocki quickly moved into a new job. After all, teachers are in short supply, especially ones that carry great recommendations from their former school principal. Wysocki went from a public school, attended by students in the greatest need of good teaching, to a school in a wealthy district in northern Virginia. 'So thanks to a highly questionable model, a poor school lost a good teacher, and a rich school, which didn't fire people on the basis of their students' scores, gained one,' O'Neil laments.[33]

It is not numbers that I am arguing against. The evidence I will use to convince you of the need to have credible expert leaders is rooted in quantitative studies. But organizations have become overly reliant on all kinds of targets and metrics. They do not pay enough attention to judgement, experience, and expertise, and this has led to the kind of crazy situation just described.

How did we land in this mess?

In trying to understand how we arrived at a place where metrics and managerialism cap expertise and experience, brothers Kenneth and William Hopper in their thought-provoking book *The Puritan Gift: Reclaiming the American Dream Amidst Global Financial Chaos* (2007) lay blame on a corporate culture that greatly deteriorated in the last third of the twentieth century. The authors trace the history of American management culture, originating in seventeenth-century New England through the 'great engine' companies, such as the railways, automobiles, and chemicals, that matured between 1870 and 1920, culminating in what they consider to be America's golden age of management between 1920 and 1970.

The traditional nineteenth-century manufacturing firm had been controlled and run by its founder and family members. As the market for goods expanded, through advances in communication and transportation, firms grew ever larger, which left the single founder boss struggling to cope. Responsibilities needed to be delegated to managers, and with this came a separation in the ownership and control of large US corporations.[34]

In a typical golden age company, senior executives often spent their whole career in the organization or industry, gaining deep knowledge about its core business, working closely and respectfully with its employees. Those who made it to senior management and up to CEO were 'from families of "moderate" means'. Most had 'worked their way' through college.

The authors single out a particular concept they believe conveys the essence of both corporate and non-corporate management during the mid twentieth century, then practised by the most successful companies:

'bottom-up' management was introduced by William B. Given in his book *People Working Together* (1949). Given wrote that it was the job of top management 'to create a sense of independence and freedom of initiative down through the middle management

levels' . . . 'if that is done successfully, the feeling spreads and the least important workers share in it'. Even the blue-collar work-force below the rank of foreman was, therefore, expected to become involved in decision-making.

What Given called 'progressive decentralization' was later claimed through the use of different terms such as 'participatory' management, 'distributed leadership', 'employee engagement', and many more. But it could have been called 'common sense management'. These early companies intuitively understood the link between high employee job satisfaction and high productivity, a link which is today supported by lots of research as well (see Chapter 5).

Importantly, under the style of management prevalent in these golden age companies, there was a clear hierarchical structure, where divisional heads were held responsible for any failures or weaknesses in return for being delegated responsibility and decision-making powers. The CEO made the corporate objectives clear, charted the strategy, and ensured it was followed. But it was also a time when the apocryphal post-boy could make it to CEO through sheer dedication and tenacity. Such a rise through the ranks is now much more unlikely in both the US and UK.

The Hopper brothers suggest that firms

'went far beyond the systematic delegation of authority that was normal and, indeed, inevitable in any well-run hierarchy; it implied that each manager was in the habit of passing some of his [sic] own responsibility for decision-making down the chain of command to the lowest level ready, willing and able to accept it' which, observed Given, 'gave a stimulating feeling of personal freedom to superintendents (factory managers), foremen, chief clerks – freedom to venture along new and untried paths; free-dom to fight back if their ideas or plans are attacked by superiors; freedom to take calculated risks; freedom to fail'.

This style of management was the norm in most of the top American companies, as the Hopper brothers write: 'IBM had defined the role of the manager as one of "assistant" to his subordinates ... [General Motors] introduced decentralized decision-making under Pierre du Pont ... Bottom-up management also flourished at Hewlett-Packard in its glory days.' Citing Dave Packard, they continue: ' "our success depends in large part on giving the responsibility to the level where it can be exercised effectively, usually on the lowest possible level of the organization, the level nearest the customer." ' Indeed, the authors suggest that the superiority of this kind of expert-managed corporation was what made America great.

Sadly, by the late 1960s the golden age identified by the Hopper brothers had come to an end under the influence of what they call 'the neo-Taylorite Cult of the (so-called) Expert'.[35]

Frederick Winslow Taylor was a management consultant, possibly even the first. Drawing on his so-called scientific management theory, Taylor had a major influence on manufacturing in the early twentieth century. He looked down on the working man, 'the factory operative was to be treated as a "grown-up child" and was "not supposed to think" '.[36] Taylorism sought to minimize the individual knowledge and skills of workers. The aim was, instead, to prepare people for mass-production processes that would be planned, supervised, and monitored by managers.[37] Rakesh Khurana, professor of sociology and leadership development at Harvard University, notes that 'Taylor's methods essentially served to cast managers as the brains of organizations and workers as the brawn, inviting all of the hierarchical implications suggested by that model.'[38]

The Hopper brothers summarize the effects neo-Taylorism had on the way organizations were managed. First, it brought about a weakening of the traditional chain of command. Second, it raised the status of (so-called) experts, the pseudo 'professional' managers who were primarily accountants. Third, benchmarks and metrics might now be used to assess and reward success, which also led to the rise of 'credentialism', where an MBA counted for more than the experience of those who had worked in a particular sector for many years. Fourth, the authors lament the loss of bottom-up management to top-down, where accountability was now so diffuse it was impossible, in Alfred Chandler's words, to 'pinpoint responsibility' so that any success was always claimed but blame was never accepted. This meant, fifthly, that without a natural line of command to hold individuals responsible, 'tsars' started to be appointed.[39] Finally, it kicked off the obsession with external management consultants. CEOs and senior executives, who did not understand the core business or the core employees, now needed to employ external 'experts' to perform the role that they could not, despite the fact that these so-called experts had never worked in the organization or managed anything themselves.[40]

The crucial core expertise and experience were gone; the whole disaggregated into countable, measurable parts, many that would soon be outsourced.

> Under the new regime, an effort would be made to evaluate and reward executives in terms of the personal contribution they had made to the success of their organization, disregarding the fact that each functioned as part of a system within a system.[41]

Knowledge and experience were reduced to a set of rules, measurements, and metrics by the new 'scientific' manager. The old holistic view of the firm narrowed into one focused entirely on profit and loss, and the emphasis on bottom-up management now became a preoccupation with the bottom line; the long view became short.

During the seventies business began to slow as the US share of world production fell from 40 to 25 per cent. American products had risen in price but declined in quality, in contrast to the superior cars, stereos, and television sets now piling in from Japan and Europe. As business slowed so traditional investors, who had been scattered and unorganized with no means of influencing senior executives, were gradually replaced by institutional investors, and this eventually led to a clash between the old management class and the new and powerful institutional bloc, which went from representing 15 per cent of the outstanding shares of companies listed on the NYSE in the 1950s to holding more than 50 per cent by the mid 1980s.[42] Today, institutions own around 80 per cent of the large cap (large market capitalization) S&P 500 index controlling $20 trillion worth of stock.

'After nearly a half-century of unchallenged supremacy,' writes Rakesh Khurana, 'senior management at many corporations faced a threat to its authority', and power was ceded from senior executives to corporate investors, who still dominate today.[43] Board directors, once loyal to incumbent executives, now caught the attention of shareholders and became central actors as institutional investors sought more control, and hiring CEOs became board directors' most important job.

By the 1980s a service industry replaced manufacturing, and deregulation created a harsher business environment that some, suggests Khurana, believed warranted a different style of headship. Focus switched to the individual CEO who was now a 'leader' instead of a mere professional manager. Thus, Khurana notes, began a new phase in succession 'that gave rise to the figure of the charismatic CEO, brought into the company from the outside, who now dominates the external CEO market'. He suggests they are a 'throwback to the swashbuckling Robber Barons of the late nineteenth century', only with sophisticated PR skills, adored by the brand new business press and army of stock market analysts. Ability was now assessed in terms of verbal skills and 'their personal characteristics or, more simply, their charisma'.[44] The 'corporate saviour' seduced and inspired, could be abrasive, brash, overconfident, and even flamboyant.

For the major corporations, insider CEOs were out of fashion, externals de rigueur – perceived to be the only ones savvy enough to cope with the fast-moving business environment that required a 'change agent'. Boards of directors, notes Khurana, were willing to pay their 'star' CEOs massive salaries, bonuses, and pensions – and golden handshakes if things didn't quite work out. Expectations were unrealistically high, so naturally failures were common. If investors became unhappy because dividends were low, pressure was immediately applied to boards to dismiss CEOs and a fresh search for the new corporation saviour began.[45] The UK followed the US. Margaret Thatcher swallowed up neo-Taylorism, and the next generation adopted managerialism, particularly Tony Blair, and neither Japan nor Europe have escaped it.[46]

Business schools have also come under attack. Some of the earliest British schools tailored their learning to the specific needs of the market for which they were providing a service. For example, the East India College (1806 to 1858) for colonial administrators, 'explicitly set out to train "civil servants", not "business people" or "managers"'.[47] A second early form, initiated in the 1900s, was the Workers' School (e.g. Mechanics' Institutes in Edinburgh and Glasgow),[48] often created by local industrialists to train their workers in scientific subjects, administration, technical drawing, reading, shorthand, book-keeping, and eventually accounting.[49] But from the 1950s onwards, observes Jerry Muller, 'the business school ideal became the general manager, equipped with a set of skills that were independent of particular industries'.[50] Domain knowledge education was replaced with general management training, designing curricula around a set of methodologies that could apparently apply to any field.[51] Thus, 'The disastrous concept of the wonderfully mobile "professional" manager – the person trained in a classroom who by definition could manage any kind of business (or indeed non-business) without knowing anything or much about it – had arrived.'[52]

Distinguished management scholars such as Henry Mintzberg, at McGill, Sumantra Ghoshal at London Business School, and Jeffrey Pfeffer at Stanford started to question the management theories being offered in business schools, arguing instead for the need to develop 'Managers, not MBAs'.[53] Mintzberg believed that the case study method 'trains people to provide the most superficial responses to problems' and, worryingly, 'it encourages managers to be disconnected with the people they are managing'.

Critiques of business schools that highlight various concerns have continued.[54] However, it is my hope that a greater recognition of the need for tailored management education is returning through the high number of master of science courses for different industries, including the leadership and management masters' for physicians that we run at Bayes Business School.

Management bla bla

Managerialism is described by business school scholars Robert Locke and J.- C. Spender as 'a phenomenon associated with membership in a specific group of managers that share specific attributes – a caste'.[55] This is reflected in the jargon used by members of the management class, who once sought to mimic the exclusive clubs associated with the many traditional professions, guilds, and trades.

Berkeley psychologist Charlan Nemeth suggests that companies inadvertently create a cult-like ethos through indoctrination, and other techniques, to try to generate loyalty and commitment.[56] Management jargon is a form of consensus programming, a tool of convergence, and the suppression of individual expression. 'Jargon masks real meaning,' says Jennifer Chatman of Haas School of Business; 'People use it as a substitute for thinking hard and clearly about their goals and the direction that they want to give others.'[57] Using management jargon is lazy. 'Think outside the box' should be firmly put into a box, locked, and buried; 'pushing the envelope' pushed out; so too 'square the circle', 'game-changing'; recently everyone is 'reaching out' and being 'impactful', which, in the view of *Journal of the American Medical Association* editors, should be reserved for instances of collision (i.e. a car crash). Does your workplace also spend money on generating organizational 'values' that you never knew existed or, worse, are not actually evident when you are at work?

The world has also developed a fixation with acronyms that denote 'I'm in the club because I know what it means'. More worryingly, they can deplete meaning from the bodies they represent. Take EDI, for example. Can there be any more important terms than 'equality, diversity, and inclusion'. When you speak these words, you can feel the emotion in your body. Yet all over the world acronyms like EDI suck out the significance and meaning, and in some cases disguise and neutralize uncomfortable truths about organizations.

Locke and Spender believe that

managerialism has done America great harm. No aspect of that harm is more pernicious than the role business schools have played in reinforcing the caste's sense of itself and the legitimacy of its predatory instincts done in the name of good management.[58]

Business schools have played their part in this unfortunate shift towards generic management. The academic field of business and management has expanded, and university researchers have had to drill down so deeply in pursuit of something new that they have sometimes become removed from the real world. Academic articles within my own field are often written in an incomprehensible style and with such complicated theories that even I don't understand, let alone the regular business people for whom the work is supposed to be relevant.[59] In recent decades leadership theorists have proffered a cornucopia of different ways in which leaders can supposedly become more effective. Based on his review of nearly a century of books, conferences, training sessions, and blogs on the topic, Stanford business professor Jeffrey Pfeffer found that most recommendations for effective leadership are based on the notion of developing certain personality and character traits. Unfortunately, in Pfeffer's view, and he is an expert academic, 'the leadership industry has failed', as 'there is precious little evidence that any of these recommendations had a positive impact'.[60]

Barbara Kellerman, from John F. Kennedy School of Government and author of *Professionalizing Leadership*, believes 'The leadership industry has failed over its roughly forty-year history to, in any major, meaningful, measurable way, improve the human condition.'[61] She has a point. A second one might be this: given the abundance of research into leadership, why is so little reliable and generalizable information known? Rarely if ever are generalizable lessons or statistical consistencies revealed that may be applicable to the majority of organizations, let alone individuals.

It is my hope that the line of research I have followed for many years, and that is explained in this book, might contribute to useful knowledge about leaders that *is* applicable to all and can be explained in one simple phrase: we need credible expert leaders.

3

The Case for Expert Leaders

I will now provide the evidence and make the empirical case for expert leadership based on over fifteen years of research in many different settings – from health care to manufacturing to elite sport to high technology; some of my research is co-authored.[1] The patterns I uncover show why we need managers and leaders who have acquired deep knowledge of their industry. To be an exceptional leader and manager requires a profound understanding of the business and a mastery of the core activity. Being able to walk the proverbial walk is critical: simply being a competent general manager is insufficient. This insight might seem an elementary one. Yet it has become lost in the fashion for generalists and generalism described in the last two chapters.

The valley of experts

In a report released in 2014, the UK headhunters Odgers Berndtson questioned whether academics 'are the right leaders of tomorrow' for universities. The search firm had no evidence to back up their shiny document and accompanying headline. Yet they were quite clear in emphasizing their unproven assertion that higher education will require leaders with skills 'honed in the business world'.[2]

If those in charge of Stanford University had taken the advice of Odgers Berndtson, it would have been a mistake on a colossal scale. Global advances in technology would be many decades behind and the consequences would eventually have been felt around the world. And here's why.

Frederick Terman grew up in an academic family that settled in Palo Alto, California, in 1910, having moved from Indiana when his father, a psychologist, took a job at Stanford. An early indicator of Terman's future career came at just seventeen when he constructed a Morse code transmitter on his own. To quote his biographer, C. S. Gillmor, 'Fred Terman built a discipline, a university, and Silicon Valley.'[3]

Terman, an extraordinary engineer who filed thirty-six patents between 1930 and 1947, was decorated by both the American and British governments after the Second World War. His Radio Research Laboratory created the technology to deflect enemy radar and communication, thus saving many lives. Terman had a stellar education, as an undergraduate at Stanford, then moving to Massachusetts Institute of Technology in 1924, to complete his PhD in electrical engineering, before returning to Stanford where he spent the rest of his academic career, holding many different leadership positions. The decision that would eventually transform the world for us all happened prior to the Second World War, when Terman convinced the university to set aside some unused land on the Stanford campus to allow industry to work in closer proximity with their engineers. Later, in 1951, when Terman was dean of the School of Engineering, he launched the Stanford Industrial Park, the precursor for what was eventually to become Silicon Valley.

William Hewlett and David Packard were graduate students in Terman's radio laboratory in the mid 1930s. Terman persuaded them to create a company and locate it at the park. Hewlett-Packard was soon joined by others including Varian Associates, Eastman Kodak, General Electric, and Lockheed Corporation.[4] David Packard recalls from his time as a graduate student:

One day Professor Terman remarked to me that many [firms] . . . had been founded by men who had little formal education. He suggested that perhaps someone with a formal engineering education and a little business training might be even more successful.[5]

Terman was describing expert leaders with a deep knowledge of engineering supported by business and management skills.

The entrepreneurs who created and ran businesses in the Stanford Industrial Park were the graduate students of the outstanding engineers Terman recruited to the university: 'here, for the first time, I saw young entrepreneurs working on new devices in firms which they themselves had established.'[6] Crucially, he believed that studying theoretical concepts alone was insufficient education; students also needed to learn how to build the electronic equipment they were studying and using.[7]

The founder of Silicon Valley had extraordinary vision, but he was *first and foremost* an academic researcher and teacher – exactly the kind of person the headhunters might have passed over. It was Terman's special kind of brilliance, in combining expert knowledge with management skill, that turned Stanford's School of Engineering and arguably the university itself into a globally recognized centre of research excellence and the envy of the world.

If Terman was the founding father of Silicon Valley, the person responsible for cementing its status and relationship with influential tech companies was John Hennessy. He was another outstanding scientist, and president of Stanford for sixteen years. 'Virtually all tablets, phones and smart devices run on a computer architecture developed by former Stanford President John Hennessy and his collaborator David Patterson,' read the Stanford News headline after the two scientists won the 2017 Turing Award.[8] Their contributions 'have proven to be fundamental to the very foundation upon which an entire industry flourished', commented Microsoft's Bill Gates.[9]

Stanford's faculty, graduates, and alumni have created just under 40,000 companies since the 1930s,[10] including globally known brands such as Nike, Cisco, Charles Schwab, Yahoo!, VMware, IDEO, Netflix, Tesla, and of course the inimitable Google, which, love it or hate it, has revolutionized the way we source information. Former Stanford graduate students and founders Sergey Brin and Larry Page have always recognized their intellectual roots. In February 2018, John Hennessy was appointed as the new chairman of Alphabet, Inc., Google's parent company.

Stanford University continues to be headed by a world-leading scholar, Dr Tessier-Lavigne, who is a specialist in brain development and repair.

Captains of scientific enterprise

Have other top universities around the world followed Stanford's example by placing great scientists at their helm? The answer is yes. I have done studies with datasets on universities around the globe. I started by looking at the position of universities in world rankings, and found a strong statistical relationship between the league table position of a university (as measured in the Academic World Ranking of Universities) and the quality and status of its president's reputation as a researcher.[11] Next, to demonstrate that the pattern wasn't accidental, I needed to be sure that the reverse relationship did not exist – that a university gets a high ranking for its research and then attracts a top scholar as president. Hence, I used data that made it possible to look at the performance of each university over a ten-year period. This allowed me to make the claim that a university performs better after it has hired a top scholar – a core business expert – to lead it. The best universities in different parts of the world – like MIT, University of Cambridge, Caltech, ETH Zurich, Nanyang Technological University – consistently hire outstanding scholars to lead them.[12] And this is why they do well and get better at what they do – producing outstanding research and teaching.

Despite these findings, some headhunters still would have us put non-experts in their place, or rely for the appointment of university presidents on academics who are diverted away from scholarship to administration at an early point in their career. In 2015 headhunters Parker Executive Search proposed for president of the research-intensive University of Iowa, Bruce Harreld, a consultant who had also worked at Kraft General Foods and Boston Market Company restaurants. Iowa's board of regents, who at the time included a social worker, a real estate developer, a retired farmer, a student, the president of an asphalt paving company, and someone from manufacturing, hired Harreld. They may well have understood their own fields, but none of them had core business knowledge of universities, teaching, or research. Yet they were given the responsibility of appointing a university president. I wonder how likely it is that a farmer or real estate developer would call on a professor of English when they had to fill an important role in their business?

Rodney Dieser, a senior academic in the School of Kinesiology, Applied Health, and Human Services at the University of Northern Iowa, argued in a local newspaper that only 'accomplished scholars understand the culture ... and know how to mentor, nurture and protect scholars so that they can conduct research'.[13] Dieser wrote:

> I have been a professor at the University of Northern Iowa for 15 years, a university quite different from University of Iowa. UNI is a teaching-oriented university, whereas the UI is a research-based university. UNI, like other teaching-based universities, is dependent on research-based institutions because teaching is founded on a body of knowledge created through basic or applied research. Textbooks, for example, capture years of research and attempt to transmit research-based knowledge in a way that makes sense to students who are beginning a vocation.[14]

Dieser and the other faculty staff who complained at the time Harreld was hired turned out to be right. An *Inside Higher Ed* headline in October 2020 read: 'Iowa president ending difficult term with early retirement'. This was following 'a controversial five-year presidency and a campus COVID-19 outbreak that sickened thousands of students, faculty members and staff members'.[15] As with so many ineffectual leaders, Harreld departed with substantial compensation, reported by a local paper to be $2.33 million.[16] Had the board of regents listened to their own faculty, this costly incident could have been avoided.

Luckily, when the board of the Australian National University (ANU) in Canberra hired its next head, it took a different approach. The university had declined in the rankings and according to

CREDIBLE

members of the academic staff had become bureaucratic and flabby. Many of its top scholars pushed the university board to appoint a great researcher. It apparently listened and duly hired as president Professor Brian Schmidt, one of Australia's most eminent scientists and winner of the 2011 Nobel Prize in Physics. Not only is Schmidt an outstanding astrophysicist; he also did his most important work at ANU.[17] The board promoted an insider to the top job, something that has become surprisingly rare in universities, partly due to the unfortunate widespread reliance on headhunters. ANU's slide down the university rankings reversed,[18] and in 2022 the QS World University Rankings placed ANU at no. 1 in the region of Oceania.

Business schools provide an interesting case study in the debate over generalist versus expert leaders as here there has been much discussion as to whether the best deans are scholars or business-people. Most MBA students assume the latter. They are attracted by the glamour of a famous businessperson and the (usually false) hope that his or her success might rub off on the school and by association their own careers. The former head of Wharton School, Patrick Harker, had little doubt, when I interviewed him, about which it should be: 'Deans from industry are a disaster. I have seen much money burned through top-down attempts to lead faculty … Unfortunately, most MBA students want Jack Welch to be dean.'[19]

My research endorses Harker's view. I looked at several business school league tables (such as the rankings published regularly in newspapers such as the *Financial Times*), and found that the best schools in the world are statistically more likely to be led by top scholars. Again, to insure against reverse causality, I used data that allowed me to look at the business school's position in the league tables years *before* a dean arrived, as with my prior work on univer-sities. And the relationship is clear – business schools go on to improve when they switch from having a dean who is a businessperson to having a dean who is a top research scholar. Deans and presidents who are at the top of their game set the bar higher for an institution, signal a focus on quality, and send an important message to other great scholars, who may be potential hires, that the culture will support them.

Harvard Business School (HBS) is possibly the most famous business school in the world. Historically, it has been led by deans who have been outstanding scholars, and as well as being home to numerous prominent management scholars, its educational programmes are heavily subscribed, and its home university, Harvard, is consistently ranked number one or two in world rankings. It is also the wealthiest business school in the world.

But can the extraordinary wealth and success of HBS really be credited to the scholars who run the place? There are those who would argue that the success of HBS is due to the fact that many of their alumni have become captains of industry who in gratitude for HBS's role in their success have sent boatloads of cash back to their endowment. But this is only partially true. If Harvard had not maintained one of the harshest tenure regimes in recruiting its faculty – where only the best receive an offer of employment – it would not have the outstanding faculty it has today. Nor would there be the mountain of celebrated scientific and medical discoveries accrued over the years, the books, research papers, etc.; and to the point raised above, nor would they have so many successful alumni able to make such large donations. Harvard's endowment is large *because* of its research success.

In 2020 HBS's revenues were $861 million on an endowment of $3.8 billion (Harvard's total endowment reached $53.2 billion at the end of 2021, sums that some people feel ethically are uncomfortably large). HBS prides itself on its commitment to fund academics' research internally. In this way, the school's faculty have 'the freedom to pursue the questions that interest them most and stay close to practice, generating insights that can help address the most pressing issues confronting businesses, organizations, and society'. The faculty, continues the school's chief financial officer, can then 'bring the learnings from these interactions back into the classroom. By informing their teaching in all the School's educational programs, their knowledge educates the next generation of leaders and influences the practice of management on a global scale.'[20] In 2021, in the middle of the pandemic, the 256 full-time faculty at HBS produced 668 cases and other course development materials, 491 books, articles, and working papers, and drew together 1,400 academics and practitioners in ten research conferences and symposia. This is the core business of academia. If the faculty didn't do this, there would be no 'product'. And if the scholarly excellence and outstanding research were absent, so too would be the stream of donations. Wealth is not a guaranteed measure of many things, including of scholarly quality. But the point I am trying to make is that the income streams, which are a marker of and in turn contribute to a university's success, have stemmed fundamentally from prior academic endeavour and brilliance.

Another important way a university president affects an institution's performance is through the quality of the people they select in the next administrative and scholarly tiers down. In universities, these include the academic departments. It is the heads of these departments who act as middle managers, overseeing the advancement of scientific knowledge on a day-to-day basis. Chairs (or 'heads of department') manage daily operations, hire faculty and administrative staff, ideally creating an empowering, supportive yet not overly regulated environment for research, which as I have found is crucial, and they work closely with senior university managers. Their role is particularly critical in research universities, which tend to be less centralized. An earlier study shows that it is management practised at the level of the academic department, not by the central HR functions, which matters most to research and teaching performance.[21] Like all line managers, they play a crucial role in supporting the scholars under them.

In our study my co-authors and I collected data on 169 chairpersons in fifty-eight US economics departments over a fifteen-year period. We looked at the change in a department's productivity *after* the chair had been appointed, to assess whether it had led to an improvement, a decline, or no change.[22] We compared this with the department head's own research output.[23] In all of our studies, where possible we try to make like-for-like comparisons on a level playing field. We do this by 'controlling' or neutralizing certain factors that might greatly affect a result. So, for example, if we were to compare the very wealthy Harvard with a less well-off institution, this would affect the result. Similarly, if one department is substantially larger than another, the results will be skewed by size.

Our research found evidence that the characteristics of an incoming chairperson have a remarkable influence on the subsequent research performance of the university department. Interestingly, it was not the quantity of articles published by the chair that mattered. Instead, and this is important, it was the quality of his or her own research work; specifically, if it had been recognized and cited by other scholars.[24] How in detail the chairperson's own high-quality research affected the work of the department will have differed across different departments. Our study could not adjudicate in a fine-grained way on that. In some cases it will have been because the high quality of the chair's own research set a standard that department members aimed to emulate; in others he or she may encourage them to produce a smaller number of outstanding articles rather than lots of papers per se, and in yet other cases the chair may have helped faculty members to secure greater resources.

In summary, prestigious universities get there by placing expert scholar leaders at the top and indeed throughout. Their presence sets the standard for the whole university. It spurs the kind of performance that can help us to avoid future financial crises, find solutions to climate change, and generate vaccines.

We will now look at the role that expert leaders can play in the important field of health care.

When physicians lead

During the peak of the pandemic the rapid development of effective vaccines helped to save lives and to alleviate some of the intense pressure clinicians and health-care organizations experienced around the world. The World Health Organization declared, in February 2020, that a vaccine against Covid-19 would likely not be available for eighteen months.[25] But with the extraordinary coming together of governments, university researchers, pharmaceutical companies, and regulatory bodies, the following month four vaccine candidates had already entered clinical trials.[26]

The pandemic pushed experts into the limelight. It also thrust them into leadership. This happened in hospitals, as many of the doctors I teach explained to me. Suddenly, clinicians were given new autonomy to make the kinds of decisions they should be making most of the time. While the coronavirus was all-consuming, Russell Durkin, then consultant in emergency medicine at the Royal Free Hospital in north London, believed that the pandemic also revitalized the National Health Service.

> Covid-19 has been the greatest example of change management that the NHS has seen since its formation. Barriers have been rapidly removed; organizations or departments have remodelled almost overnight; new ways of working have been trialled and tested; interdisciplinary specialty collaboration has emerged effortlessly.

The experts were finally at the frontline with enhanced powers and responsibilities, bureaucratic constraints were loosened to enable processes to flow more easily, there was spontaneity in the system, entrepreneurial and creative solutions were suddenly sought, the hierarchy in meetings was reduced and everyone encouraged to contribute ideas.

Sanjiv Sharma, medical director of London's Great Ormond Street Hospital for Children, has said that the pandemic tested the UK health-care system as never before, as with most countries. But he believes it is right that medical leaders were at the centre of the response. 'We have all seen good and bad examples of leadership over the past few weeks. Clinically led decision-making will need to continue when we switch services back to a new "steady state" in potentially resource-limited, Covid-19 affected environments,' he says.[27]

Sadly, in both the UK and the US physician CEOs are uncommon even though the benefit of having doctors lead hospitals can be witnessed through the extraordinary success of two physician-led hospital systems.

William Worrall Mayo was born in Salford, England, in 1818. He did chemistry at Manchester University, and eventually studied medicine in the US, where he emigrated in 1846. He started out as a pharmacist at Bellevue Hospital in New York City, but settled in the mid-west of America in Rochester, Minnesota, where he and his sons opened the now famous Mayo Clinic in 1864.[28] Nearly sixty years later, on 26 February 1921, his son William James Mayo was asked to give the keynote lecture that officially launched the now equally famed Cleveland Clinic, headquartered in Cleveland, Ohio. Toby Cosgrove, MD, its former CEO, explained in an interview that both institutions started in 'cornfields' located far away from Boston and New York, which were then the centres of health care, run by an old guard governed by traditional methods and with little interest in change. The cornfields, Cosgrove added, were also many miles from the control of central government and the main hubs for business. Thus the Mayo and Cleveland clinics were able to reinvent the delivery, research, and education of health care.

Both are non-profits. Both consistently share the top two positions in global hospital league tables such as that produced by *Newsweek* magazine.[29] But importantly, both have *always* been physician-led.[30] The relationship between being expert physician-led and high ranking is not a coincidence. On the Mayo Clinic website today are written the words: 'we are physician-led because this helps ensure a continued focus on our primary value, the needs of the patient come first.'[31] The Cleveland Clinic similarly displays: 'Since our founding ... Cleveland Clinic has been a physician-led organization because we believe this leadership structure facilitates patient-centered care.'

In *Newsweek*'s 2021 best hospitals ranking, 2,000 general hospitals are represented from twenty-five different countries. The Mayo Clinic sits at number one and the Cleveland Clinic at two.[32]

When I first examined whether those more highly rated were more likely to be led by physicians than non-medical general managers, I used the US News' Best Hospitals Ranking.[33] This separated hospitals into twelve medical specialties, and I looked at the leadership of the top 100 performers in cancer, digestive disorders, and heart and heart surgery. The personal histories of the 300 chief executive officers of these hospitals were then traced by hand and the CEOs classified into physicians and non-physician managers. I found a strong positive relationship between the ranked quality of a hospital and whether or not the CEO was a physician. Overall hospital quality scores were on average 25 per cent higher when the CEO was a physician compared with a non-medically trained manager.[34]

In 2008 Lord Ara Darzi, an influential Armenian-British surgeon at Imperial College London, produced an important report following a review of the NHS, at the request of the Labour government. Darzi put clinicians centre stage. He knew that if clinicians were not given more responsibility for the delivery of health care, and the necessary reforms, then improvements in the system would be slow to impossible.[35] Despite calls for clinical engagement in Darzi's acclaimed report, the number of medical managers in the NHS has not grown, and, remarkably, the number of physician CEOs in NHS hospitals stands at only 3 per cent.[36] And even though the Mayo and Cleveland clinics provide evidence of the value and importance of physician-led hospitals, the same is true in the US, the most expensive health-care system in the world,[37] where expenditure is now 20 per cent GDP up to $4.1 trillion or $12,530 per American.[38] Only around 4 per cent of US hospitals are led by physicians.[39] This contrasts with practices in Europe, where physician leaders make up the majority of senior managers, such as in Germany (71%), France (63%), and Italy (50%).[40]

Despite the relative absence of physician leaders in the UK and US, the empirical case in their favour has continued to grow. A group of US researchers were able to dig a bit deeper than my original study, to include various performance measures.[41] They collected data from both Medicare and US News on 115 of the largest American hospitals, and found that hospital systems led by physicians (compared with non-physician managers) have higher overall quality ratings, and across all medical specialties, but they also have better operating efficiency (e.g. use of hospital beds). Notably, the financial performance of hospitals managed by medically trained leaders was found to be just as good as those run by general managers. This is an important piece of evidence which flies in the face of the conventional wisdom that doctors should focus on patient care, and managers on the business side of things. A further study in 2014 found that the best-performing hospitals are those with a higher percentage of clinicians across multiple levels of management.[42]

The same question was put to data from Iran.[43] My co-author and I analysed the leadership of seventy-two Iranian general hospitals separated into private, public, and not-for-profit. Clinical leaders included mainly doctors but also a small number of nurses.[44] Again we found the same pattern within each type of hospital – the best performers were more likely to be led by clinicians. A 2016 study sought to review the evidence up to that point, and found that the majority of studies support the call to place clinicians into leadership, and specifically physicians (who are clinicians with a full medical degree).[45]

Hospital boards are another tier that benefit from clinical engagement. These are the bodies that govern hospitals, provide oversight, and select CEOs. The presence of physicians on boards has been shown to have a profound effect on hospital performance. Yet few are represented. The absence on boards of clinicians, and particularly physicians, is associated, empirically, with lower quality of care and patient safety, reduced overall health system performance, less efficient financial management of resources, and higher morbidity rates.[46] Even a small increase, 10 per cent, in the number of doctors had marked consequences for hospital outcomes such as higher-quality ratings and lower morbidity rates.[47]

Logic would suggest that core business experts are required on governing boards. It may be inappropriate to overfill boards with current staff,[48] but why not include great physicians, medical scientists, and nurses from other health-care systems? More and more research is now emerging that reveals how important it is to have frontline representation. There are found to be 'informational advantages'[49] that shape how strategic decisions are made when frontline experts are on boards. And it can greatly help with communication, from board members to employees and back, and can translate into cost–quality trade-offs. Importantly, if non-executive directors also include outstanding core business experts, then a board will know what questions to ask and will have a degree of autonomy. And this is the point of boards, after all: to challenge and ask difficult questions from the safety of distance, ideally with a good degree of industry knowledge. Governing boards play an influential role, but they are only as good as their membership.

Why, as I have so often observed, do public bodies fill their boards with seemingly inappropriate people in numbers that go beyond the need for democratic layperson oversight? Contrast this with the behaviour of the major management consultancies like Deloitte, McKinsey, KPMG, PwC, Boston Consulting, the same firms that non-medically trained CEOs frequently consult at high cost. Remarkably, although these firms produce numerous documents spouting the need for board diversity, there appears to be a complete absence of external non-executive directors evident in their own governance structures.[50] Because these firms misleadingly describe their employees as 'partners', it is often wrongly assumed that they are legal partnerships, which they are not.

The major consulting firms are, arguably, excessively homogeneous, but so many organizations go in the opposite direction. When experts like physicians move into executive positions, they bring with them at least a decade of medical education, and a working life of looking at issues through a patient-focused lens, understanding the intricacies, which can then feed into the development of a patient-centred strategy.

Hospitals are rapidly changing places that require knowledgeable leadership, but, as I discovered, there are even faster industries where high-performance is powered by experts.

Expert leaders in a fast-moving environment

If you have ever driven a Mercedes on the no-speed-limit autobahns of Germany, you will know that even at 85 miles an hour there will be cars going much faster than you. But the smoothness and comfort of the drive is hard to beat. This may explain why, although the first vehicles with the Mercedes-Benz badge were produced as early as 1926, by the year 2018 Mercedes-Benz became the largest seller of premium vehicles in the world when it sold 2.3 million passenger cars.

In understanding the story of this success some history is valuable. In 1976, after completing his PhD in engineering at the University of Paderborn in Germany, Dieter Zetsche was hired by Daimler-Benz. He was to spend the next four decades of his life with the same employer. In 1998 Zetsche joined Daimler's board and eventually became chair and CEO of Mercedes-Benz between 2006 and 2019. Dr Z, named in *Time* magazine's 2006 list of the 100 most influential people, reversed a decline in the fortunes of Mercedes-Benz by raising both the quality of their product and their customer satisfaction ratings. His successor, Ola Källenius, similarly began his career at Daimler-Benz in 1993 as a junior researcher. As the latest CEO and board chair, he is now responsible for the company's switch to electric vehicles.

Angela Shepherd became UK CEO for Mercedes-Benz Retail Group in 2019. She joined the company as a graduate trainee in September 1990 and worked her way up through dealer operations, aftersales, training, and network strategy. Shepherd acknowledges that 'Having been involved in sales and aftersales, worked closely with dealers, and held key leadership positions within the Mercedes-Benz brand, I'm fortunate to have gained a very broad, helicopter view of how retailers operate.'[51] This pattern of what can be described as informed internal promotion can be observed in different parts of Mercedes-Benz, including its retail arm and flagship Formula 1 or F1 Motorsport.

Formula 1 as an industry is worth approximately $6 billion in annual revenue.[52] It is made up of the organizations that construct the cars who are owned and backed by manufacturers such as Ferrari, McLaren, Mercedes, and Haas, known as constructor teams. Constructors are medium-sized companies that employ on average around 400 highly trained and highly paid people. They contract with numerous auto component suppliers because since 1981 they are obliged to build their own race car chassis, and often engines as well. Every season each team competes by entering two cars and two drivers into two championships, one for drivers, the other for constructors. Points are awarded to determine who wins the two World Championships through 'Grand Prix', reflecting its French roots dating back to 1894.

This is the most widely watched sport after the Olympics and football's World Cup, with around 500 million viewers. A higher finishing position, primarily a podium (first to third), generates more sponsorship and broadcast revenue. It is an expensive sport. Constructors need to raise around $300 million to compete in F1, and the top ten teams spend collectively around $2 billion annually.[53]

The Fédération Internationale de l'Automobile (FIA) imposes a great deal of regulatory restraint on the turbulence of F1 through the imposition of strict conditions that change every season, on all aspects of the teams: technology, resources, track, tyres, and drivers. Regulations are mainly used to increase innovation, and also to produce as level a playing field as possible for all the competing teams, especially when one is dominant in a particular season, as Ferrari and Michael Schumacher were in 2003. A key motivator for the F1 rule changes is the development of new technologies that may have a wider benefit to society, leading to improvements in road car efficiency. Earnings from the sale of spill-over technologies have benefited many of the recent teams: McLaren has an associated company, Applied Technologies, as does Team Williams.

Formula 1 racing might not seem very environmentally friendly, but because of the regulations imposed by the FIA, and the constant need to develop lighter, faster cars, the design process seeks to squeeze out every possible drop of energy from the fuel they carry. F1 cars can go from 0 to 60 mph in close to 2.6 seconds, reaching speeds of up to 223mph. To win, they have to move fast around tracks with many very sharp bends, and relatively few straights.

German engineer Ferdinand Porsche designed the first hybrid car in 1899. It used a gasoline engine to supply power to an electric motor that drove the car's front wheels. In 2014 F1 boss Bernie Ecclestone responded to accusations that motor racing showed little concern for climate change by introducing a rule that all cars must rely heavily on hybrid technologies (i.e. hybrid V6 turbo engines). 'Few people know that the current F1 hybrid power unit is the most efficient in the world, delivering more power using less fuel, and hence CO_2, than any other car,' said current head of F1 Chase Carey, when he announced that every part of F1 – the cars, on- and off-track activity – would have net zero carbon by 2030.[54]

Most of the technologies that make modern cars more fuel-efficient, and also safer, were originally developed for F1 racing. In the 1950s the Jaguar team were the first to use disc brakes, which replaced drum brakes, and now all cars have ceramic disc brakes. F1 pioneered the use of turbo charging to boost engine power. Active suspension was first used by top driver Ayrton Senna in the 1980s after being invented by Lotus founder and engineer Colin Chapman for use by his Lotus Team. Energy recovery systems, such as regenerative braking, particularly used in electric cars, enable the energy usually lost when we slow or stop a car to be used to recharge the battery. Kinetic energy recovery systems (KERS) is another energy storage technique. The McLaren team first utilized light-weight but super-strong carbon fibre in the 1980s, and the monocoque chassis, which made it possible to incorporate a vehicle's body into its chassis in a single, load-bearing piece instead of using many parts, was initiated by Lotus cars.[55]

Traction control systems help us control cars by detecting when a wheel loses its grip in adverse weather conditions. Sophisticated display systems and the incorporation of controls into steering wheels were directly lifted from F1. Williams first developed sequential gearing technology in response to Ferrari's introduction of the semi-automatic gearbox. Paddle shifters, which made gear change faster and smoother, were first used by the Williams team in 1991. Finally the extensive use of computer systems to control the management systems in our engines to improve performance and our driving experience, and to reduce both fuel consumption and emissions, has been current for years in F1.

All of these extraordinary manufacturing innovations have come out of F1 racing arguably as a result of expert leaders focusing resources on addressing the key issues which will improve perform-ance. And as a result it is perhaps not surprising that the most successful team principals are almost always expert leaders.

Torger Christian 'Toto' Wolff has been on, or close to, a racing track for his whole career as a driver, financial investor, and leader. Today he is CEO and team principal of Mercedes Petronas F1 Team and holds a 33 per cent share in it. In 2020 Mercedes F1 became the most successful team ever, surpassing the record held by Ferrari. Their British driver, Lewis Hamilton, holds F1's record for the most race wins, pole positions, and podium finishes (i.e. race finishes as one of the fastest three cars).

A principal is responsible for the day-to-day running of a constructor team, and they operate in a highly stressful environment which requires skilled and quick decision-making. The role differs across teams, but includes selecting the drivers, having the final word on technical issues such as how the car is set up, pit strategy, which gearbox or engine is used, and financial decision-making about sponsorship and team wages. Some famous principals, for example Frank Williams of Team Williams or Tony Fernandes of Team Lotus, owned and ran their own teams. Owner-leaders have extensive powers. In other cases, principals are hired by owners to manage their teams; one example is the British principal Christian Horner's relationship with the beverage company Red Bull, which invests around $83 million into the team.[56] At Red Bull, Horner has won ten F1 world titles – four World Constructors' Championships and six World Drivers' Championships.

Horner grew up around cars. He lived in Coventry, England, which was at the heart of the British motor industry, where both his grandfather and father worked. Horner was a former racing driver who like most drivers started his career in go-karts as a child before moving to professional racing. The celebrated German driver Michael Schumacher first raced around a karting track at four years old, becoming the youngest member of his karting club. British F1 rival Lewis Hamilton won his first go-kart championship at age ten. The first woman to race in F1, Suzanne Stoddart, was karting at eight.

The winning formula for success?

My colleague Ganna Pogrebna and I decided to find out who makes the best F1 team principals.[57] As with many sports, there is extensive accessible information about F1.

We collected data on the performance of every team in every Grand Prix season from the start of the industry in 1950 over six decades of the F1 World Constructors' Championship to 2011 (sixty-two seasons). This generated a total of 19,536 car entries in 858 races, from 106 constructor teams. We also collected background information on the team principals of all F1 constructors (e.g. Ferrari, McLaren, Williams, Haas, Mercedes) for the same sixty-year period, 1950–2011.

Our dataset enabled us to measure exact organizational performance linked to constructor teams and principals. We used podium positions (i.e. teams coming in at 1 to 3 in a race) because they award the highest number of points. We included the starting and final positions of all cars that participated in each race; the constructor teams; their leaders' names, personal information, and background; the drivers' personal information and background; information about each race circuit; and for some years, information on team budgets, the number of cars in each race, and the success of each constructor brand.[58]

To understand the different characteristics of principals, which then made it possible to create different measurable categories, we examined their depth of racing knowledge and prior experience in relation to their team's ultimate performance. We identified four distinct leader types:

- managers who are businesspeople and have often moved to F1 from a different, unrelated, industry
- engineers with formal degrees in fields such as mechanical engineering
- mechanics who have extensive practical technical experience in car building and mechanical repairs

- drivers who have usually raced competitively (in F1 and other competitions) from an early age.

What did we find?

Our research showed that the best way to stay in pole position (the jargon used in Formula 1 for the leading car) is to hire an F1 boss who spent his or her career in the driving seat or close to the track. Constructor teams led by drivers (followed in the ranking by mechanics) are more successful than teams headed by managers and engineers. Drivers' and mechanics' teams win more often, both in races and qualifying, and gain the fastest laps. Both types of people have spent the longest time next to the track, either on it or working beneath the bonnet.

The characteristic that is tied to the *most successful* team principals is having had a long competitive driving career. Remarkably, the leader's former experience in competitive racing is a better predictor of current organizational performance than the driving experience of the person who is actually racing for the team. Ten years of racing experience (instead of zero years) leads on average to a higher probability of the principal's team coming in first, second, or third in a race of 16 per cent. That is a huge difference, of course. And in the next chapter I discuss why and how that comes about.

From racetrack to superstar basketball

Another big-dollar sports industry is US basketball. Phil Jackson, who at 6 feet 8 inches is considerably taller than the average Formula 1 driver, is one of those basketball coaches who stands high in the fan rankings. As a basketball player he did twelve seasons in the National Basketball Association (NBA), winning NBA championships with the New York Knicks in 1970 and 1973. As a coach he has the highest winning percentage of all NBA head coaches and also holds the NBA record for the most combined championships, having won thirteen as a player and a coach. Jackson's playing has clearly informed his coaching.

Sports data are interesting for social scientists because there is little ambiguity about performance. You either win or you don't. It is also possible to find detailed data that can clarify questions that motivate heated discussions between fans, for example on the topic of who the best coaches are, those who played the sport competitively and professionally or those who did not. I sought to answer this question in US professional basketball.

In a study with Larry Kahn of Cornell University and Andrew Oswald of Warwick University, we measured the success of NBA teams in 15,000 basketball games led by sixty-eight NBA coaches in 219 coaching seasons between the years 1996 and 2003. Larry had previously found in baseball that managers (equivalent to head coaches in basketball) with the most experience and a strong past winning record, raised the performance of both teams and individual players.

Approximately one-third of the coaches in our study had never played NBA basketball; another one-third had played at that high level but were never all-stars; a further one-third had gone further and in their previous playing life had achieved the coveted all-star status. The latter category includes people like Lenny Wilkens, who is the all-time leader in wins for an NBA head coach. While all-stars are recognized as the best players, in our study we used a second measure of talent – total years of playing experience in the NBA. This is likely to be a mark of playing skill because of learning on the job, and only the best players are continually offered new playing contracts and thus the opportunity to play for many seasons.

In our comprehensive analysis we found that basketball teams won more games if they were led by coaches who were former all-star players or had long playing careers in the NBA. The effect of such expert leaders on winning percentages can be seen within the first year of a new coach arriving. For the typical team, the difference between having a coach who never played NBA basketball, and one who himself played five years of all-star basketball (approximately the average among coaches who were former all-star players), is estimated to be six extra places up the league table. In other words, hiring a former great player as a coach can create a major improvement in a team's performance.

In an innovative study that recorded 3,296 observed coaching actions by Pat Summitt, who was a former Olympic medal winner when she was a player, and one of the most successful coaches in NCAA basketball division one history, the authors Andrea Becker and Craig Wrisberg found that the single most common action chosen by her (happening 48% of the time in their sample) was 'instruction' and then 'praise' (14% of the time).[59] Thus the majority of Summitt's chosen coaching actions involved instruction, which is a clear indicator of expert leadership. It allows a former great player's knowledge to be passed through from the leader into their team's performance.

Let's now glance at the most popular sport in the world: football – also known as soccer.

Putting the boot in

During the years I have been researching expert leaders, one question routinely comes up: who are the best managers in the 'beautiful game' – a term made popular by Brazilian player Pelé – arguably the world's finest footballer. Generally the questioner already has a strong opinion, which my findings disprove. Importantly, this bears on the difference between hard evidence and anecdote. The depth of feeling held by most fans about their own clubs and their rivals naturally makes pundits of us all. But many wrongly think that it does not matter whether a manager him- or herself was a good football player. The data show that it does.

Johan Cruyff, a Dutchman and another legendary footballer, was an exemplary manager. Cruyff won an astonishing eleven trophies for Barcelona, and he is still the longest-serving boss in their history. However, his title as the club's most successful manager was topped by one of the players from his 'Dream Team',[60] Pep Guardiola, who won fifteen trophies as manager of Barca. Indeed, Guardiola, an outstanding midfield player with forty-seven Spanish caps (i.e. he was chosen to play for his country forty-seven times), is currently on track, at Manchester City, to become the most successful football manager of all time.

Pep Guardiola, and former Real Madrid boss Zinedine Zidane, typify the successful manager in world soccer. Second-rate players like José Mourinho – whom interestingly Cruyff criticized because he 'only cares about the result and doesn't care much for good football'[61] – are outliers in the world of successful soccer management. Mourinho, during a mediocre career as a player, lacked the requisite pace and power to make it to the top, and gave up to study sports science at university in Lisbon. Yet he is among the top ten football managers of recent years, having won twenty-five titles with the likes of Chelsea and Real Madrid.

Alex Ferguson, a tough Scotsman born in 1941, is arguably the world's most famous football manager. On the day he retired in 2013, after twenty-six years as manager of Manchester United FC (a record in itself), I was interviewed about him for BBC News.[62] A popular maxim is 'Those who can, do; those who can't, teach' (or manage). I was therefore prepared for the claim that Ferguson had not been a particularly good footballer. That tends to be a stock-in-trade response of critics who know of someone as a long-standing coach and yet are not old or wise enough to be aware of a person's earlier talent as a player. Yet as a player in the Scottish league, Ferguson achieved an average of *one goal every second game* throughout his professional career.[63] Such a record remains even today an extraordinary achievement.

It is a strange, but perhaps understandably human, fact that when people look at leaders (especially in as emotive a setting as elite sports), they tend to notice and overemphasize those people who are exceptions to a rule. In the case of football or basketball, onlookers also often lack the necessary depth of knowledge – partly because today's sports managers were inevitably playing decades earlier.

Look at the numbers. A back-of-an-envelope check shows that the managers of the ninety-two soccer clubs in the English football league were themselves playing professional football in senior clubs for an average of sixteen years. All, indeed, had played professionally.

Any person who makes it into a professional team is by definition an extremely talented player. Those who ascend to the pinnacle and are part of the Bundesliga in Germany, Ligue 1 in France, Serie A in Italy, or the Premier League in England are players at the top of the world's game.

Competition to become a professional football player is brutal. It starts young with a complex system of club-based and commercial football academies. The dropout rate is extraordinary. In England, only 0.5 per cent of children under the age of nine who are initially signed by elite football clubs will ever go on to play in an adult first team. Even at slightly higher ages, approximately three-quarters of the 12,500 young players, aged between thirteen and sixteen, in the English football academy system, will fail to make the grade.[64] Yet these young players are themselves among the cream of the whole English soccer-playing population. Self-evidently, only super-talented (and injury-free) players can make it as a professional foot-baller, so we should pay attention to the playing success of managers in the Premier League. If grocers and bankers (or grocer-bankers like Andy Hornby from Chapter 1) could be successful as the manager of Manchester United, they would be. But they aren't. Elite football clubs know their industry. Soccer is thus yet another area where expert leaders are crucial to success.

A kind of symmetry is worth noting here. It is between the matching of managers to clubs that they coach with similar teams for whom they previously played. When you look carefully at the facts, you notice that club managers usually end up in charge of teams that are comparable in quality and reputation to the teams in which they themselves once played. If you were a footballer in the Premier League or the so-called Championship (i.e. the Second Division of the English Football League), for example, then on average that is where you will end up being a manager. The correlation between good manager and good player was also identified in a 2002 study of British football data with 660 managers between the years 1992 and 1998.[65] It found that previous footballing experience, particularly having played internationally, seemed to significantly improve a manager's performance.

The one thing that remains a constant, however successful their track record, is that football managers are assessed by both club and fans on the basis of their most recent wins and losses, and it can take a relatively short run of poor performance by a team for its manager to be sacked. Though luckily being sacked by one club doesn't seem to put off other clubs appointing them. This in–out cycle is found in many other work settings where leaders are loved by the board one day and shown the door the next, so this is a good point at which to leave sports and look at a statistical study where there is information on almost every company manager in an entire country.

Every boss in Denmark

There is a pretty building, with walls that are mainly windows, on the Copenhagen waterfront in Denmark. It is the workshop where Gerda and Nikolai Monies run a jewellery company, Monies. Gerda and Nikolai, both classically trained goldsmiths, founded their company in 1973. Their extraordinary jewellery is bold and unconventional (and I personally spend way too much of my earnings on it). They have sons, Karl and Niels, who are both now involved in the family business, which has prospered. Not only is the company expert-led, the family has not lost its passion.

So let's look at what we can learn about expert leadership more generally in Denmark through a unique resource that allows researchers to study the details of the lives of Danish citizens and corporations. The Danish statistical agencies permit access to this data to assist valuable academic research, but before releasing the data they remove the names of people and companies. This allows researchers to analyse general patterns without being able to literally identify the name of any particular citizen X or business company Y.

It is therefore possible to follow the life course of a business (without knowing its exact identity) set up in Denmark and to find out who started it, who now leads it, the number of staff, the company's profits and losses, and more. If you want to understand commercial organizations, it is self-evidently best to gather and analyse as much information as possible about employees, up to and including the CEO. Yet that ideal is rarely possible in a typical country. However, Denmark is different, because of the way it is willing to release (carefully anonymized) data on its nation.

An increasing number of studies, across a range of social science disciplines, are today starting to make use of so-called administrative datasets and especially ones that are sometimes described as linked employer–employee databases. Such databases are only available in a tiny number of countries. Denmark is one. This kind of dataset really allows us to probe the question – Are generalists or expert leaders better for organizational performance? – because we can examine and compare each boss in every company for an entire country, and do it over many, many years.[66]

Administrative datasets have been collected for information purposes by government or quasi-government bodies. For example, the tax authorities in a country need to keep track of every person who is earning an income and every company that is making a profit. They want that information, and can legislate to get it, in order to be able to raise the tax revenue to keep the country going. Hospitals, too, need to keep track of all their past and current patients. So they create large databases for administrative reasons.

A linked employer–employee database is, again as the name implies, simply a dataset that records two kinds of information simultaneously. One is on the firms doing the employing; the other is on the people being employed. Hence information is simultaneously gathered on Person X (e.g. Gerda and Nikolai Monies) and the Company Z that employs that person (e.g. Monies Jewellery). It's the reason why these types of data sources are termed *linked*.[67]

Denmark has been more open than most in allowing researchers to use its administrative data records. It does this, however, on strict terms. Extreme confidentiality, enforced by potential legal penalties, is required from researchers. Why Denmark is OK with this, compared to most other nations, is not easy to say. Perhaps it's in the nature of a liberal society?

If we want to know who is a really good leader, and who is just OK, it is necessary to untangle the effect of the leader from the talents of the team with whom they work and the resources available to them. It is hard to make these calculations if the leader always stays put. A CEO might be blessed in the background with a brilliant team and lots of resources, so on the surface the results look good, but in reality that leader might be making little difference.

For this reason, observing so-called switchers is particularly useful. Researchers are keen on datasets – usually called longitudinal datasets because they follow people and companies through the years – that allow that. Once a CEO moves to work at a different organization, where perhaps the team is less strong and there are fewer resources, then we get a clearer snapshot of what that leader per se really adds to an organization. It is even more helpful, of course, to be able to observe a leader who moves repeatedly from one organization to another, and then on and on again. Lots of information then flows into the research. That reveals how a leader can add value – or not – across a variety of workplaces. But even if we have hundreds of leaders who only move once each, it is still possible to learn a lot more than in a dataset (say over a very short period of time) where no leaders move.

In our study of company bosses, we do not have access to the names of individual leaders, but we do know the following, among other things: a person's age, their sex, their level of education, how long they have worked in different industries in the past, whether they are Danish, and the region where they work. We also know a fair amount about the company they work for, including the number of employees, its profitability, which industry it is in, and so on.

We are, in this way, able to examine the details of all Danish firms between 2001 and 2019 in the following industrial categories: manufacturing, construction, trade and repair, hotel and restaurants, transport, financial services, business services, culture and sports. The dataset used in the study offers information on approximately 30,000 firms annually over a period of nineteen years. There is an advantage from using such a dataset. That is: generality. It is possible to draw conclusions about the statistically typical company.

To put that into perspective, this is a bit like calculating the average height or weight in Denmark. It tells you something literally true and accurate – though of course about the norm rather than the extremes. Alternatively, think of the example of research in medical statistics. That kind of research tells us how an average person is negatively affected by smoking and is positively affected by exercise and eating fruit and vegetables.

And all of that medical research is also done with anonymized datasets.

The contribution of our Danish study of business leaders is that it is the first analysis of its kind to be able to:

- control for the innate characteristics and ability of CEOs
- draw upon longitudinal data on the organizations from an entire nation (in this case the country of Denmark)
- track the career histories, and the personal details, of the CEOs studied.

So, what exactly do we end up learning? How much of an organization's profitability is due to expert leadership?

The return to expert leaders

To calculate that, we obviously need to do some form of comparison of a low-expert leader compared to a high-expert leader. This is done using statistical methods – ones almost exactly the same as medical researchers use to understand links between health and people's lifestyle choices – that make it possible to draw reliable inferences.

Our substantive finding can be stated concisely. We estimate that *every fourteen years of extra CEO industry experience adds approximately one extra percentage point to the annual rate of return on a company's assets.* Perhaps this effect – which in everyday language tells us about the consequences for bottom-line profit – does not sound particularly large. But it is. As background, to put the number into perspective, it is important to know that the typical rate of return on assets in this sample of Danish companies is approximately 4 per cent per annum. Hence one extra percentage point really matters. On this kind of calculation, one-quarter of the whole profitability of a typical Danish company can be attributed to a leader having fourteen more years of additional expertise. This is on top, naturally, of other things that go into the make-up of a profitable company (like being in an inherently booming sector, having a strong brand and a long history of success with customers, and so on). Various influences will matter. But it is remarkable that a single person (the CEO) can make such a difference. Having an expert as a leader pays a handsome return.

Now that we have an understanding of some of the research underlying expert leadership, let's examine exactly how expert leaders influence their organization's performance.

4

How Expert Leadership Works

A ship's crew which does not understand that the art of naviga-
tion demands a knowledge of the stars will stigmatise a properly
qualified pilot as a star-gazing idiot, and will prevent him from
navigating.

Plato, Republic, Book VI

The evidence underlying the principles of expert leadership clearly
shows that organizations led by specialists in the core business
perform better than those that are not. And this has been found to
be the case across all types of businesses. But *how* do expert leaders
achieve organizational performance? What are the mechanisms
through which they influence those around them? And what is the
nature of the deep expert knowledge that brings intuition and
perspective to decision-making?

To clarify, the core business is the primary or underlying activity
or purpose of an organization. The core business of a high school is
to educate students. As the world's largest seller of smartphones,
South Korean firm Samsung's core business is electronics. For
Tottenham Hotspur FC, it is to win football championships.

Teachers in schools, lawyers in law firms, journalists in newspapers, carers in care homes are all core workers, without whom
their organization simply *could not* function. Core business experts
should be running the organization, be present at board level and in
middle management. Other non-core functional areas such as HR,
IT, and finance should also be led by experts in each of these domains,
supported by adequate knowledge about the industry and the business. But ultimately they exist to support the core business, not

dictate its direction. It would be unwise to put a marketing expert at the top of a tech company, as Apple discovered to their cost.

'But what about when X led Y . . .?' I can hear you say. There will always be outliers, but the expert leader pattern is based on a great many studies. The empirical evidence is reliable and generalizable to many different work settings.

Acquiring expert knowledge

Perhaps you remember the gripping true story of the so-called Miracle on the Hudson where a veteran airline captain managed to set his engineless passenger plane safely down on the river. The pilot, Chesley Sullenberger, known as Sully, encountered a situation that was not in the books: both his engines hit a flock of geese at low altitude after taking off from New York en route to North Carolina. The US Airways flight emergency manual did not have a checklist for the loss of both engines in a fully laden Airbus A320 at low altitude over a densely populated area. Sully evaluated his options in real time, with no power to his aircraft and with many passengers in his charge in what had become the world's most frightening glider. He could either return to LaGuardia, divert to Teterboro Airport in New Jersey, or attempt a water landing on the Hudson River. All options in principle were impossible. The plane did not have the power to reach either airport. Landing the Airbus on the river was extremely risky at best, perhaps insane, but there was no other choice. It seemed inevitable that enormous numbers of people on the plane would perish.

They didn't.

Deep expertise saved them.

To say that Sully was an expert in the core business of flying would be an understatement. As a boy he had constructed model aeroplanes. He had graduated with a BSc from the US Air Force Academy, and while still training had been awarded the Outstanding Cadet in Airmanship award. He had flown Phantom jets in the US Air Force at speeds you and I can barely comprehend, and clocked up decades of flying in military and commercial service. He was an experienced glider pilot and had served on accident investigations. Perhaps it even did no harm that he was a member of Mensa, the society for high-IQ individuals, when young.

Sully had to decide, instantly and under the most extreme pressure, what to do about a situation for which there were no rules and – this is important – no training. Deep intuition took over in that crisis moment. His words, spoken later, are instructive: 'For 42 years I've been making small regular deposits in . . . [a] bank of experience . . . On January 15, 2009, the balance was sufficient . . . [that] I could make a very large withdrawal.' Experience cannot be taught. It comes from a process of trial, error, practice, learn, trial, error, practice, learn. Experience builds profound intuition, whether one is in charge of a large organization or an aeroplane full of passengers.

The concept of 'expert knowledge' is very old and was originally used in engineering and the natural sciences. It not only involves a deep understanding of the core business: when a leader has expert knowledge, decision-making is informed by hard-earned expertise, by intuition, domain knowledge and experience, and years of practice and patience.[1] It combines explicit knowledge from formal learning with tacit knowledge from experience and wisdom,[2] and it profoundly influences how the person who has it perceives the world.[3] Expertise is not an on/off mechanism. Nor can expertise be acquired by reading about what others did. It is absorbed through doing and dealing with the same or similar situations multiple times. It is what a probation officer with decades of experience working with ex-offenders calls on when he is trying to anticipate how those in his care might behave.

Experts differ from non-experts in a number of ways. Their knowledge is represented and bundled differently in the brain; and they tend to think more holistically about problems, for example to step back and think about how a small snag might be caused by a bigger problem.[4] A combination of both explicit and tacit knowledge is essential to those who become leaders and managers. It influences decision-making and, therefore, performance.

Expert knowledge is tied to the core business of an organization in two ways. First is ability in the core activity. Is the person being promoted into a line management position good at the primary role? Could the engineer who is now my boss do my job and to a high standard? This is particularly important for line managers. If people are promoted to manage others because they can talk-the-talk to the senior executives, or no one knows what else to do with them, it can have a negative effect both on the people they manage and for the business as a whole. Yet it is not uncommon. As the research on university leaders and heads of departments described in the previous chapter shows, using data spanning ten and fifteen years respectively, those heads who were the least successful scholars in the first part of their career went on to become the least success-ful leaders. Their universities and departments performed poorly compared with institutions led by good or outstanding scholars. The evidence is clear: to achieve high-performance you must train and develop your best experts into leaders.

Alan Whittle is now director of strategy and planning at Inzpire Limited, a medium-sized company that produces support systems, training programmes, and devices for airborne military missions. These products are, the company highlights, 'designed by aviators for aviators'. On their website it says that the Inzpire team collect-ively has 'in excess of 430,000 flying hours, 850 years of engineering experience and more than 4,500 years of military experience', signalling their expert knowledge. Inzpire emphasizes its credibility by advertising the fact that it was started and run by operationally experienced ex-military personnel. As the company has grown from three people to 250 employees, so its distinct business units have always been led by 'suitably qualified and experienced people'. Whittle recognizes that 'Employee morale and customer confidence remain high only when senior managers have a specialist back-ground, with deep and tacit knowledge, and fully understand the challenges of the domain they operate in.'[5]

The second component of expert knowledge is industry experi-ence, the amount of time a leader has worked in his business or within a particular sector. As I outlined earlier, until the 1980s having both industry and firm experience were prerequisites for moving into leadership. Then things changed and boards became obsessed with what Rakesh Khurana described as the quest for a charismatic leader,[6] who in the eyes of some hiring boards only ever seemed to exist outside the firm. Khurana showed that over the period 1980–96 approximately 27 per cent of CEO successions at large corporations were taken up by outsiders. By 2000 that number was close to 50 per cent, and by 2021 55 per cent of CEO replacements were external.[7] So the trend is not going away. Another factor linked to hiring charismatic external CEOs is the remarkable rise in salaries. The ratio of average CEO earnings to average workers' pay in the US went from 24:1 in 1965 to 262:1 in 2005.[8] By 2021 CEOs made 299 times more than their average workers.[9]

Prior to the eighties outsider successions were rare. The dominant principle was that CEOs needed firm-specific skills and expert knowledge. Khurana believes that 'Recourse to the external CEO market, in short, too often undermines a firm's stability, emphasizes short-term share-price increases at the expense of long-term strategy, and undermines the loyalty of the senior managers who are the most promising internal candidates.'[10] Insider CEOs are known to stay longer and leave their companies with higher shareholder returns, which is another tangible way expert knowledge contributes positively to leadership performance.[11]

The appeal of charismatic leadership is evident not only in large corporations. It has spread into many areas of employment, including the public sector. Former school head Tom Rees ran a study with researcher Jennifer Barker to analyse the terms used in advertisements placed in the UK media to hire school head teachers.[12] They found an abundance of phrases such as 'seeking dynamic, charismatic and innovative leaders' accompanied by bold and pithy statements like 'culture is king' or 'leadership starts with vision'. Instead, Rees suggests, when hiring a head of school we should be looking for a history of excellent teaching experience and educational knowledge, coupled with personal leadership and management skills. This is because 'the main purpose of school leaders is to enable effective teaching to take place. We should therefore, be looking for good teachers to become school leaders.'[13] Yet generic leadership concepts, which often mean nothing without context, have been normalized across all kinds of professions and enterprises and distract from the core business. According to this approach, it is as if the actual field or profession a manager or leader works in has become irrelevant.

Not only our research but also experience suggests otherwise.

Nick Grey is founder of Gtech, the firm that designed the first cordless vacuum cleaner. In 2012 the company had a turnover of £4 million. At this point Grey had to address a hard decision faced eventually by most entrepreneurs: whether to grow or not. He chose growth. He recruited a chief financial officer (CFO) who advised him that he needed to put a proper executive team in place, supported by additional bureaucracy and administration. Nick Grey duly followed the advice of the CFO. Gtech benefited for a few years until 2017, when Grey realized that 'bureaucratic creep' had engulfed Gtech's work environment, and at a high cost. Gtech was spending £1.7 million a month on marketing and overheads, which was turning profits into losses. Grey stepped in and restructured the company. He had allowed non-core business people to take control of Gtech's strategy and processes. Grey knew the company 'had to return to our roots and focus on customer service and the performance of our products'. In other words, it needed to let the core business once again power Gtech's corporate strategy, management processes, and work environment. And profits at Gtech have now been restored.[14]

There are, of course, many variables involved in business success and failure, including factors that may be out of our control. There are, nevertheless, identifiable empirical patterns evident in those firms that maintain success. The firms keep their eye on their core purpose and on the people necessary to achieve it.

The mechanics of expert leadership

I believe there are five main ways in which leaders and managers with expert knowledge influence the performance of teams, departments, and organizations:[15]

1. Expert leaders are able to develop a clear sense of purpose, and this shapes their organizational strategy, which is aligned with the core business.

2. They take the really long view, reflected in their investment in R&D, and pursue sustainability with a parallel commitment to excellence.

3. They create productive work environments by setting appropriate goals, giving informed feedback and evaluation, and developing employee careers. This means a work environment that is open, empathic, encouraging of innovation, and collaborative, so that employee job satisfaction is high.

4. Expert leaders themselves perform to a high standard, and this creates an exemplar that sets the bar high for existing workers, new hires, and internal promotion.

5. An expert leader signals excellence like a quality beacon to potential new talent, to non-executive directors, donors, investors, and the market.

I will now explore how these qualities and skills manifest themselves day to day.

The art of navigation

We humans have a natural tendency to want instant gratification and are often prepared to pay a premium for it. Uncertainty about the future and impatience lead us to place more weight on 'today' and less weight on 'tomorrow', but short-termism has major negative consequences, particularly when we only spend, and fail to save or invest. The climate crisis has come about in part because of this human characteristic. Despite scientists telling us what will happen if we do not act, we continue to bury our heads in the sand and let non-experts lead us into the desert.

The long view also gets short shrift from most company boards. Public companies are particularly susceptible to being pressurized by shareholders who now routinely demand quarterly dividends. This makes it hard for firms to pursue long-term strategies. Short-termism challenges the sustainability of businesses, threatens their competitiveness and puts entire economies at risk, as witnessed in the events that caused the 2008 crunch, which included financial institutions recklessly doling out sub-prime mortgages in pursuit of fast but unsustainable profits.

Investors deploy a number of tactics to enforce a swift payback, such as tying executive remuneration to short-term performance goals and removing senior managers and leaders if they fail to immediately deliver investor expectations. Among the largest listed companies in the UK, the CEO is re-elected annually.[16] That might partly explain why respondents to a survey by consulting firm EY cited short-termism 'as a significant or major impediment to the growth and development of the British business'.[17]

One of the first changes that Paul Polman made when he took over as CEO of the Anglo-Dutch company Unilever was to abolish quarterly financial reports and earnings guidance. He did so because he believed that it shortened corporate timelines. A study by the *Accounting Review* (journal of the American Accounting Association) analysed the effects on companies who were forced, by the US government, to change to quarterly financial reporting. It found that shorter reporting intervals 'engender managerial myopia which finds expression in a statistically and economically significant decline in investments along with a subsequent decline in operating efficiency and sales growth'.[18] Geoffrey James, a contributing editor of Inc.com, believes

the reason is simple. Frequent financial reporting forces executives to think short-term rather than long-term . . . By contrast, when investors are kept a bit more in the dark, executives are more likely to make wise decisions that will improve the long-term health and viability of the company.

This was exactly the motivation behind Paul Polman's decision: 'We needed to remove the temptation to work only toward the next set of numbers . . . We have moved to a more mature dialogue with our investor base.'[19]

Shareholder-imposed short-termism often means that long-horizon investments in R&D and human capital are abandoned. This can result in limited financial support for staff training and recruitment, and during economic slowdowns high levels of redundancies may be used to cut costs quickly to maintain shareholder returns.[20] In March 2022 the British CEO of P&O Ferries, Peter Hebblethwaite, sacked 800 seafarers without notice. He replaced them with cheaper agency workers. That corporate decision backfired when suddenly many of their ships were grounded due to no longer being considered seaworthy by government safety inspectors. Why? Because the ships had lost too many of their skilled seafarers to be allowed to leave port.

Taking the long view

Some firms have resisted the temptation of short-termism and have duly reaped the benefits. 'Emerson Electric (EMR) outpaces Stock Market gains', read a Nasdaq headline in April 2022. Its performance has been exemplary, with an almost uninterrupted rise in profitability over the last sixty-five years. Emerson is a $16.8 billion Fortune 500 global technology and industrial software company providing automation solutions and commercial products, for example, in heating and ventilation. It has 83,000 employees and works in 200 locations worldwide.

Emerson was established in St Louis, Missouri in 1880. There are two facts of particular note. First, the company is on only its *fourth CEO since 1954*. Each spent almost his entire career at Emerson prior to becoming CEO. And the three that preceded the current head, Lal Karsanbhai, who joined Emerson in 1995, *each did the job for twenty years*.[21] Two decades as CEO; imagine the kind of stability and opportunities to plan strategically this offers.

A second notable feature about Emerson is that, while it has greatly expanded and diversified its business, it has not moved too far from the kinds of products that it was manufacturing in 1892, when it was the first company to sell electric fans to Americans. Thus it has stayed true to its core business, as is perhaps signalled on its website through the statement, 'Success requires a deep understanding of the challenge.'[22]

An interesting contrast is provided by the story of General Electric under the leadership of Jack Welch, who trained as an engineer and was in the CEO role at GE for twenty years. Incorporated in 1889 as the Edison General Electric Company, Thomas Edison would not have recognized the company under Welch.

> GE's breath-taking growth under Welch was fueled in large part by its transformation into a financial services superpower. By 2000 nearly half of the company's revenue – $96 billion – came from GE Capital, its lending and insurance arm, and it dwarfed all of GE's other units.

So writes Quartz journalist Oliver Staley.[23] In that same year, when drawing up its list of the top 500 US companies, Fortune discovered that less than half of GE's profits came from manufacturing, and therefore reclassified it under 'financial services' over loud but unavailing protests from its then 'celebrity CEO', Welch. Welch appears to have been so removed from both his and GE's engineering roots that the company joined the high-tech revolution way too late,[24] despite acquiring a French computer company, as Kenneth and William Hopper write, 'in a bid to rival IBM in the emerging field of electronics'. Unfortunately, the general manager of GE put in charge 'spoke no French and knew nothing about computers', which cost the company $200 million. During this period GE also ran down its historic research centre at Schenectady, which for fifty years had been 'the spiritual center of the company'.[25] By 2000 there were only seven engineers among the company's 175 senior executives.[26]

Unlike what happened to GE, the guardians of Emerson successfully navigated their way through turbulence and growth over many

decades, always retaining proximity to their company's core expertise. 'Welch', writes Michael Schein, CEO, MicroFame Media,
'relentlessly hammered home the supremacy of one central concept
– the importance of change.' As his oft-cited quote suggests:
'Willingness to change is a strength, even if it means plunging part
of the company into total confusion for a while.' His obsession with
change meant that departments and people that weren't making
money were ruthlessly cut and replaced with something new and
often completely different. Schein continues:

> While it's clear that standing still is never an option, many entre-
> preneurs and business owners have used Welch's advice as license
> to get rid of their most vital processes, values and even people
> without considering the bigger picture. For example ...
> companies have gotten rid of well-functioning operational,
> marketing or sales models for no other reason than to demon-
> strate that they were engaged in change.[27]

Instead, Schein suggests to companies: 'Amplify what you already do
best.'[28] This is arguably what Emerson Electric has done.

Firms are bought, sold, die, and start up all the time. But companies
with long lives like Emerson are scarce in both the US and UK.
Since the early twentieth century, the average life span of a top
American company listed in the S&P 500 index has dropped from
sixty-seven years to just fifteen.[29] A similar pattern is seen among
British businesses, which saw the loss of three-quarters of FTSE
100 companies in thirty years.[30] Corporate short-termism is less
common in Japan, where they even have a term, *shinise*, for long-
lived companies like Honda, for example.

Soichiro Honda was born in a small village near Mount Fuji in
Japan in 1906. As a young man he fixed bicycles in his father's repair
shop, then began an apprenticeship in Tokyo when he was fifteen.
He was a talented mechanic whose technical skills flourished after
opening his own business. Soon Honda was manufacturing piston
rings for engines, and after the Second World War he created the
Honda Technical Research Institute, which is where in 1946 his

motorized bicycles became motorcycles with engines designed by him.

Soichiro Honda was intrinsically motivated. His own technical expertise, innovation, and above all love of engineering drove Honda's corporate strategy in all senses. As an expert leader he stayed centrally engaged, even test-driving new vehicles right up to his retirement, in 1973.

In Japan there are 20,000 *shinise* – firms that have existed for over 100 years, and one hotel even exceeds 1,000 years. When asked why Japanese enterprises survive so much longer, Makoto Kanda, a professor from Meiji Gakuin University, explained that the businesses tend to be small, mostly family-run, mainly Japan-based, they avoid mergers and acquisitions, and, importantly, they are focused on a 'central belief or credo that is not tied solely to making a profit'.[31] Germany has similar corporate practices and it too has numerous companies that have survived over many years; famous names such as Daimler, Siemens, Deutsche Bank, Bertelsmann, and Robert Bosch have been around since the mid nineteenth century.[32]

Innovation fuels growth in companies and national economies, and it will be required in bucketloads to slow and protect against the climate crisis. But to innovate we need to take a long view, which requires patience and time, the time to test for success and time lost on the many inevitable failures on the way. Expert leaders are more tolerant of this process. One of the primary drivers of innovation is R&D expenditure. CEOs with graduate degrees in the STEM subjects tend to invest more in R&D than those with professional degrees in law or management.[33] Expert CEOs who ascend the ranks of their companies (e.g. Microsoft's Satya Nadella and Adobe's Shantanu Narayen) use their deep industry experience to channel the fruits of such R&D spending, pioneering lucrative cloud business and digital marketing services to increase corporate growth and profitability in their companies.

Similarly, technology-based companies like 3M have harnessed this general principle to drive their results: 'In terms of product development, CEOs and top executives at 3M have usually been part of new-product management teams before advancing to the upper echelons of the firm,' affirms Vincent Barker, commenting on his study of CEO characteristics and R&D spending.[34] 'This ensures that they understand the innovative process that drives 3M's fortunes.' The continued prevalence of technically credentialled leaders has helped power Silicon Valley's dominance, while a reliance on general managers over technical experts in the American automotive industry helped it lose market share to Germany and Japan.[35] The big three – General Motors (GM), Ford, and Chrysler – collectively controlled 90 per cent of the US market in 1965, but only 45 per cent by 2015.[36] Indeed, in the first quarter of 2005, GM lost $850 million. Its stock crashed as did its revenues, and cashflow fell from a positive $2 billion to a negative $2 billion. By the 2008 financial crisis both GM and Chrysler were on the brink of bankruptcy, requiring federal government support, which topped $50 billion.[37] Today, Toyota sits at the top of the world auto ranking, with Volkswagen and Daimler placed second and third.[38]

Developing a long-term perspective, as adopted by Daimler Benz with roots going back to the 1880s, facilitates bold (but not reckless) growth strategies which are less vulnerable to financial downturns and disruptions. Expert leaders are more attuned to adopting the long view partly because they have tenacity and draw on intrinsic motivation. This notion was expressed by psychologists Beth Hennessey and Teresa Amabile as 'the drive to do something for the sheer enjoyment, interest, and personal challenge of the task itself (rather than solely for an external goal)'.[39] Passion doesn't pay the bills, however, and money is still a vital extrinsic motivation, even for the ardent expert. This is especially so if you are trying to drag an expert employee from his or her first love of engineering or graphic design, into a management role that they are unlikely to regard with the same enthusiasm. Incentives of different kinds must be built in, as we will discuss in Chapter 6.

Boss competence and performance

While General Motors followed the mantra of Alfred P. Sloan, their president in the first part of the twentieth century – 'We are not in the business of making cars, we are in the business of making money' – their competitor, Toyota, instead concentrated on making great, affordable cars.[40] Incredibly, at the end of the Second World War Japan's auto industry was almost completely destroyed. In 1949 Toyota was on the brink of bankruptcy, and in 1950 it produced only 300 vehicles.[41] Yet, less than ten years later Toyotas, Hondas, and Datsuns rolled into the US in big numbers, and by 1975 Toyota was the most popular imported car in the United States.[42] During the 1980s the success of foreign manufacturers began to bite the accountancy-infused, metric-obsessed Ford, Chrysler, and GM, who lost out hugely to foreign firms. Their competitors, headquartered primarily in Germany and Japan, instead focused on engineering and common-sense management. The senior managers in US auto firms had no knowledge of engineering, and no interest in what happened under the bonnet or 'at the coal face',[43] whereas their counterparts at Toyota spent a great deal of time there, at what was called the *gemba* or 'real place', 'the point where value was created'[44] – the place the core business happens. 'For the Japanese,' wrote the Hopper brothers, 'the key to successful *kaizen* (or continuous improvement) is to go to the *gemba*, work with the *gembutsu* (the actual thing, i.e. the relevant tools, materials, machines, parts and fixtures) and assemble the *genjitsu* (all the relevant facts).'[45] Robert Locke and J.-C. Spender, authors of *Confronting Managerialism*, note that 'Japanese engineers not only developed and designed products, but also went to the shop floor and worked with line employees to solve problems', thus,

> they gained first-hand knowledge of the manufacturing process and obtained the quick feedback necessary for close and continuous study of the relationship between machine design and the die-change process. This allowed the Japanese production

people to keep costly downtimes to a minimum and permitted them to pursue continuous improvement, fine-tuning, and product variety.[46]

Unlike their US counterparts.

There is an extraordinary irony that should be flagged. It is that the management practices so admired in Japanese firms, that promote innovation, actually came from the United States.[47] American management practices were passed on to the Japanese as part of President Franklin D. Roosevelt's post-Great Depression New Deal prior to the start of the Second World War. Joshua Murray and Michael Schwartz, authors of the book *Wrecked*, an impressive study that charts the decline of the American automobile industry, argue that before the Second World War, when US automakers applied the same form of management passed on to Japan, 'their rates of innovation were extremely high and analysts described US management culture as centrally valuing innovation and change'. Today, write Murray and Schwartz, 'The US automakers use an ossified mass production system featuring geographic dispersal of production, parts and machine rigidity, and large stockpiles . . . This system impedes the implementation of innovation.'[48]

What is their key takeaway about leadership in these Japanese firms? According to Josh Murray,

It is that leadership included the voice of labour. The Japanese and US auto firms diverged when Toyota (first, and other Japanese firms later) decided to make labour an integral part of the production decision-making process. They realized that worker trust and buy-in was key to the operation of the just-in-time system of production, AND that just-in-time was key to innovation. US leadership, in contrast, was adamant about maintaining sole discretion over production decisions and instead bought temporary peace through pay raises, while slowly dismantling their own innovative production system so as to remove structural leverage from their workforce.[49]

The wheels of organizational performance are oiled by line managers, particularly those who understand the *gemba* and work with the *gembutsu*. Line managers and middle managers make up the bulk of the world's supervisors. Bosses matter intensely. In a study with Ben Artz of the University of Wisconsin and Andrew Oswald of Warwick University we studied 35,000 American and British employees in all kinds of workplaces. A person's immediate boss has *the* largest effect on job satisfaction, which directly influences employee productivity, as we will see in the next chapter. The often-repeated aphorism that 'people don't leave bad jobs they leave bad bosses' is true more often than not.

Economists Eddie Lazear, Kathryn Shaw, and Christopher Stanton discovered the value of bosses to worker productivity when they were given access to a Californian technology-based services firm.[50] The researchers measured the effects of 2,000 bosses on 25,000 workers over four years and looked at this question: if managers generally earn more than the workers whom they super-vise, can we be sure that the productivity they generate is worth the additional pay?[51] The tasks examined were relatively simple, but the authors made five important findings:

- If a boss in the lower 10 per cent of supervisor quality is replaced with one who is in the upper 10 per cent, a team's total output increases by more than adding one worker to a nine-member team.
- The average boss is nearly twice as productive as the average worker.
- The worst bosses are more likely to leave the firm, and work-ers who are assigned to better bosses are more likely to remain.
- About one-quarter of the effect of having had a good boss remains one year after the worker leaves a particular manager to go to a different job within the company.
- Finally, the effect of good bosses on high-quality workers is greater than the effect of good bosses on lower-quality workers. Stanton explained that 'the effect of a boss is

multiplicative. If you have a better boss on a team, you get more out of each individual worker.'

As these results demonstrate, the effect of line managers on productivity is substantial. The truth is that we want a boss who is a better version of ourselves – one who can do what we do but to a higher standard; a person who fundamentally understands the nature of our work, and how we can improve.

We have known for a long time that the lens through which we comprehend the world has been shaped by our past, our upbringing and family, schooling, and personal histories. Of course, our personalities are added into the mix. We can moderate the effect of our personality through instruction but we cannot easily change it. The renowned scholar Donald Hambrick pointed out that top management teams see the world through their own highly personalized lenses. His upper echelons theory argues that executives make strategic choices which reflect their own values, their education and training, and specifically the domain in which they have been working. If, as we've seen, you put an accountant at the top of GM or a marketeer at the head of Apple, don't expect them to understand cars or technology. How could they? The business will be run solely through the lens of a profit-and-loss spreadsheet or an advertising campaign. And this is worse in companies where even more power has switched to the CEOs, as is common in the UK and the US.

In *The Puritan Gift*, Kenneth and William Hopper reflect often on the words of Florence Nightingale. She helped to establish modern nursing, was an accomplished statistician, a vocal social campaigner, and something of an organizational expert. Above all, she recognized that 'someone has to be in charge', which is evident in the way that Nightingale-inspired hospitals were subsequently run, as described by the Hopper brothers.[52]

The most important organizing structure in these hospitals was their 'line-and-staff' system, which distributes work responsibilities from senior management, through middle managers to lower-level employees. Florence Nightingale knew that real and actual responsibility must lie with individuals at the top *and* throughout the many different levels. At the very top was a senior physician, who sat directly above the medics and was supported by two 'staff' departments, one of which was headed by the matron, who was responsible for all nursing care. Ward sisters reported to the matron, and each managed one or more hospital wards. The second department was headed by the treasurer, who took the money and paid the bills, and had his line-and-staff. In Toyota-speak, the wards were collectively the *gemba*, the real place, the place where value was created. 'In the Nightingale Hospital, the management of what is now called the "core competences" was strictly in the hands of medically qualified men and women – both physicians and nurses.'[53] But, continue the Hopper brothers, after the 1970s responsibility switched to non-medically qualified general managers, who were 'remote from the ward floor and difficult to distinguish from the "number-crunchers" who were beginning to occupy senior management positions in large companies'.[54] The authors lament that from this time onwards, 'important decisions of an essentially medical nature are being made by people not qualified to do so, that is, without "domain knowledge"'.[55] Many services were outsourced to independent companies, and monitoring declined as the chains of responsibility were broken throughout. Non-medical executives were hired en masse and soon ran most hospitals. Metrics replaced clinical assessment, and in the 1990s 'cost containment' cut pay, which also cut the supply of nurses. This then led to 'replacing "RNs" (registered nurses) with "RCTs" (registered care technologists)'.[56]

In a recent survey published in the *British Medical Journal*, three out of ten NHS doctors said they felt unsupported by their management: 'driving the discontent and dissatisfaction', say the authors, 'is a lack of feeling valued and supported.'[57] The *Guardian* newspaper's headline of 9 October 2021 read: 'Nursing crisis sweeps wards as NHS battles to find recruits'. There are currently close to 40,000 vacancies for registered nurses in England alone. 'Drexit' or Doctor-exit from the UK's NHS as a result of Brexit means that it is now at breaking point. Many British doctors have moved to health systems overseas such as those in Canada, Australia, and New Zealand, and some are leaving the profession altogether. The US is no better. In

2019, the Association of American Medical Colleges projected shortages of over 100,000 physicians in the US by 2030.

Remember who the people are in CEO positions in US and UK hospitals – (in all but 5 per cent) *they are non-medically trained general managers*. Around the world, Nightingale-inspired hospitals survive in only a few places – notably, in the best-run and most advanced health-care systems that reside at the top of global hospital rankings.

My co-author Agnes Bäker and I wanted to understand more about good hospital management, so we asked hospital physicians in Australia, Switzerland, and Denmark about the behaviours and practices of their line managers. We surveyed thousands of physicians and asked them about their well-being, whether they intended to stay in both their current job and in medicine, and how they would assess the leadership behaviour and skills of their line manager. Job satisfaction and consequent performance is particularly important for clinicians because it directly affects patients' outcomes, namely their survival rates. As mentioned earlier, managers' behaviour has the greatest influence on employee well-being; it also affects resilience, burnout rates, and their intention to stay or leave health care. Finally, we asked physicians to rate the clinical ability of their own line manager (each of whom was also a physician).

We found that the most effective physician managers, rated by those they actually work with, are *expert line managers*, who are held in high esteem and rated highly as clinicians. This is because their competence in medicine makes it easier for them to understand the work of their colleagues, and in particular enables them to coach their staff to achieve a high standard.

The physicians we surveyed also told us about the aspects of their line managers' behaviour and skills they valued most highly. They are the following:[58]

- Expert line managers lead by example, and they
- motivate employees through shared values
- communicate a clear and positive vision

- empower and encourage their staff
- support staff in developing their career
- give better feedback about many aspects of doing the job
- communicate goals clearly
- consult with their teams about how work can be completed
- engage in innovative thinking
- allow more autonomy in working
- engender trust in the organization's senior management
- create a safer environment (e.g. from bullying)
- have happy employees who are then less likely to want to quit.

When you have spent years acquiring experience, and been deep in the thick of it, as an expert line manager has, you absorb through osmosis the shared culture and value systems, the work incentives and motivations of fellow employees. Core business expertise allows such bosses to step in and assist workers when necessary, and then guide from a distance, instead of micro-managing through metrics. They employ trust and mentorship to inspire their talented work-force to new performance heights.

People focused on their profession, trade, or craft – dentists, product designers, or cabinet makers, for example – are often viewed as being both reluctant leaders *and* reluctant followers because they perceive themselves as being 'autonomous competent individuals'.[59] Actually, we all see ourselves to some degree in this way. Everyone reports in surveys that they want some autonomy at work, and not too much bureaucracy. Like shoes that are ill-fitting and create pain, constrain our pace, and slow us down, management systems can impinge too tightly on employees. All too often an administrative tail is wagging a core business dog. The encroachment of manageri-alism is particularly intense in sectors that might be described as public or in receipt of government funds (e.g. social work, local government, prisons, higher and further education, health, and social care). This weight of bureaucracy is all the more galling when it is imposed by central governments, who themselves often seem to flout rules of civic engagement and process.[60]

It is exactly *because* taxpayers' money is being used that the most efficient and productive systems should be set in place rather than the imposition of ever more managerialism and bureaucracy.

One of the most damaging effects of an over-controlling management system is that it drives away top talent whose in-demand skills give them the freedom to choose where they want to work. Ideally, we need our best graduates going into areas such as social services, teaching, and health care. Sadly, if they decide to enter a noble profession motivated by the desire to help others then they soon leave due to excessive paperwork coupled with salaries that do not compensate for their intense workload and stress. Atul Gawande raised this issue in a *New Yorker* article, citing that a '2016 study found that physicians spent about two hours doing computer work for every hour spent face to face with a patient . . . In the examination room, physicians devoted half of their patient time facing the screen to do electronic tasks.'[61] All of this has led to extended working hours and frustration. And it seems to only get worse.

The priorities in US health care are laid bare when we look at how many physicians compared with administrators were hired between 1975 and 2010. The number of physicians grew by 150 per cent, in line with population growth; however, the number of health-care administrators increased by an incredible 3,200 per cent.[62] In universities, administrators now greatly exceed academics, who have also become burdened with excessive performance metrics, monitoring, and a greatly expanded bureaucracy. There are similar issues in schools as well.

Jeanet Meijs trained to be a teacher in the Netherlands when she was seventeen and is as passionate about education today as she was then. At eighty, she still rides her bike to go shopping, and is now tutoring children who have some learning challenges, as I myself did. Meijs's drawer is full of cards from appreciative former students because she is one of those people who change others' lives.

In the past decade Meijs has acquired a second passion. It is to campaign for the right of teachers to return to their focus on knowledge and teaching, instead of administration, which she says has got out of control. Meijs blames the school boards, managers, and politicians for the current mess. School heads 'aren't even teachers anymore. That's bizarre, isn't it? That the director of a biscuit factory . . . can also lead a school?'[63]

Jamie Peston has worked in London-based secondary schools for over twenty years. During that time he has also witnessed an increased reliance on technology imposed on teachers from above. In an interview with me in 2021 he said: 'Schools have invested millions of pounds in a variety of "smart" systems that were intended to alleviate workload, reduce paperwork, and improve conditions for teachers (and administrators). Instead, the reverse has happened.' He argues that many educational technology systems are mediocre at best, and says a small cabal of big players monopolize the sector, stifling innovation. 'School Management Information Systems have similarly become more complex. Again, they were supposed to reduce the reporting burden for teachers, but instead have increased it.' This is because they were not designed by the teachers who have to use them. 'It is always the teachers who are left confused, frustrated and with the extra workload which has reduced teacher well-being and increased turnover of staff.' Peston concludes that 'while the days of printing reports, folding, addressing, and stuffing envelopes have passed, in its place are endless hours of marking, logging and inputting data, and the onus has shifted from administrators directly onto teachers, increasing workload and reducing job satisfaction.' The Organisation for Economic Co-operation and Development's Teaching and Learning International Survey found that the quality of teachers' working conditions directly affects their job satisfaction and retention. In schools that reported high leadership and management scores, teacher retention was also high. This same pattern can be found in health care, social work, the police, and the criminal justice system.

Middle managers are in a challenging position, sandwiched between the staff in their department or unit and senior executives. On the one hand there are those who look up to the C-Suite and want to keep the executives happy, willing to tie their workforce up in whatever red tape gets chucked down from above. On the other, there are those who view themselves as 'umbrella carriers',[64] expert leaders who shelter subordinates from administrative spillovers, thus reducing disruption.[65] Our research has shown that expert line managers create conditions that support and promote performance, which inevitably means some pushing back against central functions and reducing the escalating effects of an imposing bureaucracy.

Evaluation, feedback, and the setting of goals are prerequisites for appraising performance. But to raise motivation, goals need to be ambitious but realistic and must align closely to the nature of the tasks.

At the time of writing, over 170,000 people have died of Covid-19 in the UK, and the number is in excess of 1,000,000 in the US.[66] Michael Lewis' book *The Premonition* examines how the US handled the pandemic, which, by most accounts, was not well. The government agency Lewis holds most responsible is the Center for Disease Control and Prevention (CDC). Lewis describes the CDC as an organization where risk aversion and excessive caution, caused by fear of losing one's job, left the CDC impotent to the point of being irresponsible. The director of the CDC is appointed by the president and can be sacked by the president, which was quite a common occurrence under Donald Trump. Thus the individual is often perceived to be a 'yes' person. Lewis points to the very different roles performed by the director of the CDC and that of Anthony Fauci, director of the National Institute of Allergy and Infectious Diseases, with whom Trump did not get along.

If Donald Trump had gotten up and said, 'Fauci, you're fired,' nothing would have happened, which is likely why he never did it . . . To fire a competent civil servant is a pain in the ass. To fire a competent presidential appointee is as easy as tweeting.[67]

Politicians may need to rely on experts during pandemics, but in general they do not like them. Experts, like Fauci, won't do as they are told. So generalists and management consultants are preferred by governing politicians. Consultants may charge exorbitantly, but they will do as they are told. Experts' behaviours and actions are informed by codes of practice tied to their trade or profession. Being committed to a set of protocols and standards makes experts harder to shift. As a result, Trump drew not only on non-experts but also family members – Ivanka Trump was an adviser to her father, the president, and her husband, Jared Kushner, was an assistant to the president and a senior adviser.[68] Meanwhile Boris Johnson's government was frequently accused of appointing to important roles through a 'chumocracy'.[69] Similarly, Canada's inadequate response to Covid-19 was blamed on the dismantling of its exceptional public health intelligence network and the replacement of experts by generalists in key positions.[70]

Why the standard-bearer must first bear the standard

It is the leader's responsibility to establish the quality threshold in an organization. If an outstanding expert is hired as CEO then the bar is automatically raised.

John Rawls, a philosopher, moved to Harvard University in 1962. Between 1962 and 1971 he produced very little published work. It caused gossip and bad feeling among his colleagues. People were beginning to wonder: had Rawls 'lost it'? During that fallow period his salary growth remained unaffected, and no dean ever called him in for a 'little talk' with expressions of concern. In 1971, after Rawls' long period of 'low productivity', he presented *A Theory of Justice*, a masterpiece considered to be the most important work in moral philosophy since the end of the Second World War. As the late Henry Rosovsky, a (former) professor of economics and dean of arts and sciences at Harvard University, pointed out in an interview, had Harvard then 'been "corporatized," we might have deprived the world of Rawls' major breakthrough'.

Patrick Harker, the former dean of the famous Wharton School of Business at the University of Pennsylvania, was at the top of his field in operations and information management, and the youngest faculty member ever to gain an endowed professorship at Wharton. Harker opened my eyes to the importance of expert leaders for hiring and raising standards when he said, 'to be credible, the standard bearer must first bear the standard.' In other words, if you want to reach a higher high for your organization, you must have reached it yourself, and be seen by others to have done so. For example, in trying to create a world-renowned biomedical research institute, dedicated to understanding the fundamental biology underlying human health and disease, the Francis Crick Institute selected Sir Paul Nurse, a geneticist and Nobel Prize winner, to head it. Expert leaders raise the bar, inspire excellence, and attract donors and investors and, importantly, the best talent, all of which translates into higher performance. Naturally, *only* being a Nobel laureate is insufficient. Paul Nurse also had to understand how to motivate people.

In a bid to help reinvigorate its stuffy and sterile department stores, US firm JCPenney hired former Apple executive Ron Johnson as its CEO in the autumn of 2011. The move was heralded as genius. After all, Johnson had created the Apple Store and the acclaimed Genius Bar. At a debut speech in 2012 Johnson announced that Penney stores were to go through a radical redesign, and J. C. Penney would once again become 'America's favorite store'. However, reported James Surowiecki, 'Fourteen months later, J. C. Penney is America's favorite cautionary tale.' Under Johnson's watch the company lost nearly $100 million, 22,000 employees lost their jobs, and there was a 60 per cent reduction in stock valuation. Business punters were shocked that the star retailer had failed so hugely. But Johnson's poor performance stemmed from a lack of specialized knowledge; he didn't actually understand Penney's customers so how could he raise any bar higher? As Mark Cohen, a professor at Columbia University and former CEO of Sears Canada, commented: 'He had never been a C.E.O., never mounted or managed a turnaround, had limited fashion-apparel experience, and had no experience in the middle-market space.'[71]

Leaders set a variety of quality thresholds throughout their organizations. Hiring and maintaining employee quality is among the most important. It is easier for a leader or a line manager to be an effective quality enforcer if they have first met the standard that is to be imposed. For example, the undergraduate backgrounds of school heads correlate highly with the undergraduate backgrounds of the teachers they hire. Those who attend the top education colleges are more likely to hire high-quality teachers who produce better student outcomes.[72]

While most CEOs and HR directors would agree that hiring the best people is central to the success of any organization, it is easier said than done. Homophily – when like is attracted to like – can help and also hinder. The best teachers are likely to hire the best teachers but recruiters can also be tempted to select those who are like themselves in other ways – without even being aware of it. Feeling an instinctive liking or sympathy for a candidate who physically looks like you or went to a similar school or university, or who comes from the same class background, can have negative repercussions, particularly in relation to diversity. 'Group think' can also take hold when, say, an interviewer who was educated at Yale University thinks that only Yale will do. If homophily guides its hiring, an organization eventually weakens. But as long as there is self-awareness and some objective measure of what constitutes the best, there are extraordinary benefits to having the best in the field on a hiring panel because they will raise the quality bar by hiring other great candidates. If little care is put into who is involved in recruitment, the opposite can happen.

An example of this that can be applied to many different settings was that of John P, a chemistry professor in an acclaimed research university that had recently hired an ambitious new president.[73] The incoming president was an outstanding political scientist, one of whose priorities was to address the rather large reputational decline the university had recently suffered. Chemistry was particularly poor. The plan was to find a top chemist to take over as head of department, a person who would set new standards for hiring faculty and carrying out research. The president took a direct interest in the appointment, and after identifying and communicating with a potentially excellent candidate, a hiring panel was convened.

The chemistry scholar being considered was an eminent researcher and highly respected in his field – so much so that several of the existing professors in the department became worried about having someone in charge whose reputation was so much better than theirs. Fearing loss of power and status, they took action. First, Professor P and his coterie tried to control who was on the hiring panel. They pushed to have as many professors as possible from their own department, and they submitted panel candidates from elsewhere in the university whom they knew they could rely on for support. But the president was fly to this trick, and took control of panel membership. So, Professor P went further. He directly contacted the president's first-choice candidate and told him that he would not be welcome in their department. Consequently, the candidate withdrew. I have heard versions of this story from many other areas including advertising, banking, and medicine.

Hiring and keeping the best people is never easy, yet failing to do so can lead to a steady decline into mediocrity. A senior physician in the NHS, interviewed for this book, explained she often feels that

in medical selection panels there is a 'culture of second best' where they don't necessarily want to select the best clinician or surgeon, because they feel threatened by the candidate's talent, particularly if it translates into acquiring private patients. If the incomer's reputation surpasses that of others in the department, their private practice may decrease. Because of this, really outstanding doctors sometimes struggle to find jobs, which is insane.

A second-best candidate is then appointed, who may be mediocre or not as driven to succeed academically or clinically. 'Sometimes in the NHS', she concludes woefully, 'it feels like it is our worst performers that establish the organizational standards and culture, not the best performers.'[74]

Professor P's behaviour is perfectly captured in a statement made by André Weil, a mid-twentieth-century French mathematician: *'First-rate people hire other first-rate people. Second-rate people hire third-rate people. Third-rate people hire fifth-rate people.'*[75]

Those who feel disgruntled with their situation, passed over or lacking in confidence, will find it hard to hire others who are better than them. Negative self-feelings are traced directly to, and are antecedents of, processes of social comparison.[76] Humans cannot avoid comparing and ranking themselves against others. Job satisfaction and happiness have also been shown to be tied to how we compare ourselves with similar others.

Envy and competitiveness may exist to some degree among us all, and those at the top of a field may be even more sensitive about their position. Personality, age, and self-awareness also matter. Nevertheless, outstanding experts, those who are A+ or A+++ players, are often not threatened, but stimulated, by hiring individuals who are better than them. Indeed, they see it not just as hiring equivalents to themselves but as a feather in their cap.[77] Importantly, it is the A++ person leading the search or on the hiring panel who will recognize other similar talent. Put outstanding expert leaders into post and they will enforce a higher standard of hiring.

Credible 'talent magnets'

When I asked Toby Cosgrove, MD, then CEO of the internationally renowned physician-led Cleveland Clinic, why he thought physician leadership was important, his response was instant: *'Credibility – peer-to-peer credibility. This is the most important factor.'* He knew that having been a respected surgeon with a long career at the clinic mattered to his core workers, other physicians. When Paul Taheri, MD arrived from the University of Vermont to start his term as CEO of Yale Medicine he said:

> I had to scrub up and wait in the hall and let folk see my name on the surgery board. While in surgery my new colleagues leaned over my shoulder to see if I could still 'cut it'. Once they were happy that I could, my credibility was established as one of them. After that no one cared anymore.

CEOs who are industry experts, like Cosgrove and Taheri, send positive signals to internal employees, especially the core workers, but also to external stakeholders, improving the perception of their organization. Cosgrove also believes that physician-leaders are more likely to 'tolerate crazy ideas' like the first coronary artery bypass, performed by René Favaloro at the Cleveland Clinic in the late 1960s. They do this, Cosgrove said, because the Cleveland Clinic unlocks talent by offering a safe space to people with extraordinary ideas and, importantly, the leadership tolerates a certain amount of failure, which is a natural part of scientific endeavour, innovation, and all progress. The idea that credibility legitimizes leaders' authority has been known for a long time. Credibility informs the social interactions between leaders and their followers. For Paul Taheri, coming from outside, to be viewed as credible in his new leadership role, he had to first demonstrate that he could perform surgery to as high a standard as his new peers. Once that was done, he could get on with his CEO job.

Being credible and demonstrating your expertise to a high standard also signals that a head understands the culture and value system, incentives, and priorities of those being led. Because expert leaders admire and pursue other highly talented people (and are less likely to feel intimidated or threatened by them), they become what business professor Sydney Finkelstein terms 'talent magnets'.

Under the helm of an expert leader, organizations can become vibrant places that attract the best talent and help inspire their optimal performance. Many expert leaders have the star quality associated with being exceptionally good at what they do, engendering loyalty on the part of their workforce and stakeholders, as they steer their companies to greater heights. They also act as a powerful signal to *potential* employees about what the work culture and environment might be like. If a firm is headed by an expert leader, it suggests to potential talent that an appropriate work environment exists, which expands the pool of high-quality applicants. It may also signal credibility to a wider audience. For example, an organization's board may choose to hire a noted expert or specialist to signal its strategic priorities to employees, and to external stakeholders such as shareholders, customers, suppliers, the media, and donors. Finally, outstanding experts can also attract new and young talent into a field they may not have previously considered. Vidal Sassoon, who wore the crown and took the glory as the world's first celebrity hairdresser, transformed styling from hair-set and hairnet to cut and blow dry. He not only inspired a whole generation of cutters, he brought young men into women's hairdressing.

I have summarized the 'mechanisms' through which experts exert their substantial influence on organizational performance. In the next chapter I take a look at how expert bosses raise the job satisfaction of employees, and why this is important to firm productivity.

5

Expert Leaders Create Productive Workplaces

Bosses matter for many reasons but we tend to forget that a fundamentally important part of their role is the kind of environment they create for those who work for their organisation. Devising strategy might be hard, but executing it is harder, and to do so effectively you need staff who are committed and engaged. Expert bosses are vital to higher organizational performance because they understand how to create the right working conditions to enable employees to do their jobs to the best of their abilities. As I have found in much of my research, it is credible bosses who make the biggest difference to the happiness of workers, which in turn affects organizational performance.

Behind a happy worker stands an expert boss

Asher Raphael and Corey Schiller were recent college graduates when they began their careers with entry-level positions at Power Home Remodeling. Located in the Chester, Pennsylvania area, it was then a modest, family-owned and operated business that replaced windows, doors, and cladding (siding). By 2014 both men were co-CEOs, and their company had transformed into the country's second-largest exterior home remodeller (growing a stunning 1,500 per cent from 2008 to 2017). It is worth noting that 90 per cent of the executive leaders at Power Home Remodeling began in entry-level positions, just like Asher and Corey, steadily accumulating expertise as they ascended the corporate ladder.

Best-place-to-work rankings are heavily used by employees looking for work. Employers, too, recognize the need to do well in such rankings in order to attract the best possible candidates. What distinguishes Power Home Remodeling, and their famously happy corporate counterparts like SAP and Southwest Airlines, are not just competitive salaries, performance-based bonuses, annual all-expenses-paid retreats, well-stocked food stations, and Pilates classes. It is the fact that employees inside these companies express themselves as being very satisfied with their jobs.

Why is this relevant? Happiness, job satisfaction, and worker well-being are of course important in their own right, but as I will explain, it has been demonstrated in numerous studies that these factors also have a very real influence on individual productivity and organizational performance. American companies that made it on to the '100 best places to work' ranking have been calculated to have on average 3.8 per cent higher stock returns, compared to competitors who fail to make the top-100 elite list.[1] Expert bosses play a major role in this. Employee job satisfaction and happiness hinge on the core business competence of leaders and line managers. Companies with expert bosses are, simply, happier. And *happiness is profitable*.

With co-authors Benjamin Artz and Andrew Oswald, in 2017 I published what we believe is the first study to show that an expert boss with technical competence and core business knowledge is the most important factor tied to employee job satisfaction and overall well-being.[2] We found there are three critical elements:

- The employee is managed by a supervisor with the skills which would enable them to perform the employee's job themselves if necessary.
- The line manager knows the business from the bottom up – or started it.
- The supervisor's level of technical competence is judged by his or her employees to be high in their area of work.

If all three criteria are satisfied then an average worker's sense of job satisfaction is most positively influenced – even more so than salary (see figure).

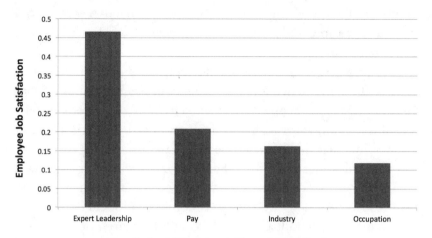

The effects of different variables on job satisfaction

What determines an employee's job satisfaction?

In terms of job satisfaction, having a technically competent boss can be worth double your salary (even when pay is high).[3]

So once again we see the power of expertise. That's almost certainly because experts are credible. Legitimate leaders, with good managerial judgement who foster creativity, provide richer feedback to employees and allow greater worker autonomy – a vital component in unleashing creativity and productivity and indeed enjoyment at work. Experts are especially compelling when they understand their own companies. That's why the famously happy start-ups that stud Silicon Valley tend to recruit, train, and promote from within their own ranks, instead of relying on outside talent or MBA degree-bearing generalists.[4]

But how do all these elements – happiness, job satisfaction, expert bosses, productivity – connect? Let's start with human happiness.

The study of happiness

Few would question the potential importance of understanding and amplifying the factors that contribute to human happiness. Philosophers and others have debated the topic for centuries.

However, the formal study of well-being is relatively recent. It uses statistical methods and large random-sample survey data as a way to better understand society and how it works.

The first-ever conference on the economics of happiness took place at the London School of Economics in England in November 1993. It was held in the fading splendour of the elderly Lionel Robbins building, a structure reminiscent of a 1950s high school. A giant rolling blackboard sat at one end of the conference room with an overhead projector at the other. The conference was organized by Andrew Clark and Andrew Oswald, then at Essex University and LSE respectively. The two young economists had spent hours walking round and round a pretty lake at the centre of the Essex University campus thinking about how the new British Household Panel Survey (BHPS) could help them understand mental well-being and job satisfaction in Britain's population. The BHPS, started in 1991, collected detailed information once a year on the same 10,300 randomly selected individuals in 5,500 households in Great Britain.[5] It was tracking these individuals' lives and recording what was happening to them. As we will see, this vital dataset would allow researchers to discover important patterns in what does and does not make individuals happy.

In the days running up to, and especially on the morning of, the November conference, Clark and Oswald put posters up all over the LSE advertising their event. They dragged 100 wooden chairs from a nearby storage room and set them out in rows. A prestigious line-up of speakers had flown in, including the psychologist and future Nobel Prize laureate Daniel Kahneman, from Princeton, and scholars from the likes of Yale, Harvard, and Cornell.

While the conference had seemed certain to be a success, it was on the surface a complete flop. Even with an all-star line-up, only four people turned up, so the speakers faced row upon row of empty chairs. Perhaps economists in the 1990s did not think human happiness was relevant to their work. Oswald later said: 'I don't think LSE economists necessarily thought the conference was a bad idea. It just did not compute.'

Clark and Oswald were ahead of their time.[6] Only Richard Easterlin, an economics professor and demographer who now works at the University of Southern California, had been sufficiently bold in a lone article in 1974 to use happiness data to argue that economic growth was *not* improving life in the way conventional wisdom assumed.[7] Standard economics believed that higher gross domestic product made a nation as a whole happier. Easterlin wanted to check if that was really true. He had the idea of looking at post-war data collected in regular happiness surveys through the years in countries like the United States and Japan. He could not detect any sign that the happiness numbers went up as countries became richer, and suggested that perhaps happiness is relative, so that when everyone has a flashy BMW, no one enjoys the status of owning a flashy vehicle because it does not stand out. This phenomenon became known as the Easterlin Paradox. The economics profession at the time did not like his empirical findings and he had trouble publishing his work in an economics journal, but eventually did so in a book. Since then the Easterlin Paradox has become a part of standard economic thinking and his 1974 paper is now a frequently cited classic.

Today, partly due to the papers presented by Clark and Oswald, Danny Blanchflower, and others at the 1993 conference,[8] the economics of happiness is a well-recognized area of research and the concept of well-being in the workplace has developed into an industry itself. The UK government today surveys its population annually to understand the nation's happiness, and a number of organizations have grouped together to produce the World Happiness Report.[9] These and other sources of similar data have allowed researchers to find out a great deal about the relationship between happiness and well-being at an individual and company level.

How satisfied are you with your life?

Just as Clark and Oswald first did in the 1990s, today economists still use large surveys to ask people how satisfied they are with their life. Most developed democratic countries report quite high levels of well-being. Only small percentages of citizens say they are unhappy, and in the United States General Social Survey, for example, approximately one-third of people say they are overall 'very happy' with their life. There was a dip during the coronavirus pandemic but levels soon bounced back. People tend to be happier and more satisfied with life if they have a high income, are married or in an intimate relationship, and are educated to a relatively high level. Overall, the statistical evidence is that children do not contribute to increased happiness, although grandchildren do raise happiness, and Oswald has been heard to say in his lectures, 'Skip the children. Go straight to grandchildren.' In individuals there is also a tendency to U-shaped happiness through the course of a person's life, where the young and the old report high levels of happiness but middle-aged people are the least happy – hence the idea of the 'midlife crisis'. Unsurprisingly, levels of happiness also fall during an economic recession.

Once wealth, education, and sex have been taken into account there are a number of important influencing factors that affect reported well-being. These include health, diet, and environment (access to green spaces and levels of air pollution), but one of the most significant is unemployment. The negative hit from unemployment is large and persistent, and the long-term unemployed do not adapt to their situation. High unemployment in a country reduces overall levels of happiness, even among those who do not lose their jobs (presumably because of the background fear that it creates). It is also important to understand that being told to leave your employer is mentally harmful for reasons that go far beyond simply the loss of wage. Reduced income is painful, of course. But the seminal work of Rainer and Liliana Winkelmann in 1998 calculated that 80 per cent of the happiness lost when someone becomes unemployed is not pecuniary in nature.[10] That large slice of induced unhappiness is mainly the result of a lower sense of identity, agency, and social capital.

Income in itself is important, but comparing your income with that of your peers matters a great deal more than the number of yen and euros themselves. Employees are acutely aware of variations in salary and of higher-wage people around them in the same firm. Workers are more satisfied when their pay is *relatively* high compared to others in the economy with identical qualifications and at the same age.[11] As humans, we are constantly looking over our shoulders and comparing what we get paid with what others earn.

Knowing the background causes of human happiness is interesting but it is also helpful when thinking about job satisfaction, because being in work (when we want it) contributes greatly to our general sense of well-being.

Job satisfaction and the well-being of workers

Most of us, when we are not sleeping, spend the largest proportion of our waking hours working. So how happy we feel *at work* really matters to our overall life satisfaction. Employees know this intuitively and many employers, from sheer observation and experience, understand the value of employee job satisfaction, and its relationship to employee performance. But they may not know how to create the right environment to foster it, which is where I hope this book may play a role. And I suspect many leaders are unaware that there is hard, statistical evidence that they themselves have the largest effect on employee well-being – specially if they are expert in their field.

To fully understand why this is the case requires an appreciation of the major influences on people's job satisfaction. This is vital for the maintenance of employee well-being, but it also matters for individual and organizational performance. Happy workers are productive workers. *And the number one influence on their job satisfaction is the quality of their boss*. I'll come back to this point later in the chapter.

People want to work – and not just because they need to. Monetary compensation is only one element of the benefit work brings; it also informs our identity, shapes our social network, and creates routine. As we will see, happier workers are more productive, less likely to quit or call in sick, and happier workplaces have more contented customers and make more money.

Since the early 1990s an enormous body of statistical evidence has built up on the determinants of well-being at work.[12] Here is a ranking of the twelve main factors that affect job satisfaction – both positive and negative – in approximate order of importance.[13] These findings, it should be emphasized, come from statistical comparisons across different kinds of people and different settings, so they tell us about average effects rather than special cases.

What makes you happy at work?

1. *Leaders, supervisors, and managers have the single largest effect on employee job satisfaction and well-being*[14]

   Your boss hugely affects how much you enjoy your work. This is because your line manager largely controls or influences your work flow, promotion prospects, your job and career development, the working environment, and much more. Our studies were some of the first to demonstrate the boss effect on job happiness, and, importantly, to be able to calculate the size of the consequences that flow from having a competent expert manager. The particular qualities your manager brings to their job and that affect your workplace happiness will vary, but most important is whether your boss actually knows what he or she is talking about. Expert bosses score high on a range of measures (as worded in surveys of employees): giving useful feedback on your work, being respectful to you as a person, being helpful in getting the job done, supporting your development, encouraging teamworking, giving you praise and recognition when you do a good job, and generally helping employees. Bad bosses score least well on 'ability to get the job done' presumably because if they haven't done the job then how can they possibly help you do yours?[15] Having a bad working relationship with your boss can, as might be guessed, greatly reduce your well-being and is frequently a key factor linked to quitting.

2. *Doing interesting work – Positive*
   Being in a job that is interesting scores high on job satisfaction – for obvious reasons. Humans need stimulation. Interesting can mean different things to different people depending on their personality. For example, intrinsically motivated people may be more likely to work in a non-profit organization, where pay is generally lower. People with extroverted personalities are more likely to choose jobs with opportunities for social interaction. Mainly, for all of us, it is a matter of trade-offs because there are always elements of our jobs that we do not love. Success therefore comes in the balance we are able to find between those factors that we really like, versus those we like less.

3. *Having job security – Positive*
   Job security is important: work gives our lives meaning, it is tied to our identity and social status, is a major source of human interaction, and provides us with a routine as well as income to live on. A threat to our job security is a potential attack on our security as a whole – our ability to feed and dress ourselves and our dependants, and have somewhere safe to live – and as such is immensely stressful. It also threatens our identity and sense of self. The importance of job security is illustrated by the enormous effect that we know both from statistical evidence and from experience, either direct or indirect, that losing it and becoming unemployed has on us. The loss of happiness caused by losing a job is shown in the data to be comparable to that caused by the death of a spouse.

4. *Employee pay (including relative pay) – Positive*
   Pay is of course important although over a certain level the relationship between pay and job satisfaction is weaker than most people think. This is because of other non-monetary factors

that are equally if not more important than income referred to above. But it still matters – especially relative pay. Job satisfaction is affected by what others in the same firm earn. Comparisons are psychologically dangerous. Knowing that others are paid more can reduce one's well-being – especially if one feels the colleague being paid more is not doing a very good job! However, if the higher salary is seen as a signal of what might come, through promotion say, it can also be a source of inspiration. There is important research that shows other forms of compensation can have a big influence on our motivation, through initiatives such as profit shares, group bonuses, and shared ownership. This 'share-capitalism effect' or buy-in is viewed favourably by employees, and it also dampens, somewhat, the negative well-being effects from those parts of our jobs that we do not like.[16]

5. *Having autonomy – Positive*
   Autonomy at work is important to job satisfaction for all kinds of employees; indeed, having even small freedoms, like being able to move our desk, raises our job satisfaction. Some professions, such as scientists and artists, require higher levels of autonomy than others. Autonomy gives us a sense of agency. In other words, we feel as if we have some control over our lives. This is why having an expert boss is crucial; an expert boss is someone who understands the nature of the work. Giving autonomy to employees is a signal of trust, but it also hands over a certain amount of responsibility. If you have a boss who does not really understand your job, it is difficult for them to assess whether the job can be done with more autonomy and if so then how much. They will also struggle to tell from afar whether you are still coping, performing adequately, or heading for a crater in the ground. Greater autonomy needs to be matched with greater recognition. So, for example, if you have been given a substantial chunk of responsibility but you feel you are not being fairly remunerated for it, or given a promotion, then it becomes less appealing. Being

self-employed, the ultimate in autonomy, is associated with relatively high job satisfaction, but is only for those who are not too risk-averse.

6. *Opportunities for promotion – Positive*
A key factor that my colleagues and I have found in our research is whether a boss can help an employee not only get the job done, but get it done better, so they can develop their career either through promotion or new opportunities. This is why everyone wants a line manager who is, professionally, a better version of themselves. They can help us improve our skills and experience and, ultimately, gain promotion, if that is what we want. Even if we don't want to be promoted, staying interested and engaged with our work requires a sense of progress and development.

7. *Doing work that is useful to society – Positive*
Humans like to feel they are doing something useful. People may judge differently how useful others' work is, but it is nevertheless a significant factor in job satisfaction. In surveys asking employees what they want from a job, a standard reply is 'doing work that is useful to society'. Yet recent research has shown that approximately 8 per cent of workers perceive their job as socially useless, while another 17 per cent are doubtful about the usefulness of their job.[17]

8. *The quality of relationships with peers at work – Positive*
Relationships at work are important and good relations are often central to why we enjoy a particular job. How we get on with our boss is particularly crucial, as mentioned above, but so too are our relationships with our co-workers, and there is a clear connection between the two. Organizational leaders and line managers not only create strategy but also the quality of the culture of a business – including the kind of behaviours to be promoted or discouraged, the type of communication and quantity of it, and the level of openness and honesty. Leaders have to

set the standards in all ways – both by example and by dealing with staff who are free riders, misbehaving, and negatively affecting other people's work. This is one of the most significant ways that leaders shape the quality of relationships within a workplace. When staff see bad behaviour being ignored and good people being treated unfairly, they become resentful and withdraw, or at worst leave.

9. *The length of working hours – Negative*
   In many parts of the workforce there is evidence that people are working longer hours, and this is reflected in the higher rates of stress and burnout being reported. Long hours are particularly hard on people who have jobs that are unrewarding, physically demanding, and highly regulated, such as call centre workers. Or where, for example, there has been a rise in bureaucracy that prevents workers focusing on what they consider to be their core competence, as has been the case with teachers and doctors, as we saw earlier. We are also less satisfied if our employer is inflexible and we are not allowed to work the hours we want or need to. The pandemic may have had a positive effect on the way we work, with firms now having a greater understanding of the importance of staff well-being, productivity, and flexible working. But it very much depends on the sector one works in.

10. *Working in large workplaces – Negative*
    Small workplaces tend to be flatter hierarchically. They allow for more autonomy and give greater responsibility, which is often also more easily awarded as the lines of accountability are shorter. In a small workplace we can really see when people are putting in effort. Plus it is easier to have a sense of collegiality, because one is acquainted with a larger number of individuals in the workforce by virtue of it being more intimate. By contrast, the larger the place of work, the easier it is to feel like a cog in a machine and that one's individuality and contribution is not recognized. Large workplaces may also offer less autonomy

because by virtue of their size they require a more standardized organization and reporting structure.

11. *Education level of the employee – Negative influence if income is held constant*
Research has shown that there is a sting in the tail from being highly educated.[18] Higher levels of education tend to make you expect more – more income, more fulfilment, more promotion – and can therefore be associated with reduced job satisfaction if expectations are not met. This is especially the case when people of equal income are examined in the data. If I have a degree from a top university, and I earn 45,000 dollars a year with no prospect of improving my earnings, I will feel dissatisfied. If I have no educational qualifications and I earn 45,000 dollars a year, I tend to be more satisfied.

12. *Intrinsic danger and stress of the kind of work – Negative*
For obvious reasons, there is a lot of evidence that people are less happy in dangerous and highly stressed workplaces, especially if they feel that their work is not sufficiently remunerated or recognized.

On the productivity effects of happiness

Instinctively, most of us might recognize that it is better for everyone concerned if employees feel content at work. But in addition to it being highly desirable, there is also a strong commercial incentive for leaders to know if their employees are happy or not. The well-being of workers has been demonstrated to greatly affect performance and productivity. There are at least two reasons for this.

The first is that unhappy workers quit. And people quitting their jobs is expensive in terms of time and money. Vacancies must be filled – with the attendant costly advertising and internal meetings, formal and informal interviews, and large amounts of HR administration. Those offered jobs can take time to accept, particularly if they are talented and have numerous offers. And in the meantime there are inevitable gaps left in the workforce, reducing outputs and increasing pressure on existing employees who must work harder. This, in itself, can create unhappiness among staff. Getting new employees onboard also requires induction time and effort and can unsettle others. Waves of dissatisfaction can result that escalate quickly and may not be initially obvious to managers but can be deeply disruptive. It becomes especially dangerous and self-fulfilling if bosses have not grasped *why* the quitters quit in the first place.

Moreover, it is possible for people to 'quit' before they actually leave the company. In other words, they can start to be resentful while they are still employees, and deliberately (sometimes even unconsciously) dial down their effort and commitment to the organization.[19] They can also feign illness and invent excuses for being absent.[20] Absenteeism can quickly become a difficult, and even contagious and widespread problem for workplaces.

The second reason is that happy employees are productive employees. As we discussed earlier, this might seem a matter of common sense but in the past some economists and businesspeople took the opposite standpoint, arguing that work was purely transactional – the exchange of labour for money – and happiness didn't come into the equation.

While these issues have been debated for more than fifty years,[21] common sense is now reinforced by a growing body of research showing that it pays to care about your employees' well-being.[22] First, satisfied workers are less likely to take a job with a competitor firm, and employers do not want lots of labour turnover, as we saw. Second, happy individuals are intrinsically more productive. One of the earliest randomized control trials in this research area showed that relatively small boosts in happiness went on, in a white-collar task, to produce 12 per cent extra in labour productivity. That effect also works in reverse: the study found that sadness, caused by illness in a person's extended family, led to the person being less productive.[23]

Exactly how or why a person's performance is improved by being happier is, paradoxically, not fully understood. One possible explanation for the happiness–performance link is that happier people may be more focused on their work and less distracted by deeper worries. They are more productive because they can keep concentrating on tasks in the workplace, rather than constantly thinking of their personal troubles and sadness.[24] A study of farmers faced with financial troubles showed how worry can overwhelm people's mental 'bandwidth'.[25] It is also known more generally that 'a wandering mind is an unhappy mind'.[26] An unhappy employee may also feel underappreciated and thus have little incentive to put extra effort or initiative into their work. For all these reasons a good boss will look the unhappiness of workers in the eye – and do something about it – if they can. Otherwise, their organization is likely to be confronted with high employee turnover, high absenteeism, low effort within the workplace, and resentful and poorly performing employees. If that goes on long enough, either bosses get the sack or the organization goes under.

Thanks to the research that is now being done, we know that greater happiness is directly linked to our individual performance and also to the quality of our outputs. Worker satisfaction is integral to organizational productivity and growth, whilst unhappy workers drive costs up. Gallup estimates that unhappy employees cost the United States between $450 and $550 *billion* annually through days off work, caused by physical and mental illness, and lower performance.

An expert line manager transforms

Having established the links between individual productivity and well-being, we need to go a step further and look at who is responsible for ensuring our well-being at work. Middle managers supervise the nuts and bolts of working life for most of us day to day and week to week. They control our jobs, put us up for promotion, allow flexible working, and consent to our vacations. They also bring either job satisfaction or despair. Make no mistake, organizational CEOs are responsible for *who* moves into important line management positions. But line managers keep the place functioning efficiently.

So how much of an expert do they need to be?

In our 2018 study of physicians in four countries – Switzerland, Australia, the United Kingdom, and Denmark – Agnes Bäker and I found the best line managers are not just able physicians, they are highly competent ones.[27] These are the bosses who exhibit what the management literature calls 'transformational leadership' styles (instead of the transactional approach commonly adopted by generalists). Transformational leadership places emphasis on motivating followers through shared values to commit to common goals, communicating a clear and positive vision, empowering, encouraging, and developing staff, engaging in innovative thinking, and leading by example – all factors that predict higher workforce job satisfaction and staff retention. To be a transformational leader you really have to understand the jobs that people you manage perform.

To attract top talent to Stanford, Silicon Valley founder and engineer Frederick Terman raised academic salaries, offered generous research and student support with top facilities, and handed over control to faculty and away from administrators. But he also crafted a leadership style advocated by many today. Hewlett-Packard co-founder David Packard remembers how many of Terman's practices were introduced into HP: the idea of 'management by walking around', encouraging managers to circulate and talk with employees to better understand people's jobs and concerns, along with the concept of encouraging others, and not taking sole credit for your own successes. Terman was modest and had integrity.

We know from similar research that high job satisfaction influences the performance of doctors and nurses, and this has a direct effect on patient care. Emma Clarey is a highly trained intensive-care nurse and clinical researcher in London. She has observed good and bad nurse managers through the years. She noticed that those who were clinically competent made better line managers.

When I was team-leading, the first question staff or agency nurses would ask when we needed to fill extra shifts was 'Who is in charge?' If they perceived the nurse manager on clinical duty to be incompetent, they would decline to come in, and consequently we found ourselves with low staffing numbers.

As a practising senior nurse, Emma is

acutely aware of the impact my actions have on others, especially young nurses. Throughout my career I have observed that inefficient nurses make inefficient managers who produce inefficient teams. Micro-managers create distrusting teams with low morale who rarely take the initiative. Absent managers and bad communicators create unmotivated teams.[28]

The quality of a hospital rests upon the morale and productivity of those who work in it. Happy nurses, physiotherapists, and physicians are more likely to deliver happy and well patients.[29] In health care as well as other settings, those who occupy middle management positions have the largest effect on employees' attitudes.[30] Job satisfaction not only reflects worker well-being and individual productivity, but also clinicians' burnout rates and quits.[31] Physicians who rate their manager's clinical expertise as high, also rate their boss as being highly effective. Importantly for their own productivity and well-being, they tick high on their own job satisfaction, and report they are less likely to want to quit their job.[32]

ETC – empathy, trust, and credibility

Dr Ash Dwivedi completed his medical training in India and took his first executive position in a New Delhi hospital before moving to London. He has devoted his life both to transforming the health of his patients and transforming health-care systems. Dwivedi believes that to change and transform organizations it is essential that senior clinicians are a central part of the design and decision-making process, and ideally are leading it. Only they understand frontline staff. 'I have witnessed management-led attempts to "impose" major structural changes on hospitals and in primary care, which left employees disengaged and angry.'[33] He elaborates: '"ETC" sums up my experience of working with frontline professionals, managers and policy makers in health care. Empathy, for me, is the number one step when connecting with patients. It creates an inconspicuous complementary channel of communication between two people.'

Trust, Dwivedi says, is a second key ingredient to making any relationship work. 'A recent poll showed again that doctors and nurses are the most trusted of all professionals in Britain. This really helps us with our clinical work.'

Credibility is his final component. 'If those you want to engage do not view you as a credible advocate, they will switch off. Being credible is the starting point.'

Dwivedi recalls a hospital stroke unit that desperately needed a redesign. It was grappling with high patient demand but lacked sufficient inpatient beds. 'The hospital's management made several attempts to bring in changes that the doctors and nurses knew would not work mainly because of the clinical risks. This was not understood by the non-clinical managers.' A well-respected stroke consultant in the unit put together a list of potential solutions that were eventually introduced successfully. 'As a stroke specialist, these insights came from his knowledge and experience of the unit and its patients, and through corridor conversations with fellow clinicians, on ward rounds, and staff breaks.'

There are concerns today about stress and psychological ill-health in workplaces.[34] Gallup reported that half of US employees say they have left a company at least once because of a bad boss.[35] Generalist managers are more likely to move from company to company with no core expertise in a particular field, as raised in Chapter 1. If you're managed by someone who doesn't really understand the systems you are using or the day-to-day tasks necessary to get your job done, they might impose new and unnecessary procedures that will cause additional stress and unhappiness. Or they might struggle to understand how best to support you during a particularly challenging period.

Managers who know their business get listened to. A leader's influence is extended if she or he has credibility. Their workers are happier and more productive. It's quite simple, really.

How, then, should organizations identify and develop their expert leaders of the future?

6

Spotting Expert Leaders[*]

I have been told more times than I can count that experts don't make good leaders. That is usually followed by assertions that experts simply do not know enough about finance, or business, or anything else but their own, narrow area of expertise, to make good managers. If I had a penny for every time I heard that, as my granny used to say, I would be rich!

As this book shows, such claims are simply not true. The research that I and my fellow co-authors carried out reveals the opposite, and there is robust evidence across a wide range of industries and professions going back decades showing that when expert leaders take on management roles there can be enormous benefits. As we saw in the previous chapter, there is increased employee engagement and better outcomes, including higher job satisfaction and improved organizational performance. But it is not always easy. Experts need to be well prepared if they are to succeed.

Experts and professionals face unique challenges in pursuing the dual track of being both a specialist and a manager. Imagine you have defined yourself as a 'techy' or 'legal advocate', 'chef' or 'editor', for many years. With that identity has come membership of a tribe you have been a part of your whole career. Then, suddenly, you are no longer just part of the expert team. You have become a manager, a boss. You are now separated from former peers by the need to make decisions on their behalf and to liaise with senior management. This has a huge effect on your psychological sense of self. No

[*] This chapter has greatly benefited from the input of Natasha Maw, Dr Jaason Geerts, and Patty Fahy, MD.

wonder that going from expert to expert leader can be a disorienting and challenging experience.

Many individuals who have acquired significant technical expertise may also have legitimate concerns about whether a management role will mean that they will not only have to give up their professional identity but also shoulder additional burdensome administrative responsibilities, or even in rare cases be required to make a short-term financial sacrifice.

In this chapter and the next we look at how to avoid hiring and promoting the wrong people, how to spot potential leaders and diverse talent, and how to do succession planning. And we outline how best to develop expert leaders.[1]

The 'golden era of management' ends

Succession planning and talent management have changed significantly over the last fifty years. Companies traditionally hand-picked and nurtured future leaders over the long term. This still happens in top management and accounting firms such as McKinsey and Deloitte. Such companies tend only to promote from within and thus rely on their own internally acquired expertise – despite the fact that they sell the opposite story to the rest of the world and consistently recommend others to hire in from outside their organization, and to seek advice from externals like themselves. Indeed, notably, the major consulting firms seem not to preach what they themselves practise.

As technology accelerated innovation, and globalization affected all parts of the labour market, so companies became less secure about their future. This coincided with the period described by Kenneth and William Hopper in *The Puritan Gift* as the end of the 'golden era of management'. A dramatic decline in the promotion of managers to the top from within was mirrored by an obsession with charismatic external CEO hires who were seen as necessary 'change agents'.[2] Hiring externally was not only happening at CEO level. Outside hires started to compete with internals for all management positions, and companies encouraged employees to take personal responsibility for their own career development.

The problem is that this created a sort of superficial democratization of leadership – 'take a training course and you too can become a leader' – without giving employees sufficient support to develop the skills they needed. It was all part of a shift towards generalism and generalists – the advent of peripatetic managers with generic business skills and degrees being promoted in a merry-go-round of management roles instead of knowledgeable executives being promoted from within the ranks. It became easier for generalists to move around, because they were not tied to a process of professional development that required constant technical learning to keep their skill sets up to date, and they could instead focus on becoming proficient in the latest leadership or management fad. This trend runs counter to one of the key arguments of this book: the best bosses are expert leaders, not generalists. Yet, to maintain their expert status, those individuals must be allowed time to continue honing their technical expertise *in tandem* with their leadership development.

When the wrong hat is thrown into the ring

One of the significant changes over the last few decades is the recognition that leaders need to have emotional intelligence. Such skills need partially to be taught – they are not instinctive, or rather instinct is not enough – and when properly developed they enhance not only the leader's own career and ambitions but also benefit all those with whom they work.

For too long the hugely important role of emotion in the workplace was ignored. Now that it is being recognized, there is an awareness that all of us need to hold a mirror up to ourselves and our behaviours in the hope that greater self-awareness can lead to improvement. But for some, behaviour change may still be unlikely, and these are the people whom we should *not* be promoting into leadership roles. So we will explore next the crucial importance of identifying correctly who has leadership potential and who does not.

An influential study published in the *Harvard Business Review* found that most executives believe their organizations are bad at spotting and developing effective leaders.[3] This might explain why one-third of management hires leave their new place of work within three years.[4] Harvard Business School professor Boris Groysberg believes that this is because most hiring practices are 'haphazard at best and ineffective at worst'.[5]

If anything in the following scenario sounds familiar, you are sadly not alone.

Your organization has no formal succession planning; instead talent spotting happens when a management position opens up, usually because someone has left.[6] HR advertises the vacancy, a job description is recycled from the archives, and everyone waits for applications with curiosity, thinking: I wonder who will apply? There is no talent pool of potentially interesting and interested candidates who have been incentivized to throw their hat into the ring. Unsurprisingly, no top-performing internal experts apply, since they are way too focused on their day job, and have no interest in more meetings or admin.[7] After all, no one goes to law school or teacher training to sit in meetings.

A hiring committee wades through the pool of applicants. The committee consists of an HR representative and someone from the department which is recruiting whose main concern may be that the new hire does not try to change too much in the department. High-flying applicants are often the most threatening, because they outshine the panel members, and if hired might suggest the level of productivity should be raised, meaning more work for everyone. In the screening process, they can be strategically dismissed as either overqualified or overconfident. Those who look most like the committee members are eventually shortlisted – unconscious bias in full flow – because diversity means dealing with the unknown and the potential for disruption.

When interviewing the shortlisted candidates, the committee members follow the standard protocol, ask the same set of generic questions, and if they are not bound to hire the most senior person, mull over their initial (gut) reactions, pondering which candidate would be the best fit – code for either are they one of us? or, which is the least likely to rock the boat?

Without a succession plan in place, which can ensure that the best core business experts are prepared through leadership development to be able to apply when management roles arise, who does show up for the job? Seven types of possible candidate are outlined in what follows. All of them present different problems as leaders.

1. The first is the *generalist or career administrator*, who is not a core business expert. He or she has not trained or practised in the area in which they will manage, but is a smooth communicator, well versed in general management principles, likeable, organized, and willing to do the work that the expert candidates (lawyers, doctors, IT specialists, designers) avoid. Some applicants have an MBA and they have learned how to 'please' in interviews.

   Another key fact is worth remembering. In the modern world of organizational democracy, where people are meant to feel 'included' and 'consulted', many non-experts will sit on the panels that make hiring choices. Humans are attracted to people who look like themselves. Deep expertise is uncommon. So the sheer power of democratic decision-making can mean that experts are (wrongly) voted down as leaders by a gaggle of non-experts on a hiring panel.

   If a generalist non-expert is selected, the department will tend to lack cohesion, and revert to siloed working, because the manager does not understand what they do. Quality will decline; bureaucracy may increase as metrics take the place of expert judgement acquired from having spent years in the trade.

2. A second possible candidate is the *mediocre professional*, who is unlikely to get promoted on core business performance alone because they are not that proficient; so, instead, they attempt to raise their status and pay by trying to get promoted into a management role. They do not mind foregoing practitioner time because

CREDIBLE

they are not that committed anyway. Much time may have been spent fraternizing with senior managers in a bid to get noticed. If hired, business resumes as usual, although then there is rarely an inspiring vision or remarkable improvement, and the top performers will feel little allegiance to their new manager, and just want them to stay out of their way.

3. Another type, which Patty Fahy, MD, a leadership consultant and former health-care executive, has written and spoken extensively about, are *narcissists*. Dr Fahy says:

> This could be a generalist too, like a certain former president or prime minister, an entitled individual driven to ascend to the top of the organization because they see themselves as special and, if only subconsciously, want the spotlight. They are the kind of person who tends to take a disagreement personally, and to have little empathy for others.

One point is especially relevant. Dr Fahy believes that 'narcissists will wreak havoc when they are part of a team, but when they reach the upper echelons of leadership (which they very often do) they will destroy the organizational culture.' She concedes that they can be bright, technically high-performing, and articulate. Therefore, dangerously, 'selection committees and upper management often interpret their self-absorption to be an appealing self-confidence' and, she adds, 'They are masters of the "kiss up, kick down" rule. Once they are ensconced in a leadership role, their unfortunate direct reports discover every move is self-serving, blame always belongs elsewhere, and the rules do not apply to them.' Narcissists are agreeable only to those who can advance their agenda – wherever those people are.[8]

4. Fourth on the list is the *overconfident under-experienced professional on the rise*. They may have proved themselves, for example as teachers or engineers, but they lack the management experience necessary for a higher role. If hired, they can burn out or fail

within the first six months, and may be reluctant to ever consider another run at management again – and indeed their failure may have been so spectacular no one else is willing to take a chance on them.

5. Next is the *veteran* candidate, who sees such a role as providing a summation or a fitting end to their career. The veteran may well have been a high-performer some time ago, but has not been professionally active for a while and has failed to maintain their core business credibility. As a result, the experts and professionals they manage view them as out of touch with the latest thinking in the field, and even though they may have lots of experience to offer, the team lacks confidence that the veteran leader can help them develop or innovate. Frustrated by what they perceive to be a lack of originality or willingness to do things differently, the young high-performers in the team can start to look for jobs elsewhere. Creativity stagnates.

6. Sixth is the *'buddy' or protégé* of someone with power, who has been given the job as a result of favouritism or nepotism. Such appointees are expected to pursue the interests and wishes of whoever has given them the job and are rarely judged by their bosses on the basis of actual competence or performance but on the basis of loyalty and malleability. In turn, the people who work for them are generally divided between those who are loyal to the leader and those who are not. Not surprisingly, outcomes and quality suffer, infighting occurs, and top performers get fed up and start to quit.

7. Finally, there is the *outsider*, an externally hired candidate, who may be professionally qualified but who lacks understanding of the organizational culture and the sensitivity required to represent staff and resonate with clients. This person may even be an outstanding expert, someone it is deemed necessary to bring in because organizational performance has declined – so the bar needs to be raised and no one within the organization is able to

do it. If they work hard to understand the people and culture, and if they surround themselves with the talent inside the department, then standards can and should, given enough time, rise. Yet there are risks. If the person neglects to foster the relationships and do the trust-building required, and is insensitive or fails to reflect on what they as an incomer do not know, then the first year can be one of blunders and new initiatives that existing staff do not support. The second year might improve, perhaps through lessons learned the hard way. However, to make all this work requires a degree of self-awareness and humility that few humans possess. While the outsider has a tough hill to climb, some of the key staff will be reluctant to wait around to see if they make it.

A culture of second best

We have described the types of candidate that are best avoided or can be problematic when promoted into leadership roles, but do individual appointments really matter as long as the organizational structure and culture are strong? Dr Michael Gardam, former chief executive officer of Health PEI for Prince Edward Island, a small province just off Canada's Atlantic coast, believes that

> Nobody's perfect and everyone needs to develop, but people who are deficient in key areas should not advance into leadership roles. I've worked with senior leaders who have had amazing strengths . . . but [also] shocking weaknesses and are terrible leaders mainly because of their poor emotional intelligence, inability to see how their actions are perceived by others and they don't listen to anyone! They're often raging workaholics, which helps them get a lot done, but by bulldozing through it. Long-term, they damage the potential of their organization, and a frightening number of talented people leave, because they create a toxic culture. [9]

Dr Patty Fahy agrees, and explains how this can have a negative impact in the health-care system. For example: 'if the work environment is toxic or the health system leaders prioritize profits over patients – then the most esteemed physicians will eschew leadership roles, because they will not compromise their professional values.' And, as she points out, 'the best of the best don't need to compromise because they have options'.[10]

Additionally, where there is minimal investment in leadership development, this signals that a physician's value is as a revenue generator, not a leader. 'This is especially noticeable', continues Fahy, 'when compared with the development opportunities offered to non-physician counterparts.'

Promoting the wrong people will also lead to a culture of second best. Or worse. A workplace that becomes dysfunctional disengages and ultimately depletes its pool of talented individuals. Brilliant people can easily find other work. Plodders find it harder.

The executive partners at one of the Big Four discovered that their traditional talent-spotting approach had left them with a group of managers who were mainly white, male, and aggressive workaholics driven by financial incentives. Their talented millennials had fled the firm – interested in greater work–life balance, more diversity, a less macho culture, and an empathetic work environment.[11] Today, that organization tries to ensure that managers and directors have the frameworks, tools, and training to be able to identify and measure all potential and recommend *different* career pathways.

Getting it wrong has serious consequences. In one major hospital system, physicians were line-managed by nurses. It seems unlikely that anyone who had any understanding of the health-care system would think such an arrangement could work. Not only do physicians have many more years of training and different expertise from nurses, but crucially physicians have the ultimate legal responsibility for patients. In one hospital system that failed to see this, many of the nurse-managers lacked the necessary knowledge to assess doctors' medical competence or understand their training needs. The result: a high turnover of physicians. As one doctor complained,

Nurse managers took the autonomy away from doctors by micromanaging the allocation of clinical tasks, because they didn't really understand what we do. This led to a chaotic work environment. Overall, doctors were disappointed by the lack of learning opportunities and concerned for the quality of patient care.[12]

Getting beyond the diversity déjà vu

While appointing the wrong candidate to a leadership role can have serious consequences for an organization, another fundamental issue which needs to be considered when hiring is diversity. You may have become bored reading headlines that continually lament the absence of diversity at the head of organizations. The problem is that the persistent lack of diversity at the top is not only inequitable, it is also inefficient. Apart from underqualified white guys, everyone is losing out.

There are two things that should be considered at the outset for the successful inclusion of diverse candidates. First, they must be *core business experts, who are credible and have the expertise and experience to succeed.* This is crucial. Placing someone in a role merely to signal an organization is ticking the diversity box can cause more harm than good, for the individual, the organization, and the diversity movement. A form of this is when women or ethnically diverse candidates are handed a poisoned chalice – the so-called glass cliff phenomenon – by being given a leadership role when the risk of failure, due to economic or company downturns, is most likely.

Second, to ensure the individuals succeed in their leadership role, ample support and development must be available. But we also need to recruit differently. Conventional selection and promotion practices assume that the 'best people will reach the top'. Yet many good candidates are often unwilling to throw their hat into the ring. Years of overt and covert discrimination can predispose women and minority candidates, for instance, to be psychologically wary of entering competitions, and more likely to suffer psychologically from failure or rejection.[13] The willingness to compete for management and leadership roles requires self-confidence, and a belief that one has a real chance in a system that is both fair and meritocratic.

On the demand side, recruiters are prone to biases and other irrationalities. Evidence from neuroscience shows that stereotype associations, which influence behaviour through unconscious biases, are hard to control. When candidates differ greatly in their characteristics, they are more difficult to compare. Research suggests that evaluations are then more likely to be implicitly influenced by prejudices, stereotypes, and in-group favouritism. So, although employers are eager to select diverse candidates, they often fail to do so.[14]

Some of the solutions that address the supply side, that is, which focus on encouraging more diverse candidates to put themselves forward, try to 'fix the woman'. The female candidate is encouraged to 'lean in' or 'ask more'. This implies that women are where they are due to lack of ambition, when in fact the evidence shows that women have been asking for higher pay and promotions for a long time, but just not getting them.[15] This is an insidious form of blaming the discriminated-against group or individual rather than looking at where the institutional discrimination comes from. Relatedly, and possibly the most ubiquitous form of bias, is homophily – selecting in your own image (mentioned in the recruitment scenario earlier) which is often practised by people who are totally unaware of what they are doing. This tendency to be attracted to versions of oneself is evident on hiring panels, across management activities, and in many social settings.

Populating middle-management with diverse expert talent is essential, because *if it is not in the middle, diversity will never reach the top*. Homogeneity harms organizations in many ways. Scott Page, a distinguished professor at the University of Michigan, has shown that there is an inclusion and 'diversity bonus' from heterogeneous teams. He found that problem solving is improved, innovation increased, adaptation made easier, and predictions are more accurate, all of which, he argues, leads to better performance and results.[16]

A recent study on gender pay found that the wage gap starts to close when the share of female managers in the workplace rises.[17] This happens, the authors found, because women's wages are more likely to go up under a female boss, while men's decline or flatten. Interestingly, the authors reveal that 'this is more pronounced when employees are paid for performance, consistent with the proposition that women are more likely to be paid equitably when managers have discretion in the way they reward performance, and those managers are women.' This suggests the need to spot and incentivize more women and diverse candidates into management.

Importantly, if we don't see anyone ahead who looks like us, we are unlikely to join the leadership track. This point was made by the historian and broadcaster David Olusoga in his keynote lecture at the Edinburgh Television Festival.[18] In discussing his previous experience at the BBC when he was a young journalist, Olusoga explained that although some efforts had been made to recruit diverse talent into the broadcaster in the early 1990s, most of those hired had not been retained. The new generation had been welcomed into the BBC, but then dumped, with careers leading nowhere. The absence of Black people in senior positions had left Olusoga feeling isolated and disempowered. This ultimately led Marvin Rees, current mayor of the English city of Bristol who started out as a BBC journalist, to quit and became a politician. Olusoga believes that the media may not have lost a generation of Black talent if someone like himself 'might have been there, or on the end of the phone, as a senior colleague, to give advice'.

What Olusoga was referring to is the informal learning and development that has to underpin an effective desire to recruit, retain, and promote diverse expert talent. Aware of its earlier failures, the BBC recently launched its most ambitious diversity strategy yet,[19] which, importantly, places most emphasis on how to develop and nurture diverse talent into management positions. It has committed to expanding its pool of diverse senior leaders and supporting their development through networking and providing role models, flexible working, and mentoring, executive coaching, and action learning (a form of group coaching that will be discussed in Chapter 8) – precisely the kind of initiatives that Olusoga was calling for.

Over the past few years the UK *Financial Times* newspaper has also altered its approach to the recruitment and development of diverse candidates. Isabel Berwick, work and careers editor at the *FT*, has been involved in the changes. As she explains, an issue for the newspaper had been a scarcity of diversity, particularly in areas of class, ethnicity, and disability, among the senior leadership:

> But we have a number of new schemes at the *FT* that go to the heart of the issues raised by David Olusoga. We have created mechanisms that help employees to be seen and heard by more senior experts within the organization. For example, we have introduced reverse mentoring, and we have a 'next generation board' that shadows our Executive Board, which has led to a cross-fertilization of ideas and advice between the two. All sorts of new ideas have emerged, for example, employee listening posts, and a peer mentoring scheme. [20]

Samira Chowdhury[21] has worked in insurance for twenty years. She is currently the HR director of an international insurer and reinsurer based in London. The firm have introduced a performance management strategy that encourages leaders to give continuous feedback. It is tailored to the individual, a process far removed from the box-ticking approach followed by many. Chowdhury says: 'We take a many-sizes-fit-all approach to career progression and development. Performance management is based on technical expertise and whether a candidate expresses the values held by the firm – such as "enjoying being different", "inspired by opportunity" and "determined to improve".' In insurance, leaders must have technical knowledge. Importantly, all the senior executives have domain expertise.

Charisse Jimenez, in charge of Physician Leadership Development at Texas Health Resources, has discovered something very interesting. She has put nearly 300 physicians through her leadership programme. Notably, over 50 per cent were nominated by their peers instead of their managers. Jimenez believes that the process of peer nomination has greatly increased diversity – in ethnicity, sex, age, experience, specialty, gender orientation, and more. 'I believe it eliminates some of the bias executives may have simply due to their limited spheres of observing physicians practising on the front line.' This method of selecting for development programmes could be easily applied in all workplaces.

Taking the horse to water – motivating experts to become leaders

In order to ensure that they choose the right people from a diverse pool of candidates, world-leading organizations develop systematic talent identification and management strategies as an integral part of their organizational strategy. Dr Verna Yiu, President and CEO of Alberta Health Services, Canada's largest health-care organization, describes her leadership journey. As a young paediatric nephrologist, she was focused on refining her clinical practice and had no grand leadership ambitions. One day, a senior leader tapped her on the shoulder and suggested that she had leadership potential. Yiu reflects, 'I didn't think of myself as a leader, but the seed was planted and it started to germinate.' In her many executive roles, she has had the opportunity to tap others on the shoulder, to let them know they are being considered for leadership and an interesting future of possibilities. Then, Yiu says, you observe how they respond.

What does she look for in promising future leaders?

For medical leaders, being an exceptional clinician is a given, along with the ability to consolidate information and communicate it effectively and succinctly, to work well with others, to make things happen, while having humility, empathy, humour, and kindness, and, of course, excellent leadership skills.

Yiu believes that getting to know people is key to talent management, because you also have to know whose shoulders *not* to tap. Endorsing the wrong person can badly hurt the reputation of those doing the promoting. Yiu says that the biggest mistake people make in hiring and promoting is

> not doing the homework and skipping over steps that are important. There are lots of charmers who are great at impressing supervisors but are horrible at managing others and being team members. Full 360-degree confidential reference checks are crucial, along with introducing candidates to the teams they would be working with, and getting their feedback, which also contributes to earning their buy-in.

Experts are inherently drawn to the acquisition of knowledge. That is why and how they became an expert in the first place. The compelling issue for organizations who want to harness the dual skills of expertise and leadership is how to attract such people into these positions.[22] As we discussed at the beginning of the chapter, these people have trained in their specialism for years, crafted their trade, and adopted an identity as a design engineer, advertising creative, or social worker, which they are often reluctant to give up. Therefore organizations must adopt a strategy tailored to their specific needs and concerns, and consider, for optimal outcomes, what would motivate a potential expert leader to make this move? Despite this logic, how many of us have ever been asked, on annual staff surveys, the simple question: what would motivate you to take a management role?

We did just that in a survey of physicians in Denmark.[23] My colleagues and I asked: would doctors be willing to lead and, if so, what might motivate them to do so? We discovered things that will likely apply to most experts, from lawyers to helicopter pilots. First, respondents said they would step forward if they could make a positive impact and explicitly 'make a difference'. Second, if their pay was increased – because it is necessary to remunerate people more to persuade them to step away from their first love, especially when

walking away means the loss of technical hours and accrued expertise that raise a physician's fees. Third, the physicians recognized that
they needed to be trained in leadership and management, and
wanted to be given enough time to do the necessary personal development work.

What were the perceived disincentives associated with taking a
job in management? Losing time for medical practice and research,
and instead spending hours on meetings and administration
(which, these days, has become overwhelming in many organizations). Respondents also felt frustrated by the siloed nature of
health care. They perceived a lack of leadership training opportunities, and of space to develop leadership skills. Not having the
resources to be able to make that all-important 'difference' is also
an issue; and finally, a rise in work pressure tied to the inevitable
fear of burnout, which is a huge problem in health care every-
where. The issues outlined by physicians in our survey are common
to many occupations.

Professionals – whether they be landscape architects, solicitors,
or chefs – identify strongly with their professional roles. That is how
they describe themselves to others and present themselves to the
world – and they also feel happiest, and safest, with others in their
own tribe who think as they do. Why would they want to lose this
association and identity, to move from team player and one of us, to
one of them, the managers? The answer lies with incentives. While
those who are intrinsically motivated by their work are less concerned
about extrinsic factors such as cash, it is important to feel that one's
skills and experience are formally recognized, and one of the problems with core business experts moving into management is often
the lack of adequate compensation for the extra work. Counter-
intuitively, many physicians are expected to actually take a pay cut
when they take on a leadership role.

A person's internal psychology also matters. The need for experts
to identify psychologically as leaders is, as we found in our research,
a significant factor. It influences how they perform as a manager, and
how those who work with them feel. We discovered that employee
job satisfaction and retention were higher among those people

whose line managers were both outstanding experts and also identified with their new identity of leader – in other words, those bosses
who were happy in their new managerial skin. Taking on the mantle
and identity of a boss is part of taking responsibility when power is
offered. It also signals to other potential expert leaders that it is okay
to classify yourself in this way.[24]

But a word of warning – as those who become leaders go upwards,
ties with their expert colleagues become looser, and the sense of
their own professional identity weakens, while their leadership
identity strengthens. Having started out as a standard-bearer for
the core business employees, they are now expected to act on behalf
of all units and departments. Hard as it might be, the expert CEO
is obliged to master the difficult balance of being a leader for all
while at the same time continuing to focus strategy around the core
functions.

Let me be clear: there are many who think that when someone,
particularly an expert, becomes a senior executive or CEO, they
must think equally about every part of the organization. Of course
they must consider the well-being of all employees, but ultimately
expert leaders have to prioritize the core business workers and
departments, even though many non-experts will try to divert them
from this approach. The expert leader may also feel uncomfortable
if the expertise they represent is deemed more important than
others' knowledge, and may therefore try to water it down or
distance themselves from the original tribe. The desire to be a CEO
whom everyone loves is strong. But it should be kept for a Walt
Disney movie, not real life. It is not possible to please all the people
all the time.

To encourage expert leaders into management requires a clear,
incentivized, attractive pathway that also offers flexibility. As
suggested, people's identity is primarily shaped by what they do. It
requires what the literature calls a dual identity to see oneself as
both expert and manager – and to feel okay about that. Sitting
comfortably within this middle ground is difficult and takes time to
adjust to. Who am I now? What will my colleagues think? And so
on.

For this reason, organizations should make it possible for core business experts to continue to perform their primary role and maintain their technical identity for as long as is necessary for them to adjust to their new management role. And of course allowing them to keep their hand in has benefits, because it maintains their credibility. Inevitably, over time, as the vision broadens and the executive takes on extra responsibility, the more removed they are going to be from frontline tasks. However, if they are experts, and able to self-reflect, they will know when the time is ripe to step back and hand the baton on to the next generation.[25]

Who should drink the water?

In the military, soldiers have to learn how to command as well as fight. Consider Britain's elite Sandhurst military academy. During the first fourteen weeks of its ten-month officer training programme an officer cadet is charged with leading a series of combat simulations. These exercises take place in safe and controlled environments, but they are physically and emotionally exhausting. They require cadets to perform efficiently on minimal sleep while facing realistic wartime challenges. After each exercise, the cadets evaluate their own performance. That is followed by an assessment by senior officers and fellow cadets. The evaluation criteria for these After Action Reviews (AARs) are based on the military's six core values – courage, discipline, respect for others, integrity, loyalty, and selfless commitment – as well as on established performance standards. Because combat leadership is about dealing with life and death situations, feedback is candid and stringent and performance at the highest level is expected.[26]

There are lessons for other industries from this approach. Indeed, the concept of leadership and its development began in the armed forces.

In the United States, the professionalization of the armed forces was set off by the Civil War of 1861–5, with the upgrade of weapons and capacity to kill on a scale previously unknown.[27] Rakesh Khurana notes in his book, *From Higher Aims to Hired Hands*, 'chivalric

conceptions of the soldier's calling, and the nation's military academies shifted their focus away from producing heroic leaders and to
the education of military "managers", often trained as engineers.'[28]
The military changed its perception of leadership and notably it
tailored its management and leadership development around the
wider needs of the armed forces.

Selection through 'theatres of observation', as is so often used in
the military, creates environments for individuals to be observed and
coached while performing their actual job. These kinds of settings
provide a forum for assessing emerging leaders in a way that is not
reflected on a resumé, such as accountability, collaborative acumen,
and self-awareness.

Major General Marc Bilodeau, MD, surgeon general of the
Canadian Armed Forces, explains that in the Canadian military,

> talent management and succession planning are systematic,
> proactive, continuous processes. The goals are to maintain an
> action-ready talent pool, to ensure that the best leaders are
> promoted, and to orchestrate the optimal alignment between
> the leaders' capacities based on their competencies, and past
> experiences, and the roles to which they are assigned.

Each year, all members of the Canadian military are assessed by
their supervisors in terms of their performance and their potential
for leadership progression.

Officers being promoted to the rank of brigadier general or
higher also undergo 360-degree assessments prior to being
promoted. Those assessments offer a fuller picture of individuals'
professional conduct and can identify blind spots that would potentially affect their ability to lead in a reliable way at higher levels.
Supervisor assessments are intense. They allow selection board
members to observe how high-potential cadets perform in different
circumstances, which in turn aids succession planning. Importantly,
the military recognizes that their best experts need to be involved in
appraisals, since experts are more likely to pick up signs of weak or
outstanding performance.

Although the military provides a very specific context for this kind of recruitment and development, such approaches can be successfully applied in other settings that require a high level of performance coupled with an extreme level of responsibility. Lynn Myers is the chief medical and quality officer at Texas Health Physicians Group in Dallas, Texas. The group includes over 600 physicians and 475 physician assistants and nurse practitioners in 200 plus hospitals and clinics. Dr Myers organizes regular networking events prior to meetings, as a kind of theatre of observation. As the event kicks off, she walks around mingling with physicians so she can observe them. She recalls noticing the behaviour of one person in particular. He was vocal in expressing his appreciation of her attention; he leaned into the conversation and almost seemed to soak up her words. His posture was open, his eye contact intentional, his response to her sincere, and he offered to help should the need ever arise. He was confident, she noticed, so she was curious about what level of expertise he truly had. Dr Myers then recalled, years before, having visited his clinic and being stunned at the technical sophistication of the man's operations. So it seemed possible that his aptitude matched his seeming confidence. Two years after their first meet-and-greet, she hired him as medical director, and today is pleased with his managerial progress and development.

Charisse Jimenez, who has been training physicians in leadership for over twenty-five years, works with Dr Myers. She says: 'These cues or behaviours may not seem like anything profound, but they are a signal of potential, and what we use to spot candidates nominated onto our physicians lead programme.' Jimenez suggests criteria such as

> exhibiting interest, or already serving, in a leadership capacity at any level, small or large; frequently asking, how can I help to make this better?, and being willing to or contributing to an improvement effort; appears to have good ideas, is innovative, may act as a change agent, and importantly, is able to influence others.

There are many ways that leadership opportunities can be used to test the capability of top performers. Employees can be asked to manage projects from conception to completion, to supervise others directly, and to work across different divisions of an organization. Delivering strong outcomes in these stretch roles can also strengthen their expert leader identity. Candidates earmarked for C-suite roles should also be involved in committees that inform decisions about strategy and finance, and be put on hiring panels.

It is a cliché to say that organizations are only as good as their people, but the best companies are aware of their reliance on expert talent – as I will discuss in Chapter 8. These are the workplaces that make you feel genuinely valued because they recognize that they are lucky to have you, not the other way around. When such workplaces encounter outstanding talent, they are not fazed if there is no vacancy available at that time. Instead, they find creative ways to engage and retain a brilliant person. Their leaders and managers are active, at all levels, in spotting, developing, and supporting top performers from the moment of recruitment throughout their career. They stay close to their best employees and work to keep them. This is not entirely altruistic: staff churn is expensive and also destabilizing.

Talent spotting, hiring talent, and HR

At Sandhurst, the best soldiers train and evaluate the best soldiers. The ideal candidates to be able to judge talent are those who have achieved a world-class standard themselves. Top performers know what great looks like. As covered in Chapter 3, our study of NBA basketball teams shows that coaches who had been all-star players, such as Bill Russell, or had long playing careers in the NBA, like Phil Jackson, typically become the most successful coaches.

Core business experts – top designers, actuaries, fund managers – should thus be involved alongside HR professionals in the selection of new recruits and in deciding on promotions, as well as in performance reviews and evaluations. This facilitates a better fit and maintains quality, but it often feels like human resource functions sit miles away from the technical talent they are trying to recruit and develop. Can HR really understand them?

Anthony 'Mac' McKeever is an NHS CEO[29] and turnaround specialist. He has worked for more than twenty-five years helping boards to deliver reform and better results in health care. He is a passionate advocate of expert clinical leadership, partly because 'professionals who can align their own clinical vision and strategy with that of an organization, improve things for patients and taxpayers'. McKeever gets frustrated about the siloed nature of HR and clinical expertise in the NHS, which he sees as detrimental to successful health care:

> HR isn't as radical as it could be. It would work much better if HR were mandated to work with clinicians. Staffing requirements could then be shaped by experience and expertise, so that clinicians can exercise control over the lion's share of resources. This means that HR would put their trust in clinical experts to reorganize their own departments to make them work better.

He gives an example:

> I visited one hospital where the surgeons' operating routines did not dovetail with those of the recovery nurses who work alongside them in the same theatres. This was because HR had determined the nurses' rotas. Staff need to be flexible and be available when patients actually come through the door, but HR were concerned not to break union agreements. If this is how key staff want to work, then change the agreements.

McKeever would like to see HR work closely with clinicians to develop workforce plans that give power, resources, and responsibility for planning to people on the frontline who can use it to best effect. 'Why don't specialist functions like HR and clinicians work more closely together? Because the organisational set-up doesn't always encourage it.'

The private sector has been quicker to realize the importance of bringing HR and organizational development personnel closer to employees in core business functions. When this alignment happens it has a direct, positive, and significant effect on organizational performance.[30] This joined-up approach ensures that the most talented are recognized and developed.

Dr Patty Fahy, the leadership consultant mentioned earlier, was given a strategic HR role after she joined the executive team of a large medical group. She was asked to lead a mission to improve culture and increase engagement among a group of about 600 physicians.

> It didn't occur to me to include 'performance management' as a central element of my HR strategy. But it became clear very quickly that a lack of clarity and accountability was a huge contributor to the poor morale. So performance management is not just about highlighting areas for improvement and development; the urgency comes from the wide-ranging impact that incompetence or toxic behaviour has on the organization.

Dr Fahy and her team launched a tiered approach to physician leadership programmes that included modules on performance management. Increasingly, the local department chiefs took on the bulk of the disciplinary issues. They consulted her only as needed. She states that she considered orientation to be the first step of leadership development and she invited every new physician to a three-day 'Introduction to Management' course. In that course, physicians learned about recruiting and selection, performance management, labour relations, and how to run meetings. This type of education paid great dividends because formal physician leaders, the chiefs and department heads, now had other physicians in their group who had some understanding of management issues.

Fahy believes it is critical to do performance management as early as possible:

> Ideally we don't bring a low performer or someone with narcissistic traits into the organization. But if we do make a

hiring mistake, we have to address it before they drive away high-performers or – heaven forbid – before they find a way into a leadership role. Physician leaders, and other experts in the core business, can do this work because they have credibility with their peers and their teams. And they understand the enormous costs of staff unhappiness and low physician morale that can arise if performance management isn't done. I think physician leadership pays enormous dividends in terms of organizational culture and ultimately the performance of the entire organization.

Many HR departments use 'capability frameworks', which define the competencies, capacities, or skills necessary for employees to perform different roles or functions. Our research suggests that organizations should modify their existing frameworks to infuse them with expertise, articulating a set of key domain capabilities that expert leaders must demonstrate to execute their roles at various stages of their careers. HR can then use their Expert Leaders Capability Frameworks as guides for creating or revising job descriptions, performance evaluations, interview questions and hiring and promotion criteria, staff development plans, and internal development programme design priorities. However, as Anthony McKeever said, organizations need to develop structures and systems which are expert-friendly and allow experts to do selection and performance management.

I have argued in this chapter that if experts take on management roles then there can be enormous benefits to the success of organizations and the well-being of workers. However, specialists need to be encouraged and motivated to go into leadership. They need to be confident that they will be developed and supported in the transition from expert to leader while being assured that they will be able to make tangible differences for the benefit of their teams, organizations, and stakeholders. Organizations also have to be adept at spotting and hiring the right people. They need to be mindful of the disruptive lure of homophily, of any lack of diversity, of the weaknesses of charismatic and narcissistic charmers, and of inadequate recruitment procedures.

But that is not easy. Organizations should focus on the skills, behaviours, and inherent talent of their home-grown experts – while integrating HR with expert-led specialist departments to ensure that the right people are noticed and encouraged.

Let us now look at exactly how to help brilliant technical experts develop into outstanding expert leaders.

7

Developing Experts into Leaders*

Anders Ericsson was described as the 'expert on experts'. He was a Swedish scholar who spent his career trying to understand how the best experts develop their skills.[1] His first famous study 'The Role of Deliberate Practice in the Acquisition of Expert Performance', published in 1993, argued: 'Many characteristics once believed to reflect innate talent are actually the result of intense practice extended for a minimum of 10 years.'[2] In this article, Ericsson and his colleagues examined violinists at the Academy of Music in Berlin. The authors discovered that those who went on to become violin teachers put in around 4,000 hours of practice, whereas very good violinists put in 8,000, and the really elite performers clocked up more than 10,000 hours. This is where Malcolm Gladwell's so-called 10,000-hour rule as described in *Outliers* came from, although Ericsson viewed it as an oversimplification of his work.[3]

Ericsson went on to scrutinize the lives of chess masters, basketball players, ballerinas, surgeons, and runners. In all of these different areas of expertise, he showed that deliberate practice was a necessary component but that, unsurprisingly, natural ability also played a central role. Subsequently, researchers like Fredrik Ullen, Zachary Hambrick and Miriam Mosing have argued that peak performance is more likely due to innate talent and intelligence than practice.[4] Whichever direction causality goes – that is, the most talented are the most motivated because they have the greatest chance of success, or the most motivated become the most talented

* As with the previous chapter, this one has greatly benefited from the input of Natasha Maw, Dr Jaason Geerts, and Patty Fahy, MD.

because of their hard work – Ericsson's 'deliberate practice', involving immediate feedback, clear goals, and focus on technique, is a necessary part of rising to the highest skill levels in whatever the field.

As an approximation, it is the best 10 to 20 per cent of performers who should make up the pool of suitable candidates for senior leadership roles. Their talent and experience ensures that the putative leader can set the benchmark for what needs to be achieved, can mentor others, and can give strategic direction (as outlined in Chapter 3).

As the above suggests, experts have a very particular set of qualities. These enable them to drill deeply within a relatively narrow field of knowledge: the qualities include tenacity, commitment, self-belief, focus. The downside of this may be the presence of hubris; they have excelled in one area, therefore they may assume that they are pretty good at everything else. This could lead to a certain level of arrogance, or, if one is being kinder, a lack of self-awareness about their own skills and competencies outside their area of expertise. That gap in perception can be particularly obvious in their dealings with others.

As a manager this is a serious problem and can undermine a leader's credibility. Experts can be overly confident and sometimes even psychologically inept with other human beings.

Charisse Jimenez, from Texas Health Resources, told us she finds it

> interesting that the very qualities that draw attention to potential leaders can also cause their demise. Passion, commitment, and deep expertise can cross over into speaking up too much, or with arrogance, or at the wrong time. Also, there is a capability gap between the capacity to present intelligent insight or ideas and turning those into results. This type of development occurs through coaching or supporting relationships.

Those difficult conversations

Another issue that we have identified in the leadership training we have done with doctors is that they tend to be good at difficult conversations only if the topic relates to their field. They are routinely less comfortable if the topic is outside that area of expertise. Doctors can inform patients about life-threatening health conditions and advise them on their options. Likewise, lawyers are happy to give their clients a realistic analysis of their prospects of winning or losing a legal battle. In both cases the information that is being shared is grounded in experience, previous precedent, the letter of the law, or in science.

But ask an expert to have an emotive conversation with a problematic work colleague, and many will do their utmost to avoid tackling the issues. They will beat about the bush to avoid a direct confrontation – with the result that the problematic behaviour is not addressed. That can affect the whole team and lead to the most brilliant members of a work group leaving. It is also not uncommon for an unscrupulous person who is behaving badly to recognize that others are keen to avoid direct conflict and to use that to their own advantage. They will threaten to make a complaint to HR before their work colleagues or managers can, in a bid to shut them up. Senior managers and colleagues alike may fear that it will be a negative mark on their record, thereby impeding their chances of promotion – not to mention the time and energy taken up by dealing with the complaint procedures and subsequent investigations. In this way, the disruptive staff member may effectively ensure they are never challenged, with dire consequences for everyone involved, and especially the success of the business.

It is therefore essential that expert leaders are capable of having difficult conversations. That usually means having them with difficult people. It is our collective responsibility to call out bad behaviour, and expert leaders need to understand and deploy the skills and capabilities necessary to do so.

Becoming emotionally intelligent

James Stoller, MD, chair of the Education Institute at the Cleveland Clinic, believes that expert leaders have to excel in areas such as sensitivity to others' feelings, willingness to listen, emotional intelligence, ability to work with diverse people, and understanding the motivations of other employees, which requires an ongoing, collaborative process of feedback and dialogue with regular performance management touchpoints. Stoller, who is also an organizational development scholar, has spent years training physicians to be leaders. He strongly believes that 'emotional intelligence is a core competency for health-care leaders. Ample evidence and experience demonstrate that self-awareness, to deeply listen, to be socially aware, and to manage relationships are absolutely critical for a leader's success.'[5]

Emotional intelligence is 'the ability to process information about your own emotions and other people's. It's also the ability to use this information to guide your thoughts and behavior.'[6] Daniel Goleman popularized the term in his book *Emotional Intelligence – Why It Can Matter More Than IQ.*[7] He later illuminated the importance of EI to leadership, demonstrating that the best leaders use self-awareness, self-regulation, motivation, empathy, and social skills to maximize not only their own performance but that of their followers.[8]

A recent act, in June 2020, of truth-telling and empathy – both essential components of emotional intelligence – was witnessed when the most senior enlisted member of the US Air Force, Kaleth Wright, asked a question on Twitter: 'Who am I?'

His response went viral and pushed Air Force leaders into responding to the latest act of police brutality – an act they had been slow to comment on. 'I am a Black man,' said Wright, 'who happens to be the Chief Master Sergeant of the Air Force. I am George Floyd ... I am Philando Castile, I am Michael Brown, I am Alton Sterling, I am Tamir Rice,' all the names of Black men killed by police officers.[9] This was the first time that a senior leader in the Defense Department had spoken publicly about the death of George Floyd.

The need to demonstrate emotional intelligence (EI) as a key leadership competency, and speaking the truth is being more widely called for in military circles (as well as in many businesses). There is also greater awareness of the need to manage and reduce the number of toxic leaders – defined as those 'who embody dysfunctional characteristics, exhibit destructive behavior and so generate a poisonous effect on the organizations and individuals they lead'.[10]

In 2010, then Brigadier General Pete Bayer asked anthropologist and psychologist Dave Matsuda to advise US commanders on why thirty soldiers in Iraq had committed or attempted suicide in just one year. 'Whenever a soldier committed suicide,' Bayer said, 'a team of Army investigators would essentially ask the same questions: What was wrong with the individual soldier?' A troubled childhood, mental health problems, the end of a relationship, or debts? Bayer reported that the answer was often yes, but he also recognized that something else was going on, and sure enough there was more. Matsuda uncovered that personal problems were evident but that 'the victims also had a leader who made their lives hell – sometimes a couple of leaders',[11] and this is what made the life-or-death difference. Toxic leadership was also blamed for the high number of sexual assaults in the military.

In 2009 the Center for Army Leadership at Fort Leavenworth in Kansas surveyed 22,000 troops to try to assess the quality of its commanders. Although many received high ratings, an astonishing 20 per cent of soldiers reported that they had toxic leaders. In 2012 the army articulated clearly in its Army Doctrine Publication that 'Toxic leadership', in summary, 'is a combination of self-centered attitudes, motivations, and behaviors that have adverse effects on subordinates, the organization, and mission performance.'[12] The British Army Leadership Doctrine now also includes a similar text.[13]

George Reed, previously director of Command and Leadership Studies at the US War College, believes that toxic behaviour derives from a leader's own feelings of inferiority, often combined with narcissism. At one end of the toxic spectrum are the psychopaths with personality disorders, and at the other, suggests Reed, sit those whose behaviour can be corrected or lessened through various development programmes.[14] But holding up the proverbial mirror in front of ourselves is hard. Fixing our own behaviour is the most testing of challenges. Nevertheless, learning and training courses designed to help us change undesirable behaviours are now commonplace. They are spreading into industries and organizations, like the army, once considered conservative and previously resistant.

When they don't want to be trained

Josh Saxby is divisional director of Clarkson plc, one of the oldest shipping services companies in the world, established in 1852, with a market capitalization of over £1 billion.

> The issue with the current generation of leaders in shipbroking is that they are often also the most successful revenue earners, and have little or no interest in the practice of leading itself; they therefore continue to service their own portfolio of business. As a result, little heed is given to people development, strategic decision-making or around improving their own abilities to lead.[15]

Saxby considers the industry to be somewhat 'self-interested', with individuals chasing their next deal to enlarge their annual bonus. 'Whilst this is no bad thing, a balance needs to be struck. It is important for the industry that those with credibility in their field step forward to become leaders and managers.'

Boutique asset management businesses have also been slow to recognize the benefits of developing their leaders. Sebastian Stewart, partner and head of client services at Somerset Capital Management, explained that

> boutiques are typically established by small groups of experi-enced investment professionals who want to create unbureau-cratic businesses that can focus on capitalizing on the founders' investment expertise. Developing teams and future leaders is rarely a priority. This has meant that leadership development is often overlooked, that is until it is brought into focus when the founders want to diversify their offering or think about succes-sion. By that stage, it can be too late. Those boutiques who have not invested in their staff can face significant financial costs and uncertainty in making external appointments, and it can even be a death blow for some.[16]

Tim Liversedge, a paediatric anaesthetist at Great Ormond Street Children's Hospital in London, and an alumnus of our physician MSc, described how leadership presents a challenge to the mindset of a physician:

> The path to becoming a medical expert is long, resolutely focused on the acquisition of knowledge and clinical skills over many years. Both medical school and post-graduate specialty training are highly competitive with individuals ranked against each other in examinations; collaborative working is learned on the job, but as a self-developed coping strategy rather than a specific focus of training.

He laments that little or no time is allowed for leadership devel-opment, teamworking, or understanding career paths in health care, and that governance structures in hospitals and in the NHS are not explained. 'The predictable end result is solitary practi-tioners, deeply rooted in independent day-to-day practices with a lack of understanding, and a disengagement or distrust of management process.' He suggests that 'Often they settle for a role which is, in the main, psychologically safe, as the expert in the room, where they are both experienced and clinically confident.'

Tim's story could apply to many kinds of expert and professional. Yet, the evidence is clear. These are exactly the kind of people who should be going into leadership at all levels.

As core business experts progress in their line of business, and widen their lens at each career stage, they must be supported through leadership development programmes that broaden their awareness and increase their desire and knowledge to recognize the larger system around their own practice. Executive leader Dr Lynn Myers recognizes that

> physicians may be the most intelligent in the room, but they often lack business knowledge and are weak in the area of influencing others. This creates a challenge for physicians who realize that people believe they are more capable than they actually are.

This unspoken pressure, suggests Charisse Jimenez, at the same Texas Health provider, 'makes peer-based, physician-led development programmes a perfect way to bridge any gaps, providing a safe place to learn, explore, and experiment'. This was why we created the Executive Masters in Medical Leadership, which is tailored to physicians' specific requirements. The programme prepares mid-career professionals to become future expert leaders by helping them develop leadership qualities such as self-reflection, showing vulnerability, bravery and truth-telling, teamwork and emotional intelligence. This happens at a middle-management career point, after doctors have spent five to ten years acquiring a bedrock of expertise, and when they are poised to pursue a dual track of clinician *and* manager.

Experts benefit from bespoke leadership training

It is estimated that companies spend some $50 billion globally on leadership development programmes. And for good reason: recent evidence finds that such interventions improve both the leadership capabilities of individuals as well as organizational performance.[17] Yet companies also waste money on leadership training programmes that are too generic, poorly conceived, not based on the latest scientific evidence, and which are ill-equipped to nurture expert leaders. At one university, for instance, the top team sought to move more females into executive positions. Their Organizational Development team offered a leadership programme intended specifically for women from both the administration and the faculty. But the team who designed the course failed to do their research into the type of course that female scholars would find useful. Generic decisions were made about course content and importantly the amount of time required to undertake the training, which was viewed as too long for academics. As a result, only women who worked in the administrative departments of the university enrolled, and the organization failed to cultivate a corps of expert female academic leaders.

Leadership development should be available to all. But we need to recognize that different professional groups also have diverse developmental needs. It should be tailored – as common sense suggests – to the requirements that each situation demands.

In his research into school leadership, Matthew Evans, himself an experienced school head, writes that teachers have domain-specific knowledge – 'the technical, social and cultural knowledge which relates to the task in hand. Even communication skills, often cited to be domain-independent, are almost entirely dependent on contextual knowledge.'[18] It is a fallacy to think that there are generic skills which all experts can add to their leadership toolkit and apply across the board, regardless of context. In fact, Evans continues, 'Leaders don't bring skills to the task, they develop fluid execution through repeated application of domain-specific knowledge.' My research confirms this. What expert leadership brings to the task is a deep understanding of the domain and an ability, learned over many years, to navigate and understand what's really going on.

Evans also makes the good point that leadership development should be fashioned not merely around specific professional groups but also to particular domains, such as curriculum leadership, for example. He believes that a whole raft of problems result from the myth of generic leadership skills, including, in particular, complacency on the part of those who feel they have 'mastered' leadership, and the notion that a generic skills toolkit, based on abstract models and process, can be used across multiple contexts at the expense of decision-making based on 'deep knowledge of the leadership domain'.[19]

We have certainly discovered that professionals want high-quality tailored programmes taught by researchers and experts in partnership. They want the instructors to draw on contextually specific issues that relate directly to their work, and to learn methods that are optimal and supported by data. Academics, particularly in the top business schools, have been slow to recognize the importance of adding personal development to curricula: helping students examine their own behaviour, demonstrate weakness, ask pertinent questions, open up, speak candidly, and critique, all within a private and protected environment. But this is now changing.

Training should be done on the job and alongside the job

Part of effective management and leadership education is encouraging the trainees to draw from live, real-time situations and issues at work, and to collaborate with their peers on the course to find imaginative solutions. Employers have a responsibility to find ways to facilitate this and to think about how they will progress their newly tooled potential manager. There is little point in developing and empowering your experts if you have failed to create an outlet for their progression. If options for practising new skills are opened then you have incentivized the nascent and potentially reluctant expert leader to channel new skills, and, importantly, to be helpful to the organization. However, if firms whet the appetite through development but do nothing to help them practise their new selves, this will create frustration in the potential expert leader, and they will look elsewhere to fulfil their expectations.

There is a distinction between formal learning and offering ongoing support through mentoring, exposure to the top team, job shadowing, and rotating on buddying schemes. The latter set of activities is critical – and even more important as remote and hybrid work become common. Budgets for formal programmes are often tight, and many people feel too overburdened or burnt out for heavy commitments to formal training.

Programmes need to be evaluated and measured against outputs

Most development programmes fail to measure *actual* outcomes. This is very different from the mechanical listing of 'teaching and learning outcomes' that typically end up in unwieldy documents, full of jargon, that almost no one including the students can understand. Our research suggests that key questions need to be asked before a programme is even designed. What we want to achieve is determined beforehand through dialogue with participants, programme faculty, HR professionals, and internal experts. Outcomes based on these criteria can then be assessed with a full return on investment (ROI) of programmes.[20]

Ideally, we would evaluate at different time points (e.g. before or at the beginning of the programme, once during, at the conclusion, and a year after the development intervention). We would include subjective and objective outcome measures, at different levels (individual, team, organizational, such as increased staff engagement, benefit to clients/users, economic), and, if not too difficult, involve different raters (self, peer participant, line manager, faculty, supervisor, etc.). This kind of assessment can be adjusted depending on time and resources, but just chucking cash at programmes and students, without properly assessing their learning outcomes and ROI, is a waste of money.

The capabilities experts need to lead

The capabilities that a trained expert leader will ideally demonstrate are as follows.

1. *Self-awareness and commitment to personal growth*
   This is emotional-intelligence work. It is the hard graft of self-knowledge, reflective practice, and the management of oneself in relation to others. This includes awareness of how others perceive you, how you adapt to different contexts and stakeholders, a commitment to continuous personal development, and an openness to feedback. When we train experts we have found that this is foundational work because it feeds into all future learning and also the ability to develop others. To appreciate the role of leader, we all are required to start with an understanding of ourselves and only then is it possible properly to encourage self-reflection, curiosity, and personal growth in others. As I have said before, the expert leader is a standard-bearer, not only in terms of their technical skill and expertise but also in their behaviour. In this way, they embody the attributes of expert leadership.

2. *Interpersonal communication skills*
   Effective interpersonal communication is central to teamwork and also to the ability to motivate others. We know that happy, engaged workers are more likely to have a boss who is an expert, has good listening skills, gives constructive and informed feedback, and who allows for autonomy and innovation. We teach experts the principles of coaching techniques, active listening, and Socratic questioning. These skills describe an expert leader who is also a coach – someone who mentors and guides others,

who is respectful, who is empathetic, who enables rather than controls, and who listens attentively. Michael West calls this kind of listening 'attending':

> The first element of compassionate leadership is being present with, and attending to, those we lead. Leaders who attend will model being present with those they lead and 'listening with fascination'. Listening is probably the most important skill of leadership and involves taking time to listen to the challenges, obstacles, frustrations, and hurts of staff experience, as well as the successes and pleasures.[21]

3. *Speaking the truth*

Expert leaders must speak fearlessly and honestly. That is how trust and credibility are painstakingly built.[22] They must also encourage others to do likewise by promoting a culture of psychological safety in their teams and organizations. Amy Edmondson defines this as 'the shared belief held by members of a team that the team is safe for interpersonal risk-taking'.[23] This is the sweet spot identified by Timothy Clarke, where there is high intellectual friction and low social friction, where people feel safe enough to debate, argue, and think creatively.[24] West links the quality of teamworking to a climate of psychological safety:

> The influences on such climates include a clear shared vision, values and goals: support for reflection, learning and innovation; frequent and positive contact between team members; team members valuing diversity; difference (e.g. of opinion) and positive conflict; and relationships based on mutual support, compassion and humility.[25]

Speaking truthfully also means a willingness to hold others to account and to reduce toxic behaviour in a workplace. Whatever the setting – on a day-to-day basis or in a meeting – a leader must be able to confront behaviour that harms and silences others and that might thereby derail the organization from its mission. So leaders need to be brave. That is not easy in life. But bosses have to call out bad practice and challenge bad decisions. Performance management is part of optimal leadership because if poor behaviour goes unchecked then it can produce tendrils of harmful consequences that work their way through the organization.

4. *Navigating diverse stakeholders and systems*
Nurturing professional relationships with a diverse set of stakeholders is integral to expert leadership. Bosses do not operate in a social vacuum. Leaders need to understand the systems within which they work (systems which often have competing interests, such as operational, leadership, governance, quality improvement, etc.) so that they can collaborate, cope with complexity, and foster change. Somehow they have to shepherd together a mix of people who will also often have competing interests. This requires an awareness of the agendas of different kinds of stakeholder – whom are they accountable to, their financial incentives, and their strategic priorities – while seeing opportunities to build coalitions of interest. Resilience, the ability to negotiate, and persuasive non-confrontational communication skills; all these are part of successful stakeholder management.

5. *Continuous learning and flexibility*
Expert leaders must learn to put the curiosity and hard work that initially made them an expert to use in areas that may not greatly interest them. These might include understanding finance; the current economic and business environment, particularly as it relates to their own industry; labour relations, HR laws, and compliance regulations; and, leadership skills such as performance management. As I mentioned in the last chapter, experts need intellectual flexibility and commitment. That will often be taxing.

I began this chapter with Ericsson's notion of 'deliberate practice'. It underpins excellence and is dependent on immediate feedback, clear goals, and a focus on technique. There is a symbiotic relationship between the leaders and the culture of an organization. In the final chapter I explore the fundamental components of an expert-friendly organization.

8

The Expert-Friendly Organization

As we approach the end of this book it is useful to stand back and remind ourselves why it is important to have leaders with high levels of expert knowledge – truly credible leaders.

The 1980s saw the rational execution of management start to derail. Individual investors who wished to make money from solid long-run bets were replaced by giant, risk-seeking institutional investors.[1] A new style of investment manager, with bonuses tied to annual profits, tried to outstrip one another. They were incentivized by a focus on short-run returns. Decision-making became distorted. Companies' figures began to be gamed – to reach quarterly targets.[2] 'The shrunken time horizon', notes Jerry Muller, 'creates a temptation to boost immediate profits at the expense of longer-term investments, whether in research and development or in improving the skills of the company's workforce.'[3] Performance metrics were used to 'squeeze assets in the short term at the expense of long-term consequences'.[4] Added to this mix was the spread of eye-watering remuneration among the new generalist 'charismatic' CEOs, who were seen as 'change agents' by impatient board directors and expected to 'turn the ship' around in a matter of months or be shown the door.

This still describes many of today's Fortune 500 and FTSE 100 companies, and while the phenomenon started in the United States, it has gone global. Yet a short-termist culture is counter to the tradition of an expert-friendly organization, and, crucially, to our desire for sustainability. We just cannot run our world like this any more. That means we must fashion a way of life that affirms the value of expertise and goes on to support employee well-being and sustainable performance.

Life for expert workers in a poorly designed company becomes particularly demoralizing. And when your core employees have the kind of skills and brainpower that make them easily employable elsewhere, they can melt away. One positive development in the modern world is that subtle assets such as human happiness, employee job satisfaction, corporate reputation, motivation, and trust are now more easily measured, and, as we saw in Chapter 5, there is greater awareness of their importance. As this book has shown, the credibility of expert leaders and managers is a strong predictor of long-term performance outcomes.

What expertopia looks like

The principles of expert leadership covered so far have, I hope, clarified that an organization's core business should determine its leader; that expert leaders are needed throughout the organization, including on the board, but are especially important at the top; finally, that being an expert is not a proxy for having leadership and management skills. All leaders must also learn to be a good boss.

In Chapter 4 I looked at *how* expert leadership works. It happens by developing strategy that is aligned with the core business, and one that takes the long view regarding investment and sustainability; by creating productive work environments that raise employee job satisfaction through suitable management practices, such as appropriate goal-setting, feedback, and development; by being light on metrics and bureaucracy; and through raised standards in hiring and promotion that are set by expert leaders who are themselves exemplars of high quality.

In this chapter I examine the kinds of organizations that *are* expert-friendly, because they do all of the above and more . . . and it is the more I will focus on here. From my own research and the outstanding examples I explore below, it is clear that the most effective organizations share a set of additional characteristics:

1. The best organizations have built a company philosophy that affirms the value of expertise and actively seeks to grow it. Culture is used as a tool to allow expertise to permeate up and down the organization.

2. They enable autonomy, organizational flexibility, and ideally profit sharing, and they allow *minimal* bureaucracy. Expert line managers are given considerable freedom and responsibility, and in return must be accountable.

3. They are focused but diverse, organized but disruptive to encourage divergent thinking and experimentation, which means being tolerant of some failure.

4. They develop an environment that fosters informed dissent. (Yes-men and yes-women need not apply.)

5. They create physical spaces where experts collide, which facilitates unplanned interaction and collaborations, and provides a stimulating workplace that reminds employees why they want to be there.

6. They build a culture of curiosity and questioning, and promote continuous learning.

This is a challenging set of goals to aspire to. But it is how thriving ideas-led workplaces operate. If we think it through, there are many experts in organizations, including in marketing, finance, HR, and beyond. All are important and should have some input into organizational decision-making.

Yet the core business functions are king. They define the purpose and dictate the general direction and strategy. This does not mean that finance or marketing are not listened to; they just should not lead the show.

Hundreds of years ago human wealth came in a particularly simple and direct way. It was either mined from the ground (gold and coal), sucked up from the depth of the earth (oil), pulled from the oceans and rivers (fish), or grown in the fields (corn and rice). Wealth could be acquired in an elementary and immediate way, provided one had sufficient freedom, resources, and energy to amass it.

Wealth today is different. It comes predominantly from brain-power – from people's heads bashing up, metaphorically, with other people's heads. At the time of writing, the three most valuable companies in the US stock market are Apple, Microsoft, and Alphabet (Google). They were built upon sophisticated science and sheer originality of thought.[5]

If we want to understand how future corporations should operate, we need to *think expert*.

Learn from the (very, very) best

At the end of the nineteenth century the United States lagged behind Europe in many areas of science. Germany was particularly strong in scientific medicine, and became a magnet for medical students from around the world. Between 1870 and 1914 over 15,000 Americans studied in German universities, and it was those students who eventually transformed clinical medicine in the United States.[6] At the time that they were returning home with superior medical knowledge, their country's economy was also transforming. Some individuals were becoming wealthy on a scale never seen before. One of these was John D. Rockefeller Sr, who was motivated by two great passions: making money – and giving it away. He began his philanthropic voyage at the age of just sixteen, by giving 6 per cent of his earnings to charity.[7]

Said to have been the richest person in modern history,[8] Rockefeller Sr decided to donate to medical research, in part motivated by the death of his grandson from scarlet fever. At that time, most American medical schools were commercially run and did not invest in research, unlike the Institut Pasteur in Paris and Robert Koch's institute in Berlin, which were developing new treatments for tuberculosis, diphtheria, and typhoid fever.[9] In 1901, in part modelled on these institutions, J. D. Rockefeller Sr established the first biomedical research centre in the United States – the Rockefeller Institute.

Today, 120 years later, the Rockefeller Institute is a private graduate college in New York City. It is tiny, with just over eighty in its faculty, and by some standards it is only moderately endowed. Yet Rockefeller has made more twentieth-century discoveries in biomedical research than nearly all of its well-capitalized global peers, such as Harvard, Oxford, and the Max Planck Institute. How has it maintained this standard for more than a century?[10] J. R. Hollingsworth, from the University of Wisconsin–Madison, undertook an extraordinary piece of research to try to uncover Rockefeller's success.[11] He found an organizational culture built on unsurpassed excellence, which produces transformative science that is applied to the critical medical challenges facing the world. For example, the discovery that deoxyribonucleic acid (DNA) carries genetic information, and that cancer can be caused by a virus.

Most organizations begin life with the same ambition as Rockefeller, namely, to be the best at what they do. But they typically swing from good to mediocre and if they are lucky back again. Or they go into major decline, which is reflected in figures on average firm life span: a US S&P 500 company's length of life has dropped from sixty-seven to fifteen years, and within the UK FTSE 100, after thirty years 76 per cent of companies have disappeared.[12] Rockefeller is small, of course, so it should be easier to control quality, though many equivalently sized institutes have not. Its practices, however, are relevant to all organizations, indeed many have been adopted by the world's largest companies, such as Microsoft, and older ones, like the Royal Shakespeare Company, that first opened its theatre in Stratford, Shakespeare's birthplace, in 1879.[13]

To achieve the pinnacle in anything we must observe and learn from outstanding examples. The principles of optimum performance used by Rockefeller, and uncovered by Hollingsworth, are, as we will see, common in today's most successful firms.

Give autonomy, be flexible, kill bureaucracy, and share profits

Organizational autonomy gave Rockefeller 'exceptional freedom of inquiry' to be able to respond quickly to an urgent problem – a new strain of virus, for example. Because 'knowledge changes rapidly, and if an organization is to be continuously at the frontiers of fundamental new knowledge, it must be highly flexible'.[14] The ability to adapt is necessary for all industries. Constantly changing technologies, new instrumentation and tools, fluctuations in government policies and regulations, changes to funding sources and market positions, governance and shareholder pressures, political and economic volatility, climate change, and demographic alterations; these all require a responsive fluidity.

Rockefeller created its own flexible structure and processes so that it could react quickly to new challenges. Unlike most universities and businesses, housed in entrenched department structures, Rockefeller was and is laboratory-based and largely unconstrained by disciplinary siloes. It also has an on-site research hospital, which makes it possible for biomedical scientists to take their discoveries from the lab bench to the bedside. Its process of putting research into practice means the organization is less likely to become stale and inert. Rockefeller will create almost instantly a new lab when deemed necessary, and populate it with scientific appointments from any field. It is less constrained by externally imposed norms of credentialling, is relatively free from regulations imposed by state bureaucracies (a burden felt in much of higher education), and as a result, it can appoint people to any position it chooses.[15]

Importantly, and this is part of the nuts and bolts of adaptability, the organization describes itself as having 'minimal administrative bureaucracy', which allows its funds to go more directly to research.[16] This sets Rockefeller apart from the weaker laboratories and research bodies. In those, creativity is suppressed by hierarchical authority, an imposing bureaucracy, with centralized decision-making and more formal and standardized rules and procedures, that are usually, Hollingsworth noted, more prevalent among larger organizations. This will sound familiar to many.

Process and structures have to fit the core workers. In other words, before implementation they need to be expert-tested. There is no point adding a complex new system at great cost only to discover that it is reducing the productivity of your core workers, or that they are simply ignoring it. Here is an example from a different, but also important, arena of life.

Fatma Makalo is the manager of Bridgeside Lodge Care Home in north London. Her organization is consistently rated as Outstanding by government inspectors at the Care Quality Commission, and in August 2022 Fatma was awarded the UK Chief Nursing Officer Silver Award. Fatma says:

> Nobody is born a leader, but we create our own paths, and mine is based on an understanding of the people I work with, and an understanding of myself. I get my hands dirty. I have the respect of my staff because of my own expertise as a clinician, but also because I will challenge senior leadership, if I think it is to the detriment of the staff or residents.[17]

Fatma did challenge the leadership just before the government inspectors were about to assess the facility. She was told by the CEO that the care home would fail the inspection if she did not implement a very long list, which he had drawn up, of more than fifty 'improvements' that would involve burdensome bureaucracy. 'I was furious but read the suggestions with an open mind and realized I could not implement his recommendations.' Fatma knew she risked losing her job, but felt the CEO had concentrated only on process and box-ticking while ignoring the needs of staff and their relationships. 'I felt that if I had taken on board his suggestions, I would lose the respect of my staff, and the strong bond unifying the teams I had built, would be broken.' So, she decided not to tell the CEO of her decision until the inspection was over. 'It was a nerve-racking three days followed by two weeks of waiting for the results.' The Care Quality Commission awarded her care home an Outstanding and she grudgingly won the respect of the CEO, who left her in charge. 'So often I see staff and morale destroyed by ill-thought-through procedures and processes, but I feel very strongly that you should not work for the system, instead let the system work for you.'

In some countries, the bodies created by governments to fund scientific research – for example, the UK's Economic and Social

Research Council (ESRC) – have created so many procedural boxes to tick that the best scholars do not bother trying to get their research funded. One highly cited disillusioned professor told me:

> Oh, I gave up on the ESRC many years ago. It's all about show and bureaucracy. To get funding it would be necessary to put in a second-rate project stuffed with old ideas, and with the required silly jargon and buzzwords. Then there would be endless ridiculous meetings, long forms that would be looked at by people who *do not understand the science*, and time-consuming and unpleasant annual reports to ESRC committees that we all know will never be read anyway. If I were to put in for a grant for really original work, I wouldn't have a chance. I just accept it now.

Is this unfair? Isn't it natural that larger organizations need more bureaucratic systems and processes? Wilmot Reed Hastings Jr, co-founder, chairman, and co-chief executive officer of Netflix, once thought so too. But not any more.

The subscription streaming service, film and TV production company Netflix launched in 1997. As of 2021 it has over 214 million subscribers in 190 countries, with just under 10,000 full-time employees.[18] It has earned seventeen Golden Globes and numerous BAFTA nominations, and was ranked number one in 2019 by the Reputation Institute[19] as the most highly regarded company in America.[20] The fortunes of Netflix differ markedly from those of Hastings' first start-up. The fledgling Pure Software began with a dozen people, and each was given a lot of freedom to make decisions with few constraints. As the company expanded, inevitably, such employee autonomy also meant there were some mistakes. 'Each time this happened, I put a process in place to prevent that mistake from occurring again.'[21] And over time, as in so many of our organizations, layer upon layer of rules and restrictions followed. In the opening section of his book *No Rules Rules* with Erin Meyer from INSEAD Business School, Hastings notes that 'Policies and control processes became so foundational to our work that those who were great at coloring within the lines were promoted, while many creative mavericks felt stifled and went to work elsewhere.'[22]

Hastings thought that the layering of processes and rules was just what you did when a company grew. On reflection, he noticed two things happened at Pure Software:

The first is that we failed to innovate quickly. We had become increasingly efficient and decreasingly creative. In order to grow we had to purchase other companies that did have innovative products. That led to more business complexity, which in turn led to more rules and process.[23]

(This is an important point also about the potential weaknesses of outsourcing versus growing your own.) His second observation related to when the market shifted from C++ to Java, a different program language: 'To survive, we needed to change. But we had selected and conditioned our employees to follow process, not to think freshly or shift fast. We were unable to adapt and, in 1997, ended up selling the company to our largest competitor.'[24]

Three years later, in 2000, Hastings, joined by Netflix co-founder Marc Randolph, schlepped to the Dallas headquarters of Blockbuster, cap in hand, to ask for much needed investment. That year the struggling Netflix incurred losses of $57 million while Blockbuster was *the* $6 billion home entertainment giant. Hastings and Randolph were politely, but flatly, turned down. Blockbuster declared bankruptcy ten years later.

The advice to organizations offered by Reed Hastings today is stark. It is: reduce controls. 'Start by ripping pages from the employee handbook. Travel policies, expense policies, vacation policies – these can all go.'[25] As the organization's talent grows, and the culture becomes more embedded and feedback more fluid, you can remove approval processes throughout the organization, teaching your managers principles like, 'Lead with context, not control,' and coaching your employees using such guidelines as, 'Don't seek to please your boss.' Handing over so much power to employees reflects a deep trust in them. Removing controls creates a culture of 'freedom and responsibility'. Hastings believes this both attracts top talent, for whom autonomy is a must, and has transformed innovation at Netflix to a level unmatched by most companies. He cautions, in his book, that the removal of controls needs time to fully evolve; it cannot happen overnight.[26] Many will view handing over so much control to staff as too radical, especially in areas of the public sector or more conservative kinds of businesses. But is it?

Svenska Handelsbanken, based in Sweden, provides banking services and insurance for consumers and businesses, investment banking, and trading. It greatly values autonomy and accountability through its devolved structure,[27] and is recognized by financial experts as having 'outperformed the market for the past four decades ever since it moved to a decentralised model'.[28] It is among Europe's thirty biggest banks by assets, and regularly tops customer satisfaction and loyalty ratings. That tells us why its customer base continues to grow. The bank's success is largely attributable to its unique organizational strategy of extensive decentralization and the autonomy given to branch managers. 'The branch is the Bank' is the motto of Handelsbanken. Bank managers, who interestingly have worked there for an average of twenty-three years, are the people who make decisions about loans and interest rates. Importantly, there are *no* call centres. Bureaucracy at the bank is scaled back and managers function through a 'church spire principle – under which a branch manager should be able to see all their customers from the top of a tower'.[29] Regional managers, responsible for between twenty-five and ninety branches each, mentor and coach more junior branch managers to help them improve decision-making. This investment in branch autonomy raises managers' motivation and sense of entrepreneurship. One customer told me:

> I love Handelsbanken. I really do. OK I pay £30 a month, but for that I just email my 'individual banking manager', and she replies by personal email that day. She knows my name and my family. I never wait fuming on an automated telephone queue and then get asked the name of my late mother's second dog. Handelsbanken keeps my blood pressure low.

Handelsbanken has no sales targets and it pays no bonuses. Its staff are awarded an equal share of profits in every year that the bank's return on equity outperforms its rivals'.[30] This is paid into a foundation, called Oktogonen, which invests mostly in Handelsbanken shares and owns a 10 per cent stake in the bank. Employees cannot withdraw their holding until they are age sixty, and everyone is given the same amount irrespective of position or rank. When the bank does well, the employees also benefit. Indeed, in good years employees have retired with up to a £1 million lump sum.[31]

Humans like sharing, especially if it is accompanied by a sense of reliable fairness. Profit and equity sharing is the norm in the large and small companies that inhabit the world's tech hubs, which are almost always expert-led. Richard Freeman at Harvard has for many years probed the effects of various forms of employee engagement in profits and ownership. It can take many forms. For example, the UK department store chain John Lewis Partnership is employee-owned, whereas the Chinese appliance maker Haier uses a combination of bonuses, dividends, and profit sharing. Through the empirical research of Freeman and colleagues it is possible to understand the benefits of these practices to individual performance and firm productivity.[32]

- First, employees are incentivized to put in more effort, to co-operate and share information with each other. They are also more likely to innovate.
- Second, workplaces can be more harmonious with everyone working towards genuinely shared outcomes that go beyond a mere mission statement.
- Third, sharing profits also requires greater corporate transparency and openness with employees, who often have to participate in workplace decisions, and therefore need to understand what exactly is going on.
- Fourth, the positive effect of worker autonomy upon employee job satisfaction and performance is enhanced when some form of profit sharing is included – the

argument being that having autonomy to make decisions makes me work harder, but if I feel that my efforts also benefit my pocket then I put in even more effort. Notably, this effect is greater when the financial gains are shared with a team instead of just going to the individual.

- Finally, the authors suggest that at a time when inequality has increased in the world, leading to social exclusion and despair,[33] a system of employee stock ownership and profit sharing can contribute to feelings of equity, engagement, and commitment, which in turn, they argue, enhances democracy.[34]

Handelsbanken has thrived through decentralized decision-making. It puts emphasis on 'dialogue over metrics', branch autonomy, a strong but local customer focus, a parsimonious use of financial incentives, much weight on employee well-being, and a slow but steady approach to growth. Leaders are also promoted from within the bank. Carina Åkerström became Handelsbanken's first female CEO in 2019. At that point she had been with the bank for thirty-three years. Her arrival in this position coincided with a Covid-19 pandemic that shook up retail dramatically. It also altered most people's working practices. Handelsbanken prides itself on having numerous physical branches, and thus for a long time resisted losing its high-street presence. But by 2020 the organization had to follow other banks and increase its online side. Branches and jobs have been cut to boost the bank's digital offering,[35] but Handelsbanken has said that the remaining branches will be given *'an even greater degree of decision-making authority'* along with access to specialist advice.[36]

Hollingsworth has shown that autonomy, around lab design and hiring, was a key reason why Rockefeller led the world in biomedical innovations. But an even more radical approach to worker autonomy was adopted by the appliance maker Haier, based in Qingdao, China.

Thirty years ago Haier was a sluggish state-owned enterprise making low-quality products. Today it is the world's largest producer of appliances such as washing machines, refrigerators, dishwashers, and air conditioners, with revenues of $35 billion and 75,000 world-wide employees. In a very different market compared with film-making, IT, or banking, it competes with Whirlpool, LG, and Electrolux. Business writers Gary Hamel and Michele Zanini told the story of Haier in an interesting article about the 'end of bureaucracy'.[37]

The authors explain how Haier transformed its fortunes in a decade. This all happened under a 'renegade CEO' Zhang Ruimin, who stripped out the old management structures with their authoritarian bureaucracy and hierarchies, and converted the company into a 'start-up factory' with 'just two layers of management between frontline teams and the CEO'.[38] Ruimin saw bureaucracy as a major liability to success, slowing innovation and creating barriers for employee achievement. His goal, '*to let everyone become their own CEO – to help everyone realize their potential*',[39] mimicked start-ups – offering autonomy coupled with accountability, a tolerance of failure, openness, and a plasticity to change when needed, where employees are more like owners, because they have equity or their own capital invested; and, finally, a set-up that better suits an internet age. So, Haier's audacious CEO decided to emulate a start-up but on a massive scale.[40]

Hamel and Zanini summarized what Haier looks like today.[41] The most interesting change in the firm was its evolution into 4,000 micro-enterprises – small autonomous businesses with an average of ten to fifteen employees, unless involved in manufacturing. The micro-enterprises, or MEs, are separated into three categories: 'transforming' MEs, which are market-facing; 'incubating' MEs, which are like new businesses; and 'node' MEs 'which sell component products and services such as design, manufacturing, and human resource support to Haier's market-facing MEs'.[42] These micro-enterprises are given a lot of freedom in the direction they chose, and in their form, but they share core organizing components. They decide their own strategy of what to pursue and how, and who they wish to partner with, internal MEs or externals. They make their own hiring decisions and define working relationships, and they can set their own pay and bonuses. Hamel and Zanini describe how Haier, through its micro-enterprises, has created 'an organizational model that mimics the architecture of the internet', diverse and yet still coherent, or, citing Harvard technologist David Weinberger, 'small pieces, loosely joined'.[43]

This decentralized super-start-up has produced innumerable innovations and in breakneck delivery times. Their approach will not suit everyone, and personally I think it is unduly target-driven. Nevertheless, Hamel and Zanini believe that *'Haier's empowering, energizing management model is the product of a relentless quest to free human beings at work from the shackles of bureaucracy.'*[44] Arguably, it shows what can be done without bureaucracy.

Private companies have the freedom to do things differently, especially before they go public and enlarge their stakeholder pool. Haier was a state-owned behemoth converted into a groundbreaking organization, and it is common to hear that when taxpayers' money is involved, everything becomes wrapped up in red tape. Why is this the case? Is it not exactly *because* taxpayer funds are involved that management practices should incur less bureaucracy and cost, and be a great deal more efficient? Our modern world is litigious, which has made accountability more important and risk-taking harder, but this applies to all organizations, private, public, and not-for-profit. I can see that borrowing Netflix's approach to expenses might be difficult to implement for a high school. But claiming expenses has for many of us become so complex and time-consuming that it is sometimes easier and cheaper not to seek reimbursement. Recall in Chapter 4 Atul Gawande highlighting a study that shows 'physicians spent about two hours doing computer work for every hour spent face to face with a patient'? Bureaucratization and managerialism exist across many sectors, but there is surely a case to be made that wherever any public funds are involved, it is more important than ever to avoid excessively bureaucratic and inefficient processes and management.

Be focused but diverse, organized but disruptive,
experimental and failure-tolerant

Employees must feel invested in the organization and its core mission, and be ready to fight its corner. Trust, openness, and honesty is the ideal, combined with accountability and responsibility, as noted above. But there is not a one-size-fits-all personality. And brilliant people, especially those focused enough to want to become the best experts, may not always be the most self-aware of people. It is necessary to work with those people, in the ways described in Chapter 7, to help them with communication and a bit of self-reflection, so that they can understand how their behaviour might affect others. That is an important element in helping technical experts to develop into expert managers and leaders.

Rockefeller secured its place at the top by selecting diverse people and ideas – thereby protecting itself against becoming too narrowly focused or entrenched. To stay ready to respond to new health problems, and guard against uniformity of thought, teams are made up of contrasting researchers.

Teams have become the norm in most workplaces. Research looking at R&D productivity, by Ben Jones at the Kellogg School of Management, Northwestern University, suggests that teamwork makes it possible to aggregate more efficiently the knowledge which has grown exponentially across all fields. To make his point, Jones uses the example of aviation. In 1903 two men, the Wright brothers, designed, built, and flew the first heavier-than-air aircraft. But today, to design and manufacture just the jet engines alone requires the attention of thirty different engineering specialties.[45] Highest-performing teams are those made up of people who may differ in their sex, race, or cultural identity, but who are approximately the same in their professional, cognitive, or scientific ability, which contrasts with the idea that efficiency is most improved by spreading the best people across different quality teams.[46]

For the best outputs we want people in teams to be different from each other, but not *too* different. This type of team selection facilitates a kind of organized disruption, and ensures a level of informed dissent, thus creating new ways of thinking. When teams are unduly cohesive, they are less innovative and more likely to suffer from groupthink, a term inspired by Orwell's 'doublethink' in *1984* and used by psychologist Irving Janis, who argued that too much uniformity will 'suppress critical inquiry and result in faulty decision making'.[47] But if they are too widely separated in their field, again, innovation is decreased.

The doctors involved in my leadership and management master's degree course are diverse in all hues of identity, sex, race, seniority, and medical specialism. Thus, the voices and perspectives are distinct and complementary. But they share one thing in common: they are all medically trained. Thus, they fit the moderate diversity requirement. As a non-medical person teaching physicians, you cannot fail to notice that there is a 'medical mindset' – a way of thinking, a cognitive pathway, that is distinct. As former student and critical care doctor Ruth McCabe explained to me, 'Medical students and doctors expect to be tested to the very edge of our knowledge. And it doesn't matter how much you know, you are always close to potential failure, because the line between knowing and not, is so thin.' And failure can have devastating consequences. A cardiothoracic surgeon explained the stress tied to failure 'when you have an 18-year-old bleeding to death on the table in front of you, and there is nothing you can do about it, and you have to tell this to the distraught parents waiting outside the room. A management meeting can be taken in your stride after that event.'[48]

This is what differentiates doctors from other health-care professionals. The contrast is particularly sharp with non-clinical managers.

The proverbial buck really does stop with doctors. As Ruth McCabe explains, 'They are, crucially, diagnosticians who have to work out what is going on and decide what to do about it, so the decision-making comes as the other side of the diagnostic/problem-solving coin.' Clinicians have responsibility for their actions (and inactions) and must be prepared to defend them in court if needed. And, adds Ruth, 'no matter what you are "told to do", you will always

THE EXPERT-FRIENDLY ORGANIZATION

have that personal responsibility and must act accordingly. This includes challenging within your own hierarchy and within your own organisation and profession.' The General Medical Council, with which all UK medical practitioners must register, advocates and regulates that for all physicians, 'the care of the patient is your first consideration, you should challenge other professions including management'.

This is why experts are not usually popular with politicians. Experts do not make good yes-people.

There is a peculiar paradox apparent here. Diversity is being called for, shouted from the rooftops, and rightly so. Diversity is fair – and individuals not being the same has many measurable benefits. However, this also requires us to acknowledge that difference needs to be accommodated differently. One size fits only the few, and treating everybody the same does not allow diversity to be acknowledged, or for the ability to adapt to differing needs.

Foster informed dissent

Adapting to change is necessary for all. Whether it is the arrival of the latest virus or a new code for software or the market appearance of a competitor, organizations need to be ready to modify and modernize.

Berkeley psychologist Charlan Nemeth has spent her career examining the value to organizations of allowing dissent.

> Good decision-making, at its heart, is divergent thinking. When we think divergently, we think in multiple directions, seek information, and consider facts on all sides of the issue, and think about the cons as well as the pros. Bad decision-making is the reverse. Thinking convergently, we focus more narrowly, usually in one direction.[49]

And she adds, we tend to seek out information and facts that support our initial preference. Through her many experiments, Nemeth has shown that 'biased focus' inhibits both problem solving and innovation, and paraphrasing the philosopher John Stuart Mill, she argues: 'when dissent is suppressed, the group and organization suffer ... With consensus, our minds go on automatic pilot. Our fears about speaking up sometimes lead us to turn a blind eye to bad decisions or ethical violations.'[50]

In an article for the *Financial Times* newspaper in December 2020, I argued that diversity is critical for effective crisis leadership. Prime Minister Boris Johnson's top team, his cabinet, were among the least experienced politicians to occupy their roles, having recently sailed in on the Brexit boat. Capability was traded for compliance, as dissenting voices from the older Tory ranks, representing decades of political and policy experience, were silenced, and shown the door. Apart from a dearth of political experience, Johnson's team also lacked diversity. It was predominantly male, privately schooled and mainly educated in the humanities – Boris himself having studied the classics. In the battle to push Britons behind Brexit, in defiance of much expert opinion from economists and others, Michael Gove, Johnson's right hand, had famously declared his distaste of experts.[51]

And then came Covid-19. The UK government ignored warnings as it spread first in China, then suddenly much closer to home in northern Italy, until 'Quick, find me an expert!' could be heard as it landed on British shores. Public health advisory bodies were activated. The UK government relied on its Scientific Advisory Group for Emergencies – or SAGE – which for a long time also lacked disciplinary diversity. Gus O'Donnell, former cabinet secretary to three prime ministers and former head of the Civil Service, pointed out that SAGE was too heavily drawn from the medical sciences, and failed to take account of views from other parts of the scientific community, particularly the social sciences. Indeed, expert representatives from economics, the field most likely to be called upon to deal with the £300 billion of public borrowing to cope with the effects of the pandemic, were almost entirely excluded from SAGE discussions. Yet the pandemic posed the biggest problem in health economics since the last world war. This shortage of scientific diversity created an inherent problem: deviation was not tolerated, which led to an emotional war between the unquestioning advocates of lockdown policies and those from disciplines who were calling for the inclusion of other ideas – in particular, much needed analyses of the costs and benefits of the dominant policies.

Where Britain was seemingly ahead of many countries was in its early development and efficient distribution of a vaccine. This was made possible through the extraordinary medical distribution facility, the National Health Service, and developed in a scientific setting that would have incorporated much intense testing, trial and error, and debating among experts.

Where there is insufficient heterogeneity within a general area, there is also an absence of radical or highly innovative thinking about existing problems. This was found by Hollingsworth in his study of medical discoveries, and learned by Reed Hastings from his pre-Netflix experience with Pure Software.

A fear of being ridiculed and/or of reprisal by managers is the primary barrier to feeling able to voice ideas or opinions in group environments. This, Nemeth found, is greater in companies with higher levels of homogeneity or cohesion. In a now widely read *New Yorker* article by Jonah Lehrer in 2012 titled 'Groupthink: the brainstorming myth', Nemeth's work is used to argue that conventional forms of brainstorming just don't work: 'There's this Pollyannaish notion that the most important thing to do when working together is stay positive and get along,' Nemeth says.[52] 'Well, that's just wrong. Maybe debate is going to be less pleasant, but it will always be more productive.' This is because 'dissent stimulates thought that is broader, that takes in more information and that, on balance, leads to better decisions and more creative solutions'.[53] This contrasts with most corporate cultures, she adds, that believe it is not right to critique another's ideas. The opposite is true in Netflix, which strives to *increase* candour. Similar to the approach long adopted at Rockefeller, Hastings believes that 'Talented employees have an enormous amount to learn from one another ... When talented staff members get into the feedback habit, they all get better at what they do while becoming implicitly accountable to one another, further reducing the need for traditional controls.'[54]

What is, understandably, hard to grasp for non-experts or generalist managers is this: R&D innovation requires constant failures coupled with repeated testing. How many attempts did it take Pfizer or AstraZeneca to produce a Covid-19 vaccine that worked? Amazon emerged out of a long period of seeming failure, which is recognized by CEO Jeff Bezos: 'If you're going to take bold bets, they're going to be experiments,' he said after buying Whole Foods. 'And if they're experiments, you don't know ahead of time if they're going to work. Experiments are by their very nature prone to failure. But a few big successes compensate for dozens and dozens of things that didn't work.'[55]

Netflix CEO Reed Hastings similarly told attendees at a conference that he was worried about the high success rate of their TV shows, with few being cancelled: 'Our hit ratio is too high right now. We have to take more risk . . . to try more crazy things . . . we should have a higher cancel rate overall.'[56]

Create space for unplanned interaction

Expert-friendly organizations have physical space that facilitates 'unplanned collaborations', which is the kind of workspace that Steve Jobs fostered when he worked at Pixar in the 1990s, when the norm for offices was walls of cubicles. The creatives at Pixar were given the ability to design their own workspace, but Jobs believed this:

> If a building doesn't encourage [collaboration], you'll lose a lot of innovation and the magic that's sparked by serendipity. So we designed the building to make people get out of their offices and mingle in the central atrium with people they might not otherwise see.[57]

There is a tendency for experts to hunker down alone. Collaboration spaces were created throughout Pixar's headquarters including close to people's personal offices. Jobs understood, as Rockefeller did much earlier, that originality of thinking is sparked when different worlds rub up against each other, and also that opportunities need to be fostered for that to happen.

Coronavirus may have finally pushed humanity into adopting more fluid ways of working. Even so, physical connections will still be required.[58] Much has been learned by those of us who, due to Covid-19, have spent months and months working from home instead of an office, Zooming, Teaming, Skyping ... to excess. Relationship building is still possible, but it excludes the random conversations, real eye contact, and the emotional engagement of being together in a three-dimensional space. Over the last few decades many companies have followed Pixar and designed office space that encourages collaboration through networking and promotes creativity. Pixar's main campus building locates its common areas at the centre of the building, which increases chance encounters. After computer scientists Sergey Brin and Larry Page founded Google in 1998, they created such a culture in their Mountain View-based 'Googleplex' in a similar fashion. There, employees substituted office chairs for bouncy balls and enjoyed the companionship of their dogs and free meals by top chefs. According to Professor David Garvin, 'the culture was designed to encourage collegiality and to break down barriers to the rapid development of ideas'. Such relaxed workplaces allow experts the necessary freedom and autonomy to collaborate, experiment, and innovate.

Constructing the right conditions for organized disruption and dissent facilitates what have become known as 'knowledge spill-overs'. That was the term first coined by American-Canadian urbanist and activist Jane Jacobs, author of *The Death and Life of Great American Cities*. She observed, in the study of urban environments, that cities are made up of dense networks of diverse kinds of firms housed near to each other, and this affects how knowledge travels to benefit innovation and economic growth. This idea was further advanced empirically by a group of economists, who showed, in many settings, that the major spillovers happen among firms from a *common industry*.[59] When companies whose purpose is approximately similar rub up against each other in close proximity, employees exchange ideas and innovations. That interaction leads to new products and methods. Firms also compete intensively, which further cultivates greater innovation and speedy adoption of new ideas. This is why business parks exist. Indian film producers and actors flock to Bombay's Bollywood, Chinese tech start-ups head to Shanghai or Beijing, and cyber companies flock to Tel Aviv, the city that is now ranked second for innovation by the World Economic Forum.[60]

Hospitals originally used to offer networking space for their physicians. When Peter Lees began his career as a surgeon in Britain's National Health Service (NHS) in the 1970s, he devoted gruelling hours to mastering his craft but also benefited from a culture that supported expertise. He received sustained mentorship from senior physicians and got perks such as a staff dining room and a bar where he and his fellow experts could share ideas and knowledge. Beds were also available for those doctors who were performing night shifts. Today, the surgeons often put in the same gruelling hours, but in a very different environment focused on targets, cost-cutting, and the bottom line. Permanent mentor relationships are rare, teams are transient, and doctors have few opportunities to rest, socialize, and compare notes. No surprise, then, that physicians are increasingly unhappy and burnt out.

Those who have been lucky enough to benefit from it will immediately recognize the importance of an informal space for the sharing of knowledge and ideas. I can remember many initiatives emerging from discussions over lunch at the London School of Economics' bustling faculty dining room – a space that still exists. Facilities for faculty networking remain common among some North American research universities – Toronto, Boston, Brandeis, Cornell, Rice – and they exist in a small number of European universities, such as Leiden, Zurich, and the colleges of Oxford, Cambridge, and Durham. But in most countries, and particularly in the UK, university dining rooms, where faculty are encouraged to mingle and integrate, have been largely left to decline into obscurity. This was partly because they were viewed as 'elitist'. Thus, the culture of lunchtime networking has disappeared from most universities, and facilities have been made 'equal' in a bid to imagine that we are all the same. These days, faculty and professional staff queue next to undergrad students for average-quality takeaway food that mimics the high street. Reducing the space for faculty to network within their institution only deepens siloes. Ironically, this takes place against the repeated mantras of outgoing then incoming university presidents telling us that we *need* to be more interdisciplinary. Yet they fail to create space for this to happen.

The decline within universities of pleasant spaces to meet and eat and exchange ideas sits in harsh contrast with practices at many top firms. Those routinely take pride in offering good-quality facilities for staff (and particularly experts in the core business) to integrate and network. The interchange of ideas does not happen through randomness. Culture cannot exist in a void. It needs a physical manifestation and a nice one – at least some of the time. It was the creation of this kind of facility that enabled the cross-fertilization of ideas that has helped the modest Rockefeller to achieve more scientific breakthroughs than its peers over many years.

Build a culture of curiosity and continuous learning

Reginald 'Reg' Revans, born in 1907, was exposed to many interesting events and people in his ninety-five years.[61] In 1910, with his mother, he attended the memorial service for Florence Nightingale. While at his home in Portsmouth, a representative of the seamen lost in the sinking of the *Titanic* visited his father, who was a marine surveyor and member of the *Titanic* inquiry panel. Revans' father had been informed by several engineers who worked on the *Titanic* that the ship was not ready to be launched. As with Boeing's Dreamliner and Max aeroplanes, the engineers' concerns had been ignored by both Harland & Wolff, the shipyard in Belfast that built the *Titanic*, and the British shipping company, White Star Line. This fact stuck with Revans for the rest of his life.

In his early twenties Reg Revans represented Britain as a long-jumper in the 1928 Amsterdam Olympics, while a doctoral student in astrophysics at the University of Cambridge. In 1930 he won a scholarship to study at the University of Michigan and later he returned to the Cavendish Laboratory at Cambridge. The laboratory was not your everyday lab. It housed five Nobel Prize laureates. Despite their success, Revans found them humble – they were still able to listen and to share ideas.[62] This chimed with the words of another extraordinary person Revans met and always remembered: Albert Einstein, who told him: 'If you think you understand a problem, make sure you are not deceiving yourself.'[63]

These Nobel Prize laureates were experts in the extreme. Yet they retained open and questioning minds, primed for continuous learning. Revans carried this with him as he developed into a 'rare original British business thinker', as Simon Caulkin of the *Guardian* newspaper described him in an obituary in 2003.[64] With extraordinary insight, Revans realized that 'for an organisation to survive, its rate of learning must be at least equal to the rate of change in its external environment'. This became known as Revans' Law: $L = P + Q$ (learning = programmed knowledge + questioning insight) – or put differently, success requires expert knowledge and experience, the ingredients of expert leaders.

Revans was not a fan of relying solely on expertise obtained through formal training. He recognized that experience gained through practice was crucial: 'problem solving, distinguishing between knowledge and wisdom'.[65] However, he also understood that learning was hard. He wanted individuals in organizations to share their problems with each other – to listen, question, problem-solve. To do this he created Action Learning, an ingenious process experienced through small groups where one participant shares and studies an issue or problem, their behaviour, action and experience, with others in so-called Action Learning Groups.[66] They work in a special, one-sided way. At the centre is a learner, who has an issue to resolve. Group members are permitted to use only questions, *never* the giving of advice, to try to help the issue-holder examine the problem differently, and their role in it. This is followed by an expectation of 'action'. Revans understood the power of being honest and of revealing one's own ignorance and weaknesses. He recognized, too, that traditional learning methods could not always solve practical problems.

In the 1940s and 1950s he created what became Action Learning, working with the UK National Coal Board and the NHS. From first-hand observation down pits and on hospital wards, he was able to show that pits in which managers paid close attention to their men were safer and more efficient than others, while patients in hospital recovered faster when doctors listened to nurses. In all cases, people learned better, faster, and more enduringly from their own problems than from management 'experts' importing 'prefabricated' knowledge.[67] Caulkin described 'his grounded idea of management as something pragmatic, concrete and rooted in experience – the very opposite of the prevailing, wheeling-and-dealing, short-termist Anglo-Saxon model'. Physicist and scientist Reg Revans pioneered now common concepts of 'group coaching' and 'active listening'.

Notably, Revans drew from his early experience in research laboratories. He knew that scientists shared problems, compared notes, and exchanged ideas. He then applied the same principles to management development programmes. Hollingsworth attributes Rockefeller's success to an unusually rich learning environment where scientists educate each other across their various scientific fields. 'In short, the Institute had developed a culture of continuous learning for its scientists' and 'the pursuit to learn more and differently persists and prevails'.[68]

In a world where intellect and technical expertise will produce new wealth, we must follow the example of an organization like Rockefeller that has been uncompromisingly willing to analyse itself through an honest and truthful lens. It has resisted letting non-experts and generalists talk it into being a fat unfocused organization. It has adapted when necessary but, crucially, it has not tried to hang on to traditional processes that no longer work.

Expert leaders foster those subtle cultural elements that allow a company and a workforce to flourish. They serve the fortunes of their companies most effectively.

A call to arms

I hope the contents of this book have provoked a call to arms. The evidence for the power of credible leadership – expert leadership – is compelling. We need to find our way back to common sense. This is a critical juncture in history for our environment, the world economy, Earth's resources, and the sustainability of species. If we are to survive on a happy and liveable planet, human society has to take the long view, and we must listen to and empower experts, and importantly support their leadership. It will be a challenging time to be at the head of organizations. But good leadership is needed more now, in my judgement, than at any time since the Second World War. So, what are we going to do about it and where do we start? I hope I have offered the material for us to take both small and large steps to an expert-led world.

Acknowledgements

This was a book I felt I had to write – but only when I had the necessary evidence to make a generalizable case for expert leadership.

I have worked with many inspirational people in getting to this point. I would like to thank them here.

For his patience and love, I need to begin with thanks to my partner in life Andrew Oswald for his encouragement and support throughout this process.

For our friendship, our shared publications, and endlessly talking through the many possible permutations of how expert leaders have their extraordinary effect, I thank Agnes Bäker at the Vrije Universiteit Amsterdam. So much of what is in this book has come from our joint work.

For his extensive research assistance, I am very grateful to Toby Houston-Sime, and I look forward to our next project.

Natasha Maw and I go back many years. Our first professional endeavour, in the early 1990s, was to produce a comedy series for BBC Radio 5. Unfortunately, soon after it launched, it was shut down, apparently for being too risqué. My radio career ended at that point, but Natasha went on to became a successful producer. Many years later she moved into the field of leadership development and professional coaching, and we again collaborated. Natasha has contributed a great deal to this book (and especially in Chapters 6 and 7). She also helped me create a remarkable master's degree in leadership and management designed for medical doctors at Bayes Business School. Chapters 6 and 7 have also benefited considerably from the ideas and research of Jaason Geerts and Patty Fahy. Jaason, Director of Research and Leadership Development at the Canadian

College of Health Leaders, is an expert in the science behind training leaders. Patty is an internal medicine physician and former senior health-care executive who, over the last twenty years, has been coaching and supporting physicians into leadership.

Two special women believed in this project from the start, and eventually helped bring it to life. They are Sarah Caro, my editor at Basic Books, who has been a supportive and erudite guide, and my literary agent Clare Grist-Taylor, who has walked me through this process with constant reassurance and care. I am very grateful to you both. Thanks also goes to John Mahaney at Public Affairs for his helpful comments throughout, to Caroline Westmore and the whole team at John Murray Press.

This book has benefited from a wealth of first-hand observations and comment from expert leaders and professionals in different work settings. My thanks go to Anthony 'Mac' McKeever, an NHS CEO and turn-around specialist; Tom Rees and Jennifer Barker from the Ambition Institute for School Leadership; Alan Whittle, Director of Strategy, Inzpire Limited; Isabel Berwick, Work & Careers editor, *Financial Times*; Fatma Makalo, manager of Bridgeside Lodge Care Home; Lynn Elliot, Certified Leadership Coach & Consultant; Emma Clarey, critical care nurse at King's College London; Anthony Finkelstein, President of City, University of London; Stephen-Andrew Whyte, senior pharmacist at Great Ormond Street Hospital; Darryl Carlton, IT project management specialist, Australia; Verna Yiu, Alberta Health Services; at Texas Health Resources, Lynn Myers, and Charisse Jimenez, who has been developing physician leaders for decades; Peter Lees, CEO and Medical Director, and Kirsten Armit, COO, of the Faculty of Medical Leaders and Managers, which has brought the importance of placing doctors into leadership into the heart of the NHS; physician leader Ash Dwivedi; Simon Clinton, Save Wild Tigers; Magnus Spence, Managing Director, Broadridge; my former MBA students Sebastian Stewart at Somerset Capital Management, Josh Saxby at Clarkson plc and Jamie Peston, Ed Tech Entrepreneur; Lisa Boudreau, Harvard Medical School; Stephanie Robertson, CEO, SiMPACT; Claire Ladwa, UK HR

Director, Convex Insurance; Julian le Grand, London School of Economics; Martin Hoare, Director for International Business Development, Raytheon Company; Matthew Evans, Headteacher, Farmor's School; and Peter Angood, CEO, American Association for Physician Leadership.

I have learned so much from the wonderful physicians who have been through our Executive Master's in Medical Leadership (EMML) programme. They have come from numerous NHS trusts, Health Corporation of America and Priory Group hospitals, and beyond. Some of those who show up in this book include Sanjiv Sharma, Russell Durkin, Bansri Lakhani, Ruth McCabe, Nick Prince, and Tim Liversedge. I also owe a great deal to Victoria Oriade, Ruth Velenski, and the wonderful EMML team.

Special thanks go to James Stoller, a specialist in pulmonary medicine and chairman of the education institute at the Cleveland Clinic. Jamie has been an exceptional friend, a co-author, and a great supporter of our Master's in Medical Leadership. Thanks also to Tarun Bastiampillai and Stephen Allison, psychiatrists in Adelaide, with whom I have worked closely. They were early champions of the 'theory of expert leadership', and turned around psychiatry services in South Australia.

A number of friends kindly read early versions of chapters or contributed helpful comments. They include Alison Cheevers-Jongejan, Judith Higgin, Sara Brailsford, Nigel Barnes, Martin Hoare, Felicity Oswald-Nichols, Wil Nichols, Nikki Racklin-Asher, Lucy Rees, Jayne Pollard, David Longdon, Serena Evans, Michele Brailsford, Susan Hill, Bill Dixon, Sarah Mullis, Ian Kirkpatrick, and my brother Mark Goodall. Thanks are also owed to Lorin Rees and Seth Schulman who got me started down this route some years ago.

I am grateful to the many other co-authors who have helped me and us to build the evidence that is used in this book, among them Ben Artz, Larry Kahn, Ganna Pogrebna, John McDowell, Larry Singell, David Berger, Alice Tsai, Susanne Maigaard Axelsen, Henrik Ullum, Marie Krabbe, Edris Kakemam, Maria Schlier, Morten Bennedsen, Margit Osterloh, Mickael Bech, Christian Bøtcher Jacobsen, and Lars Dahl Pedersen.

It is a joy being at a research-intensive university. We are given the freedom to research where our interests take us, to develop new and experimental teaching, and are encouraged to have an impact in the world. In addition, the collegiality at Bayes Business School (formerly Cass), part of City, University of London, is extraordinary. I would like to thank for their support the expert leaders at the school, including our dean André Spicer and Caroline Wiertz, Rich Payne, Lilian De Menezes, Bobby Banerjee, Amit Nigam, and Cliff Oswick, and also my wonderful academic and professional colleagues for their intellectual stimulation and support.

Before I go, I wish to thank my friends among 'the bitches' and 'the together group', who have done their best to keep me social and sane during the writing process; Jacki Sime, with whom I am launching the Pembrokeshire Seal Research Trust, and also my dear parents, for giving me chutzpah. Finally, I am grateful to the authors and journalists whose work I was able to draw on throughout the book. Thank goodness for a free press.

Notes

Chapter 1: When Non-experts Fly the Plane

1. House of Commons, Minutes of evidence taken before Treasury Committee, 20 February 2009, https://publications.parliament.uk/pa/cm200809/cmselect/cmtreasy/uc144_vii/uc14402.htm
2. Ramzan Karmali, 'HBOS' Demise', BBC News, 19 November 2015, https://www.bbc.co.uk/news/business-34859067
3. Kenneth Hopper and William Hopper, *The Puritan Gift: Reclaiming the American Dream Amidst Global Financial Chaos*, Bloomsbury, 2009, Kindle edition.
4. Ibid.
5. Ibid.
6. William D. Cohan, 'How Citigroup Escaped Financial Disaster in 2008', *New York Times*, 6 August 2018, https://www.nytimes.com/2018/08/06/books/review/james-freeman-vern-mckinley-borrowed-time.html
7. 'Rubin Says Not to Blame for Citi's Troubles: Report', Reuters, 29 November 2008, https://www.reuters.com/article/us-citi-idUSTRE4ASoC320081129
8. Jill Treanor, 'Bank Managers Getting Younger', *Guardian*, 19 February 2005, https://www.theguardian.com/business/2005/feb/19/3
9. Martin Wolf, 'Truss's Growth Plan is Nothing but a Magic Potion', *Financial Times*, 2 October 2022, https://www.ft.com/content/510948e9-3c33-42c5-929e-b97c953dc767
10. Chris Giles and Delphine Strauss, 'Trussonomics Abandoned as UK Re-embraces Financial Orthodoxy', *Financial Times*, 17 October 2022, https://www.ft.com/content/34ab7ff5-a891-4725-9a7b-fdf3b27d2f6c

11. Martin Wolf, 'What Really Went Wrong in the 2008 Financial Crisis?', *Financial Times*, 17 July 2018, https://www.ft.com/content/e5ea9f2a-8528-11e8-a29d-73e3d454535d

12. Ibid.

13. Two interesting journalistic accounts of the banking crisis are Gillian Tett's *Fool's Gold* (Little, Brown, 2009) and Andrew Ross Sorkin's *Too Big to Fail* (Penguin, 2009).

14. Karen Jacobs, 'Home Depot's Nardelli Out after Year of Criticism', Reuters, 21 January 2007, https://www.reuters.com/article/us-home-depot-nardelli-idUSN03383942200701 03

15. Claudio Fernández-Aráoz, 'Jack Welch's Approach to Leadership', *Harvard Business Review*, 3 March 2020, https://hbr.org/2020/03/jack-welchs-approach-to-leadership

16. Noel M. Tichy, *Succession: Mastering the Make or Break Process of Leadership Transition*, Penguin, 2014.

17. Ibid.

18. Joe Flaherty, 'How Home Depot Copied Apple to Build an Ingenious New Bucket', *Wired*, 31 December 2013, https://www.wired.com/2013/12/home-depot-reinvents-buckets/

19. 'Nardelli's Strategy for Getting Home Depot Moving', RetailWire, 30 March 2005, https://retailwire.com/nardellis-strategy-for-getting-home-depot-moving/

20. Joe Flaherty, 'How Home Depot Copied Apple to Build an Ingenious New Bucket', *Wired*, 31 December 2013, https://www.wired.com/2013/12/home-depot-reinvents-buckets/

21. Joann S. Lublin, Ann Zimmerman, and Chad Terhune; Joann S. Lublin, 'Behind Nardelli's Abrupt Exit', *Wall Street Journal*, 4 January 2007, https://www.wsj.com/articles/SB116782948407565911

22. Joe Flaherty, 'How Home Depot Copied Apple to Build an Ingenious New Bucket', *Wired*, 31 December 2013, https://www.wired.com/2013/12/home-depot-reinvents-buckets/

23. Brian Grow, 'Out at Home Depot', Bloomberg UK, 4 January 2007, https://www.bloomberg.com/news/articles/2007-01-04/out-at-home-depotbusinessweek-business-news-stock-market-and-financial-advice?leadSource=uverify%20wall

24. TheStreet is a financial news and financial literacy website. Robert Holmes, 'Who Will Bob Nardelli Fail Next?', TheStreet, 4 May 2009, https://www.thestreet.com/opinion/who-will-bob-nardelli-fail-next-10495716

25. Miles Weiss and Sonja Elmquist, 'Cerberus's Freedom Group Withdraws Plans for IPO', Bloomberg UK, 1 April 2011, https://www. bloomberg.com/news/articles/2011-04-01/cerberus-s-feinberg-with-draws-ipo-of-remington-arms-owner-freedom-group#xj4y7vzkg Michael J. de la Merced, 'Nardelli Steps Down from Most of His Cerberus Roles', DealBook, *New York Times*, 9 March 2012, https://archive.nytimes.com/dealbook.nytimes.com/2012/03/09/nardelli-steps-down-at-cerberus/

26. Booz & Company, CEO Succession Report: 12th Annual Global CEO Succession Study, 2011.

27. 'Let's Stop Rewarding Failed CEOs', *New York Times*, 1 October 2011, https://www.nytimes.com/2011/10/01/business/lets-stop-rewarding-failed-ceos-common-sense.html

28. 'Yahoo CEO Marissa Mayer Will Walk Away With a $23 Million Golden Parachute', Techlear, 13 March 2017, https://www.techlear.com/blog/2017/03/13/yahoo-ceo-marissa-mayer-will-walk-away-with-a-23-million-golden-parachute/

29. Michael Hiltzik, 'Marissa Mayer's $23-Million Severance from Yahoo May Look Obscene. But It's Even Worse', *Los Angeles Times*, 17 March 2017, https://www.latimes.com/business/hiltzik/la-fi-hiltzik-mayer-severance-20170317-story.html

30. Rob Davies, 'Andy Hornby: Reinvention of Man With Infamous Role in Banking Crisis', *Guardian*, 2 May 2019, https://www.theguardian.com/business/2019/may/02/andy-hornby-the-one-time-boss-of-hbos

31. Ibid.

32. Steve Jobs' birth mother was Joanne Carole Schieble and his father was Abdulfattah Jandali. He was adopted by Clara (née Hagopian) and Paul Reinhold Jobs as a baby.

33. Apple Computer Company was created on 1 April 1976 by Steve Jobs, Steve Wozniak, and Ronald Wayne. Owen W. Linzmayer, *Apple Confidential 2.0: The Definitive History of the World's Most Colorful Company*, No Starch Press, 2004.

34. Andrew Orlowski, 'Apple Sues Itself in the Foot (Again)', The Register, 4 May 2006, https://www.theregister.com/2006/05/04/apple_sa_deep_links/

35. Nivedita Balu and Noel Randewich, 'Apple Becomes First Company to Hit $3 Trillion Market Value, Then Slips', Reuters, 4 January 2022, https://www.reuters.com/markets/europe/apple-gets-closer-3-trillion-market-value-2022-01-03/

36. Andy Hertzfeld, Designer, Macintosh Development Team, http://www.pbs.org/nerds/part3.html

37. Mary Bellis, 'Who Actually Invented the Macintosh Computer?', ThoughtCo, 26 August 2020, https://www.thoughtco.com/who-invented-the-macintosh-4072884

38. Steven Pearlstein, 'Jonathan Sculley Steps Down as Chairman of Apple', *Washington Post*, 16 October 1993, https://www.washington-post.com/wp-srv/business/longterm/apple/sculley.htm

39. Stephen Silver, '25 Years Ago, Apple's Board of Directors Pushed Out CEO John Sculley', AppleInsider, 18 June 2018, https://appleinsider.com/articles/18/06/18/25-years-ago-apples-board-of-directors-pushed-out-ceo-john-sculley

40. Tom Hornby, 'Michael Spindler: The Peter Principle at Apple', Low End Mac, 17 August 2013, https://lowendmac.com/2013/michael-spindler-peter-principle-apple/

41. Clifton L. Boyd, 'Why Was Steve Jobs Fired from Apple?', Wyde Theme, 1 March 2022, https://wydetheme.com/why-was-steve-jobs-fired-from-apple/

42. Koka Sexton, 'The History of Apple CEOs', Customer Think, 25 August 2011, https://customerthink.com/the_history_of_apple_ceos/

43. In his speech at the 1998 Macworld conference.

44. Evan Carmichael, 'The Real Genius of Steve Jobs', YouTube, 28 February 2015, https://www.youtube.com/watch?v=rQKis2Cfpeo&t=8s

45. Ibid.

46. Darryl Carlton was head of IT Strategy for Telstra, head of Business Process Engineering for Optus, chief executive officer for BizTone.com, chief information officer for the Environment Protection Agency, IT strategy adviser to several government departments, and head of Applications Development for one of the world's largest internet service providers. He is an Industry Fellow in the School of Business, Technology and Entrepreneurship at Swinburne University of Technology and completed his PhD in 2019 on the subject of 'Situational Incompetence: An Investigation Into the Causes of Failure of a Large Scale IT Project' at RMIT University. He has a master's in Business Information Technology and a master's in Commerce, and is a graduate of the Australian Institute of Company Directors and a member of the Australian Institute of Project Management.

47. Patrick Thibodeau, 'Pennsylvania Sues IBM Over Troubled $110M IT Upgrade', ComputerWorld, 13 March 2017, https://www.computerworld.com/article/3180325/pennsylvania-sues-ibm-over-troubled-110m-it-upgrade.html

48. Murad Ahmed, 'Five Corporate IT Failures that Caused Huge Disruption', *Financial Times*, 28 May 2017, https://www.ft.com/content/270563ee-43b9-11e7-8d27-59b4dd6296b8

49. Okoro Chima Okereke, *Achieving Successful and Sustainable Project Delivery in Africa: How to Implement Effective and Efficient Project Management Practices and Policies*, Routledge, Taylor & Francis, 2020.

50. It was originally signed off by Prime Minister Tony Blair's Labour government in 2002.

51. Rajeev Syal, 'Abandoned NHS IT System Has Cost £10bn So Far', *Guardian*, 18 September 2013, https://www.theguardian.com/society/2013/sep/18/nhs-records-system-10bn; 'NHS IT System One of "Worst Fiascos Ever", Say MPs', BBC News, 18 September 2013, https://www.bbc.co.uk/news/uk-politics-24130684; Justinia Taghreed, 'The UK's National Programme for IT: Why Was It Dismantled?', *Health Services Management Research*, 30(1), 2016, https://doi.org/10.1177/0951484816662492. An interesting study (unpublished) is O. Campion-Awwad, A. Hayton, L. Smith, and M. Vuaran, 'The National Programme for IT in the NHS: A Case History' MPhil, University of Cambridge, https://www.readkong.com/page/the-national-programme-for-it-in-the-nhs-7669255

52. Among them, support from senior management, clear and realistic goals, a strong and detailed plan that is kept up to date, good communication and feedback, the involvement of both clients and users, suitably qualified staff and sufficient resources, effective change management, and good governance.

53. 'Lack of Technical Knowledge in Leadership is a Key Reason Why So Many IT Projects Fail', The Conversation, 10 September 2018, https://theconversation.com/lack-of-technical-knowledge-in-leadership-is-a-key-reason-why-so-many-it-projects-fail-101889

54. For Carlton's research publications see https://swinburne.academia.edu/DarrylCarlton

55. Anna Garland, 'Five of the Biggest Outsourcing Failures', ITProPortal, 9 March 2022, https://www.itproportal.com/2015/12/19/five-of-the-biggest-outsourcing-failures/

56. Ibid.

57. D. Carlton and K. Peszynski, 'Situational Incompetence: The Failure of Governance in the Management of Large Scale IT Projects', in *International Working Conference on Transfer and Diffusion of IT*, Springer, June 2018, pp. 224–44. https://www.researchgate.net/profile/Darryl-Carlton/publication/329473871_Situational_Incompetence_The_Failure_of_Governance_in_the_Management_of_Large_Scale_IT_Projects_IFIP_WG_86_International_Conference_on_Transfer_and_Diffusion_of_IT_TDIT_2018_Portsmouth_UK_June_25_2018/links/5c582b37458515a4c757137f/Situational-Incompetence-The-Failure-of-Governance-in-the-Management-of-Large-Scale-IT-Projects-IFIP-WG-86-International-Conference-on-Transfer-and-Diffusion-of-IT-TDIT-2018-Portsmouth-UK-June-25.pdf?origin=searchReact&_iepl%5BgeneralViewId%5D=6iyAk3T Gt3lyvn8uWKc4PkoDvo71j53LdJGw&_iepl%5Bcontexts%5D%5B0%5D=searchReact&_iepl%5BviewId%5D=zFttAOYoq8bV7fqDhH opLfNRSoosjpYYCBh8&_iepl%5BsearchType%5D=publication&_iepl%5Bdata%5D%5BcountLessEqual20%5D=1&_iepl%5Bdata%5D%5BinteractedWithPosition2%5D=1&_iepl%5Bdata%5D%5BwithoutEnrichment%5D=1&_iepl%5Bposition%5D=2&_iepl%5BrgKey%5D=PB%3A329473871&_iepl%5BinteractionType%5D=publicationDownload

58. D. Carlton, 'Situational Incompetence: An Investigation into the Causes of Failure of a Large-Scale IT Project', in *Dark Sides of Organizational Behavior and Leadership*, D. Carlton and K. Peszynski, 'Situational Incompetence: The Failure of Governance in the Management of Large Scale IT Projects', in *International Working Conference on Transfer and Diffusion of IT*, Springer, June 2018, pp. 224–44m. https://www.researchgate.net/profile/Darryl-Carlton/publication/329473871_Situational_Incompetence_The_Failure_of_Governance_in_the_Management_of_Large_Scale_IT_Projects_IFIP_WG_86_International_Conference_on_Transfer_and_Diffusion_of_IT_TDIT_2018_Portsmouth_UK_June_25_2018/links/5c582b37458515a4c757137f/Situational-Incompetence-The-Failure-of-Governance-in-the-Management-of-Large-Scale-IT-Projects-IFIP-WG-86-International-Conference-on-Transfer-and-Diffusion-of-IT-TDIT-2018-Portsmouth-UK-June-25.pdf?origin=searchReact&_iepl%5BgeneralViewId%5D=6iyAk3T

Gt3lyvn8uWKc4PkoDvo71j53LdJGw&_iepl%5Bcontexts%5B
o%5D=searchReact&_iepl%5BviewId%5D=zFttAOYoq8bV7fqDhH
opLfNRSoosjpYYCBh8&_iepl%5BsearchType%5D=publication&_
iepl%5Bdata%5D%5BcountLessEqual20%5D=1&_iepl%5Bdata%5
D%5BinteractedWithPosition2%5D=1&_iepl%5Bdata%5D%5Bwit
houtEnrichment%5D=1&_iepl%5Bposition%5D=2&_
iepl%5BrgKey%5D=PB%3A329473871&_iepl%5BinteractionType
%5D=publicationDownload

59. Y. K. Dwivedi, D. Wastell, S. Laumer et al., 'Research on Information Systems Failures and Successes: Status Update and Future Directions', *Information Systems Frontiers*, 17 (2015): 143–57, 149 https://www.researchgate.net/profile/Amany-Elbanna-4/publication/273482112_Research_on_information_systems_failures_and_successes_Status_update_and_future_directions/links/552653e30cf295bf160ed3e6/Research-on-information-systems-failures-and-successes-Status-update-and-future-directions.pdf?origin=searchReact&_iepl%5BgeneralViewId%5D=NFD4E1NSx18T91gLhp9kV3jpXZvvSWuOcN89&_iepl%5Bcontexts%5D%5B0%5D=searchReact&_iepl%5BviewId%5D=TaTGoNbNzzJnMjYC6emkvqpz73t6IripW2er&_iepl%5BsearchType%5D=publication&_iepl%5Bdata%5D%5BcountLessEqual20%5D=1&_iepl%5Bdata%5D%5BinteractedWithPosition1%5D=1&_iepl%5Bdata%5D%5BwithEnrichment%5D=1&_iepl%5Bposition%5D=1&_iepl%5BrgKey%5D=PB%3A273482112&_iepl%5BinteractionType%5D=publicationDownload

60. 'Lack of Technical Knowledge in Leadership Is a Key Reason Why So Many IT Projects Fail', The Conversation, 10 September 2018, https://theconversation.com/lack-of-technical-knowledge-in-leadership-is-a-key-reason-why-so-many-it-projects-fail-101889

61. Ibid.

62. Grant Robertson, '"We Are Not Prepared": The Flaws Inside Public Health that Hurt Canada's Readiness for COVID-19', *Globe and Mail*, 26 December 2020, online edition, updated 3 February 2021, https://www.theglobeandmail.com/canada/article-we-are-not-prepared-the-flaws-inside-public-health-that-hurt-canadas/

63. In emails obtained by the *Globe* newspaper.

64. 'Canada Spent $624.2 Billion on COVID-19 Pandemic: Report', True North Wire, 1 June 2021, https://tnc.news/2021/06/01/canada-spent

-624-2-billion-on-covid-19-pandemic-report/. The study was conducted by the *Toronto Star* in association with economists from the University of Toronto, the Canadian Centre for Policy Alternatives and the Macdonald-Laurier Institute (MLI).

65. R. Gunderman and S. L. Kanter, 'Perspective: Educating Physicians to Lead Hospitals', *Academic Medicine*, 84(10), 2009, https://journals.lww. com/academicmedicine/Fulltext/2009/10000/Perspective_Educating _Physicians_to_Lead.16.aspx

66. Ayla Ellison, 'Cleveland Clinic's Operating Income Rebounds to $330M', Beckers Hospital Review, 1 March 2018, https://www.becker-shospitalreview.com/finance/cleveland-clinic-s-operating-income-rebounds-to-330m.html

67. Ian Kirkpatrick, Ali Altanlar, and Gianluca Veronesi, 'Hybrid Professional Managers in Healthcare: An Expanding or Thwarted Occupational Interest?', *Public Management Review*, 25 October 2021, https://www.tandfonline.com/doi/pdf/10.1080/ 14719037.2021.1996777

68. I. Kirkpatrick, B. Bullinger, F. Lega, and M. Dent, 'The Translation of Hospital Management Models in European Health Systems: A Framework for Comparison', *British Journal of Management*, 24, 2013, S48–S61, https://www.researchgate.net/profile/Mike-Dent/publica-tion/264399206_The_Translation_of_Hospital_Management_ Models_in_European_Health_Systems_A_Framework_for_ Comparison/links/5702c58608aeade57a246916/The-Translation-of-Hospital-Management-Models-in-European-Health-Systems-A-Framework-for-Comparison.pdf

69. Ian Kirkpatrick, Ali Altanlar, and Gianluca Veronesi, 'Hybrid Professional Managers in Healthcare: An Expanding or Thwarted Occupational Interest?', *Public Management Review*, 25 October 2021, https://www.tandfonline.com/doi/pdf/10.1080/ 14719037.2021.1996777

70. Cleveland Clinic, 'Caregiver Engagement', https://my.clevelandclinic. org/about/community/sustainability/sustainability-global-citizenship /caregivers/caregiver-engagement

71. 'Boeing Knew About Safety-Alert Problem for a Year Before Telling FAA, Airlines', *Wall Street Journal*, Appeared in the May 5, 2019, print edition as 'Boeing Knew of Problem for a Year'. Updated 5 May 2019, https://www.wsj.com/articles/boeing-knew-about-safety-alert

-problem-for-a-year-before-telling-faa-airlines-11557087129; 'Boeing Knew About Safety-Alert Problems, Didn't Tell Airlines', Fox Business Network, 6 May 2019, https://www.youtube.com/watch?v=ad8QNlA23sM

72. Kenneth Hopper and William Hopper, *The Puritan Gift: Reclaiming the American Dream Amidst Global Financial Chaos*, Bloomsbury, 2009, Kindle edition.

73. James Surowiecki, 'Requiem for a Dreamliner?', *New Yorker*, 4 February 2013, https://www.newyorker.com/magazine/2013/02/04/requiem-for-a-dreamliner. The term *outsourcing*, meaning 'outside resourcing', originated in the early 1980s: see Stuart Rosenberg, *The Global Supply Chain and Risk Management*, Business Expert Press, 2018.

74. James Surowiecki, 'Requiem for a Dreamliner?', *New Yorker*, 4 February 2013, https://www.newyorker.com/magazine/2013/02/04/requiem-for-a-dreamliner

75. Ibid.

76. Ibid.

77. Peter Robison, 'Boeing's 737 Max Software Outsourced to $9-an-Hour Engineers', Bloomberg UK, 28 June 2019, https://www.bloomberg.com/news/articles/2019-06-28/boeing-s-737-max-software-outsourced-to-9-an-hour-engineers

78. Ibid.

79. Daniel Thomas, 'Boeing: Directors to Face Investor Lawsuit over Fatal Crashes', BBC News, 8 September 2021, https://www.bbc.co.uk/news/business-58483150

80. 'Boeing to Pay $2.5bn over 737 Max Conspiracy', BBC News, 8 January 2021, https://www.bbc.co.uk/news/business-55582496

81. Chris Isidore, 'A 737 Crashed in China: What We know about the Plane', CNN Business, 22 March 2022, https://edition.cnn.com/2022/03/21/business/boeing-jet-crash/index.html

82. Mitchell Osak, 'Lessons from Kodak's Demise:Beware of Outsourcing Too Much of Your Secret Sauce', Financial Post, 15 August 2014, https://financialpost.com/executive/c-suite/lesson-from-kodaks-demise-beware-of-outsourcing-too-much-of-your-secret-sauce

83. Ibid.

84. Ibid.

85. Emma Youle, 'Revealed: Who Profited from the Government's Coronavirus Spending Boom', HuffPost, 19 August 2020, updated 22

August 2020, https://www.huffingtonpost.co.uk/entry/who-profits-coronavirus - government - spending - boom _ uk _ 5f089c0c5b63a72c3413817

86. Tabby Kinder, Gill Plimmer, and Jim Pickard, 'Watchdog Criticises Government over Awarding of £17bn Covid Contracts', *Financial Times*, 18 November 2020, https://www.ft.com/content/ee4f2220-9b22-4a4d-87c2-85e8034f8e8c

87. Ibid.

88. House of Commons Committee of Public Accounts, 'Initial Lessons from the Government's Response to the COVID-19 Pandemic', Thirteenth Report of Session 2021–22, 19 July 2021, https://committees.parliament.uk/publications/6954/documents/73046/default/

89. Interview on BBC Radio 4 news.

90. Lord Rose, *Better Leadership for Tomorrow: NHS Leadership Review*, June 2015, https://assets.publishing.service.gov.uk/government/uploads/system/uploads/attachment_data/file/445738/Lord_Rose_NHS_Report_acc.pdf. In the UK a physician is a type of doctor, hence *doctor* is the generic term used.

91. Jagit S. Chadha, *The UK's Productivity Puzzle: Labour, Investment and Finance*, NIESR General Election 2017 – Briefing No. 7, National Institute for Economic and Social Research, 1 June 2017 https://www.niesr.ac.uk/sites/default/files/publications/The%20UK%20Productivity%20Puzzle%20NIESR%20DP%20448_0.pdf

Chapter 2: The Death of Expertise

1. Will McPhail, *New Yorker*, 6 March 2017.

2. E.g. Nigel Farage, Boris Johnson and Brexit, Marie le Pen in France, Hugo Chávez in Venezuela, Viktor Orbán in Hungary, Jair Bolsonaro in Brazil, AMLO in Mexico, Narendra Modi in India, and Recep Tayyip Erdoğan in Turkey.

3. M. J. Goodwin and O. Heath, 'The 2016 Referendum, Brexit and the Left Behind: An Aggregate-Level Analysis of the Result', *Political Quarterly*, 87(3), 2016, pp. 323–32, https://kar.kent.ac.uk/60236/3/Political%20Quarterly%20Version%201%208%20%25282%2529.pdf; D. G. Blanchflower and A. J. Oswald, 'Trends in Extreme Distress in the United States, 1993–2019', *American Journal of Public Health*,

110(10), 2020, pp. 1538–44, https://www.andrewoswald.com/docs/AJPHAbstractBlanchflowerandOswald2020.pdf

4. T. Nichols, *The Death of Expertise: The Campaign against Established Knowledge and Why it Matters*, Oxford University Press, 2017, p. 5.

5. Ibid., Preface.

6. Henry Mance, 'Britain Has Had Enough of Experts, Says Gove', *Financial Times*, 3 June 2016, https://www.ft.com/content/3be49734-29cb-11e6-83e4-abc22d5d108c

7. Recently changed to Advance HE.

8. 'About Us', AdvanceHE, https://www.advance-he.ac.uk/about-us#meetadvancehe

9. Edward Malnick, 'Boris Johnson to "Restore a Smaller State" as Part of No. 10 "Reset", Says Steve Barclay', *Sunday Telegraph*, 12 February 2022, https://www.telegraph.co.uk/politics/2022/02/12/boris-johnson-restore-smaller-state-part-no-10-reset-says-steve/; Zachary B. Wolf, 'Trump Wants Radically Less Government. Here's What That Looks Like', CNN, 15 June 2019, https://edition.cnn.com/2019/04/12/politics/trump-deregulation/index.html

10. Ian MacDougall, 'How McKinsey is Making $100 Million (and Counting) Advising on the Government's Bumbling Coronavirus Response', ProPublica, 15 July 2020, https://www.propublica.org/article/how-mckinsey-is-making-100-million-and-counting-advising-on-the-governments-bumbling-coronavirus-response

11. Lawrence Dunhill and Rajeev Syal, 'Whitehall "Infantilised" by Reliance on Consultants, Minister Claims', *Guardian*, 29 September 2020, https://www.theguardian.com/politics/2020/sep/29/whitehall-infantilised-by-reliance-on-consultants-minister-claims

12. Ibid.

13. Ibid.

14. Siddarth Shrikanth, 'Government Use of Consultants Soars in India', *Financial Times*, 26 June 2019, https://www.ft.com/content/76f530ae-787e-11e9-boec-7dff87b9a4a2

15. Michael O'Dwyer, 'UK Public Spending on Consultants More Than Doubles', *Financial Times*, 24 October 2021, https://www.ft.com/content/efdcaccf-a535-4ae8-afdo-8dod70b1ed4b

16. Data sourced from Federal Procurement Data System at fpds.gov, accessed 9 April 2022. The exact number of contracts awarded to Deloitte and McKinsey is unclear because 15,000 contracts in total

were listed as being awarded but a number of these had $0 attached, which is confusing. The total number of contracts (with a value of $1 or more) awarded to either Deloitte or McKinsey was listed as 8,428.

17. Ian MacDougall, 'How McKinsey is Making $100 Million (and Counting) Advising on the Government's Bumbling Coronavirus Response', ProPublica, 15 July 2020, https://www.propublica.org/article/how-mckinsey-is-making-100-million-and-counting-advising-on-the-governments-bumbling-coronavirus-response

18. Ibid.

19. Michael O'Dwyer, 'UK Public Spending on Consultants More Than Doubles', *Financial Times*, 24 October 2021, https://www.ft.com/content/efdcaccf-a535-4ae8-afd0-8d0d70b1ed4b

20. Siddarth Shrikanth, 'Government Use of Consultants Soars in India', *Financial Times*, 26 June 2019, https://www.ft.com/content/76f530ae-787e-11e9-b0ec-7dff87b9a4a2

21. Ibid., e.g. Clean India and Digital India.

22. Ian MacDougall, 'How McKinsey is Making $100 Million (and Counting) Advising on the Government's Bumbling Coronavirus Response', ProPublica, 15 July 2020, https://www.propublica.org/article/how-mckinsey-is-making-100-million-and-counting-advising-on-the-governments-bumbling-coronavirus-response

23. Ibid.

24. Finkelstein interview, 7 January 2022. In 2021 he became president of City, University of London.

25. In her campaign to be the next UK Conservative Party leader, contender Liz Truss attacked the civil service and threatened to cut their pay and numbers. It beggars belief to consider a boss attacking his or her own employees, and then being surprised when morale sinks and top talent heads for the door. See e.g. Heather Stewart and Aubrey Allegretti, 'Liz Truss Plan to Cut £11bn in Whitehall Waste "Ludicrous"', *Guardian*, 1 August 2022, https://www.theguardian.com/politics/2022/aug/01/liz-truss-plan-to-cut-11bn-in-whitehall-waste-ludicrous

26. Jerry Z. Muller, *The Tyranny of Metrics*, Princeton University Press, 2019, Kindle edition, p. 41.

27. P. K. Howard, *The Death of Common Sense: How Law Is Suffocating America*, Random House, 1995. See also P. K. Howard, *The Rule of Nobody: Saving America from Dead Laws and Broken Government*, W. W. Norton, 2014.

28. P. K. Howard, *The Death of Common Sense: How Law Is Suffocating America*, Random House, 1995.
29. Jerry Z. Muller, *The Tyranny of Metrics*, Princeton University Press, Kindle edition, pp. 34–5.
30. Ibid.
31. Cathy O'Neil, *Weapons of Math Destruction*, Penguin, 2016, Kindle edition.
32. Ibid.
33. Ibid.
34. Rakesh Khurana, *Searching for a Corporate Savior*, Princeton University Press, 2011, Kindle edition, p. 57.
35. Kenneth Hopper and William Hopper, *The Puritan Gift: Reclaiming the American Dream Amidst Global Financial Chaos*, Bloomsbury, 2009, Kindle edition, pp. 37, 166, 33 (citing W. B. Given Jr, *Bottom-Up Management: People Working Together*, New York: Harper, 1949), 103, 107.
36. Ibid., p. 76.
37. Jerry Z. Muller, *The Tyranny of Metrics*, Princeton University Press, 2019, Kindle edition.
38. Rakesh Khurana, *From Higher Aims to Hired Hands: The Social Transformation of American Business Schools and the Unfulfilled Promise of Management as a Profession*, Princeton University Press, 2007, p. 30.
39. Kenneth Hopper and William Hopper, *The Puritan Gift: Reclaiming the American Dream Amidst Global Financial Chaos*, Bloomsbury, 2009, Kindle edition, p.134.
40. Ibid.
41. Ibid., p. 135.
42. Rakesh Khurana, *Searching for a Corporate Savior*, Princeton University Press, 2011, Kindle edition, p. 57.
43. Ibid.
44. Ibid., p. 69.
45. Ibid.
46. Kenneth Hopper and William Hopper, *The Puritan Gift: Reclaiming the American Dream Amidst Global Financial Chaos*, Bloomsbury, 2009, Kindle edition.
47. A. Spicer, Z. Jaser, and C. Wiertz, 'The Future of the Business School: Finding Hope in Alternative Pasts', *Academy of Management Learning and Education*, 20(3), 2021, pp. 459–66. https://openaccess.city.ac.uk/id/eprint/26313/1/

48. Ibid.
49. T. Hopper, D. Otley, and B. Scapens, 'British Management Accounting Research: Whence and Whither – Opinions and Recollections', *British Accounting Review*, 33, 2001, pp. 263–91, https://www.researchgate.net /profile/Trevor-Hopper/publication/247309218_British_ Management_Accounting_Research_Whence_and_Whither_ Opinions_and_Recollections/links/563c971708ae405111aa2bf3/ British-Management-Accounting-Research-Whence-and-Whither-Opinions-and-Recollections?origin=searchReact&_iepl%5BgeneralV iewId%5D=gHq48ar3XJsKxEmTY3F5WYoHdAooNQR5aPGn&_ iepl%5Bcontexts%5D%5Bo%5D=searchReact&_iepl%5BviewId%5 D=1Ub8vivlpvGbLgYElaCw3JZD6k6Dq3utG3N8&_iepl%5Bsearc hType%5D=publication&_iepl%5Bdata%5D%5BcountLessEqual20 %5D=1&_iepl%5Bdata%5D%5BinteractedWithPosition1%5D=1& _iepl%5Bdata%5D%5BwithoutEnrichment%5D=1&_ iepl%5Bposition%5D=1&_iepl%5BrgKey%5D=PB% 3A247309218&_iepl%5BinteractionType%5D=publicationDownl oad .
50. Jerry Z. Muller, *The Tyranny of Metrics*, Princeton University Press, 2019, p. 34.
51. Rakesh Khurana, *From Higher Aims to Hired Hands: The Social Transformation of American Business Schools and the Unfulfilled Promise of Management as a Profession*, Princeton University Press, 2007, Kindle edition, p. 30.
52. Kenneth Hopper and William Hopper, *The Puritan Gift: Reclaiming the American Dream Amidst Global Financial Chaos*, Bloomsbury, 2009, Kindle edition, p. 146.
53. H. Mintzberg, 'Managers Not MBSs', *Management Today*, 20(7), 2004, pp. 10–13.
54. E.g. Dennis Tourish, *Management Studies in Crisis*, Cambridge University Press, 2019, Kindle edition, p. 5.
55. R. R. Locke and J.-C. Spender, *Confronting Managerialism: How the Business Elite and Their Schools Threw Our Lives Out of Balance*, Bloomsbury, 2011, p. 88.
56. Charlan Nemeth, *In Defense of Troublemakers: The Power of Dissent in Life and Business*, New York: Basic Books, retitled in the UK as *No!: The Power of Disagreement in a World that Wants to Get Along*, Atlantic, 2018, Kindle edition, p. 3.

57. Max Mallet, Brett Nelson, and Chris Steiner, 'The Most Annoying, Pretentious and Useless Business Jargon', *Forbes*, 26 January 2012, https://www.forbes.com/sites/groupthink/2012/01/26/the-most-annoying-pretentious-and-useless-business-jargon/

58. R. R. Locke and J.-C. Spender, *Confronting Managerialism: How the Business Elite and Their Schools Threw Our Lives Out of Balance*, Bloomsbury, 2011.

59. For a full understanding of the issues see Dennis Tourish, *Management Studies in Crisis*, Cambridge University Press, Kindle edition, p. 6.

60. J. Pfeffer, *Leadership BS: Fixing Workplaces and Careers One Truth at a Time*, HarperCollins, 2015, p. 4.

61. B. Kellerman, *Professionalizing Leadership*, Oxford University Press, 2018.

Chapter 3: The Case for Expert Leaders

1. All quotations within this chapter without citations are from personal communication with the author.

2. John Morgan, 'Are Scholars or Executives Best Suited to Lead Universities?', *Times Higher Education*, 16 January 2014, https://www.timeshighereducation.com/news/are-scholars-or-executives-best-suited-to-lead-universities/2010478.article

3. C. Stewart Gillmor, *Fred Terman at Stanford: Building a Discipline, a University, and Silicon Valley*, Stanford University Press, 2004, cited in https://physicstoday.scitation.org/doi/full/10.1063/1.2138426

4. Ed Sharpe, 'The Life of Frederick Terman', *SMEC Vintage Electrics*, 3(1), 1991 (now *SMECC*), https://www.smecc.org/frederick_terman_-_by_ed_sharpe.htm

5. Stewart W. Leslie, 'From Backwater to Powerhouse', *Stanford Magazine*, March 1990, reproduced in ibid.

6. Ibid.

7. Ibid.

8. Amy Adams, 'Former Stanford President Wins Turing Award for Contributions to Computing', Stanford News Service, 21 March 2018, https://news.stanford.edu/press-releases/2018/03/21/hennessy-wins-tuutions-computing/

9. John L. Hennessy, lecture video, 2017, https://amturing.acm.org/vp/hennessy_1426931.cfm

10. 'Frederick Terman: The Silicon Valley Pioneer Who Shared His Success', *Guardian*, 4 October 2016, https://www.theguardian.com/personal-investments/ng-interactive/2016/oct/04/frederick-terman-silicon-valley-mentor-stanford-hp

11. As measured by number of lifetime research citations. See 2021 Academic Ranking of World Universities, Shanghai Ranking, https://www.shanghairanking.com/rankings/arwu/2021

12. Amanda Goodall, *Socrates in the Boardroom*, Princeton University Press, 2009. A. H. Goodall, 'Should Top Universities Be Led by Top Researchers, and Are They? A Citations Analysis', *Journal of Documentation*, 62, 2006, pp. 388–411; https://amandagoodall.com/wp-content/uploads/2021/12/JDocAGversionMay06.pdf; A. H. Goodall, 'Highly Cited Leaders and the Performance of Research Universities', *Research Policy*, 38, 2009, pp. 1079–92. https://amandagoodall.com/wp-content/uploads/2022/01/LeadershipPerformanceRP09.pdf

13. Rodney B. Dieser, 'Research Absent from Debate over Harreld's Hiring at UI', *Des Moines Register*, 10 July 2016, https://eu.desmoinesregister.com/story/opinion/columnists/iowa-view/2016/07/10/research-absent-debate-over-harrelds-hiring-ui/86860366/

14. Ibid.

15. Emma Whitford, 'Iowa President Ending Difficult Term with Early Retirement', *Inside Higher Ed*, 2 October 2020, https://www.insidehighered.com/news/2020/10/02/university-iowa-president-will-retire-early-capping-five-year-tenure-started-rocks

16. Vanessa Miller, 'University of Iowa President Bruce Harreld Retiring Early', *The Gazette*, 1 October 2020, https://www.thegazette.com/subject/news/education/university-of-iowa-president-bruce-harreld-retiring-retirement-leaving-job-20201001

17. 'About Professor Brian P. Schmidt AC FAA FRS, Vice-Chancellor and President, Australian National University', https://www.anu.edu.au/about/university-executive/professor-brian-p-schmidt-ac-faa-frs

18. Emma Macdonald, 'ANU Ranking Slides on Respected Global Research League Table', *Canberra Times*, 15 August 2014, updated 23 April 2018, https://www.canberratimes.com.au/story/6137299/anu-ranking-slides-on-respected-global-research-league-table/

19. Businessman Robin Buchanan stepped down as dean of London Business School after sixteen months.

20. 'From the CFO', Harvard Business School, 2021 Annual Report, https://www.hbs.edu/about/annualreport/2021/financials/from-the-cfo/

21. J. McCormack, C. Propper, and S. Smith, 'Herding Cats? Management and University Performance', *Economic Journal*, 124(578), 2014, pp. F534–F564. https://onlinelibrary.wiley.com/doi/epdf/10.1111/ecoj.12105

22. These were located in research universities so research output was the measure we used. Specifically, departmental research success is calculated as the share of total US weighted economics publications over a three-year moving average. We use publications data collected annually (over the years 1995 through 2010) from eleven of the most selective economics journals (*American Economic Review, Econometrica, Economic Journal, Economica, International Economic Review, Journal of Economic Theory, Journal of Monetary Economics, Journal of Political Economy, Quarterly Journal of Economics, Review of Economics and Statistics,* and the *Review of Economic Studies*).

23. The department chair's own citations and publications measured in a number of different ways.

24. A. H. Goodall, J. M. McDowell, and L. D. Singell, 'Do Economics Departments Improve after They Appoint a Top Scholar as Chairperson?', *Kyklos* 70(4), 2017, pp. 546–64. https://amandagoodall.com/wp-content/uploads/2022/01/MASTERGoodalletalAugust28.pdf

25. R. Grenfell and T. Drew, 'Here's Why the WHO Says a Coronavirus Vaccine is 18 Months Away', The Conversation, 14 February 2020, retrieved 11 November 2020, https://theconversation.com/heres-why-the-who-says-a-coronavirus-vaccine-is-18-months-away-131213

26. T. Thanh Le, Z. Andreadakis, A. Kumar et al., 'The COVID-19 Vaccine Development Landscape', *Nature Reviews Drug Discovery*, 19(5), 9 April 2020, pp. 305–6, https://www1.cgmh.org.tw/library_s/2020/paper/P-0428%20The%20COVID-19%20vaccine%20development%20landscape.pdf

27. Featured in A. H. Goodall, 'How the Coronavirus Pandemic Has Tested UK Doctors' Leadership Skills', *Financial Times*, 20 May 2020, https://www.ft.com/content/d2596f10-98fc-11ea-871b-edeb99a20c6e

28. Mayo Clinic Timeline, https://history.mayoclinic.org/timelines/history-timeline.php

29. Nancy Cooper, 'World's Best Hospitals 2021', *Newsweek*, https://www.newsweek.com/best-hospitals-2021

30. I will use the term *physician* to mean 'medical doctor', i.e. those medically trained.

31. Alyssa Frank, 'The CEOs of Mayo Clinic #ThrowbackThursday', Mayo Clinic Laboratories, 21 September 2017, https://news.mayocliniclabs.com/2017/09/21/ceos-mayo-clinic-throwbackthursday/

32. Nancy Cooper, 'World's Best Hospitals 2021', *Newsweek*, https://www.newsweek.com/best-hospitals-2021

33. 'US News Best Hospitals', https://health.usnews.com/best-hospitals

34. A. H. Goodall, 'Physician-Leaders and Hospital Performance: Is There an Association?', *Social Science and Medicine*, 73(4), 2011, pp. 535–9, https://amandagoodall.com/wp-content/uploads/2022/01/SocialScienceMedicinePublished.pdf

35. See also James Mountford and Caroline Webb, 'When clinicians lead', *The McKinsey Quarterly*, 1, 2009.

36. I. Kirkpatrick, A. Altanlar, and G. Veronesi, 'Hybrid Professional Managers in Healthcare: An Expanding or Thwarted Occupational Interest?', *Public Management Review*, 25 October 2021, pp. 1–20, https://www.tandfonline.com/doi/pdf/10.1080/14719037.2021.1996777

37. Harvard T. H. Chan School of Public Health, 'The Most Expensive Health Care System in the World', https://www.hsph.harvard.edu/news/hsph-in-the-news/the-most-expensive-health-care-system-in-the-world/

38. Centers for Medicare & Medicaid Services, 'NHE Fact Sheet', last modified 12 August 2022, https://www.cms.gov/Research-Statistics-Data-and-Systems/Statistics-Trends-and-Reports/NationalHealthExpendData/NHE-Fact-Sheet

39. R. Gunderman and S. L. Kanter, 'Perspective: Educating Physicians to Lead Hospitals', *Academic Medicine*, 84(10), October 2009, https://journals.lww.com/academicmedicine/Fulltext/2009/10000/Perspective__Educating_Physicians_to_Lead.16.aspx

40. S. Dorgan, D. Layton, N. Bloom et al., *Management in Healthcare: Why Good Practice Really Matters*, McKinsey & Co. and LSE (CEP), 2010, https://www.researchgate.net/profile/Stephen-Dorgan/publication/350441477_Management_in_Healthcare_Why_Good_Practice_Really_Matters/links/605f7465a6fdccbfeaof5048/Management-in-Healthcare-Why-Good-Practice-Really-Matters.pdf?origin=searchReact&_iepl%5BgeneralViewId%5D=6QHoYWU1gV7EFW4LeAFUOKoV7xulBAW51PJT&_iepl%5Bcontexts%5D

%5B0%5D=searchReact&_iepl%5BviewId%5D=aP3wNBzAooqFh
VHZdeSd1TbAbWWTbeDJ5yFR&_iepl%5BsearchType%5D=publ
ication&_iepl%5Bdata%5D%5BcountLessEqual20%5D=1&_iepl%
5Bdata%5D%5BinteractedWithPosition1%5D=1&_iepl%5Bdata%5
D%5BwithoutEnrichment%5D=1&_iepl%5Bposition%5D=1&_
iepl%5BrgKey%5D=PB%3A350441477&_iepl%5BinteractionType
%5D=publicationDownload

41. M. Tasi, A. Keswani, and K. Bozic, 'Does Physician Leadership Affect Hospital Quality, Operational Efficiency, and Financial Performance?', *Health Care Management Review*, 44(3), July/September 2019, pp. 256–62, https://doi.org/10.1097/hmr.0000000000000173

42. N. Bloom, R. Sadun, and J. Van Reenen, *Does Management Matter in Healthcare?*, Stanford University Press, 2014, https://prod-edxapp.edx -cdn.org/assets/courseware/v1/dd428dcc44daa742d5c5c91aeb9dcd21 /c4x/HarvardX/PH555x/asset/Management_Healthcare_June2014. pdf

43. E. Kakemam and A. H. Goodall, 'Hospital Performance and Physician Leadership: New Evidence from Iran', *BMJ Leader*, 11 October 2019, https://amandagoodall.com/wp-content/uploads/2022/01/ IranianHospitals.pdf

44. Some studies look at clinical leadership, which includes nurses, physicians, physiotherapists, etc. My studies focus mainly on physicians.

45. F. Sarto and G. Veronesi, 'Clinical Leadership and Hospital Performance: Assessing the Evidence Base', *BMC Health Services Research*, 16(2), 24 May 2016, pp. 85–97, https://link.springer.com/ content/pdf/10.1186/s12913-016-1395-5.pdf

46. E.g. H. Jiang, C. Lockee, K. Bass et al., 'Board Oversight of Quality: Any Differences in Process of Care and Mortality', *Journal of Healthcare Management*, 54(1), January/February 2009, pp.15–29, https://www. researchgate.net/profile/H-Joanna-Jiang/publication/24025775_ Board_Oversight_of_Quality_Any_Differences_in_Process_of_Care_ and_Mortality/links/00b7d52600cb156ced000000/Board-Oversight- of-Quality-Any-Differences-in-Process-of-Care-and-Mortality.pdf; G. Veronesi, I. Kirkpatrick, and F. Vallascas, 'Clinicians on the Board: What Difference Does it Make?', *Social Science & Medicine*, 77, January 2013, pp. 147–55, https://doi.org/10.1016/j.socscimed.2012.11.019; K. E. Reimold, M. K. Faridi, P. S. Pekow et al., 'The Relationship between Governing Board Composition and Medicare Shared Savings Program

Accountable Care Organizations Outcomes: An Observational Study', *Journal of General Internal Medicine*, September 2021, pp.1–7, https://link.springer.com/content/pdf/10.1007/s11606-021-07053-4.pdf

47. G. Veronesi, I. Kirkpatrick, and F. Vallascas, 'Clinicians on the Board: What Difference Does it Make?', *Social Science & Medicine*, 77, January 2013, pp. 147–55, https://doi.org/10.1016/j.socscimed.2012.11.019

48. In the US the Sarbanes-Oxley Act of 2002 requires public hospital boards to have a majority of independent directors.

49. C. Molinari, L. Morlock, J. Alexander, and C. A. Lyles, 'Hospital Board Effectiveness: Relationships Between Governing Board Composition and Hospital Financial Viability', *Health Services Research*, 28(3), 1993, pp. 358, 361, https://www.ncbi.nlm.nih.gov/pmc/articles/PMC1069940/pdf/hsresearch00060-0095.pdf

50. The Deloitte website reads, 'Deloitte is a leader because our leaders are committed to exemplary governance'. Further, it states that its 'Board composition is diverse' yet also claims, in the same section: 'Except for the Deloitte Global CEO and Deloitte Global Chair, all Deloitte Global Board members are active member firm partners. No Deloitte Global Board members hold any other significant positions and commitments in other commercial organizations.' How is this diverse?, https://www2.deloitte.com/global/en/pages/about-deloitte/articles/leadership-governance.html

51. 'Angela Shephard Appointed UK CEO for Mercedes-Benz Retail Group', Mercedes-Benz, 16 December 2019, https://www.mercedes-benz-media.co.uk/en-gb/releases/1341

52. A. H. Goodall and G. Pogrebna, 'Expert Leaders in a Fast-Moving Environment', *Leadership Quarterly*, 26 (2), April 2015, pp. 123–42, https://amandagoodall.com/wp-content/uploads/2022/04/Expert-leaders-in-a-fast-moving-environment-LQ-version-F1.pdf

53. In the 2021 F1 season a $175 million budget cap was introduced.

54. 'Formula 1 Announces Plan to Be Net Zero Carbon by 2030', Formula 1 World Championship Limited, 12 November 2019, https://www.formula1.com/en/latest/article.formula-1-announces-plan-to-be-net-zero-carbon-by-2030.5IaX2AZHyy7jqxl6wra6CZ.html

55. Sam Collins, 'Formula 1 and the Environment', *Racecar Engineering*, https://www.racecar-engineering.com/tech-explained/formula-1-and-the-environment/

56. Christian Sylt, 'Red Bull Reveals How Much It Really Costs to Run an F1 Team', *Forbes*, 14 January 2020, https://www.forbes.com/sites/csylt/2020/01/14/red-bull-reveals-how-much-it-really-costs-to-run-an-f1-team/

57. A. H. Goodall and G. Pogrebna, 'Expert Leaders in a Fast-Moving Environment', *Leadership Quarterly*, 26(2), April 2015, pp. 123–42, https://amandagoodall.com/wp-content/uploads/2022/04/Expert-leaders-in-a-fast-moving-environment-LQ-version-F1.pdf

58. For example, it might be that Ferrari or McLaren often out-perform others not because they have successful leaders but because they have a long history of competing in F1 and thus traditionally had better facilities, more sponsorship money, a high level of public support, and highly experienced human resources.

59. A. J. Becker and C. A. Wrisberg, 'Effective Coaching in Action: Observations of Legendary Collegiate Basketball Coach Pat Summitt', *Sport Psychologist*, 22(2), pp. 197–211, https://doi.org/10.1123/tsp.22.2.197

60. Johan Cruyff's dream team won the club's first European Cup in 1992 and four successive Spanish league titles from 1991 to 1994, https://www.dafato.com/en/history/biographies/johan-cruyff

61. 'Negative Mourinho Doesn't Care about Football! Barcelona Hero Cruyff Slams Real Madrid Manager', *Daily Mail*, 18 April 2011, https://www.dailymail.co.uk/sport/football/article-1378041/Johan-Cruyff-slams-negative-Jose-Mourinho.html

62. 'Sir Alex Ferguson "Expert Manager and Player"', BBC News, 8 May 2018, https://www.bbc.co.uk/news/av/business-22449102

63. FootyForAllLauren, 'Sir Alex Ferguson: Playing Years and Early Managing Career', FutbolPulse, 23 May 2013, http://futbolpulse.com/2013/05/23/sir-alex-ferguson-playing-years-and-early-managing-career/

64. Alistair Magowan, 'Football Talent Spotting: Are Clubs Getting it Wrong with Kids?', BBC News, 22 December 2015, https://www.bbc.co.uk/sport/football/35054310

65. P. Dawson and S. Dobson, 'Managerial Efficiency and Human Capital: An Application to English Association Football', *Managerial and Decision Economics*, 23(8), December 2002, pp. 471–86, https://doi.org/10.1002/mde.1098

66. The Danish government's statistical agencies have, for reasons of individual confidentiality, removed the names attached to each firm.

67. Traditionally, these kinds of information sources were viewed as highly confidential. They were assumed to be too sensitive to allow them to be made available to researchers. Yet it has come to be recognized that, as the American Economic Association has itself argued, the policy relevance of social science research could be increased substantially with better access to administrative records on federal government programme participants or those who report to government entities. Administrative data can also help in the evaluation of public programmes. Yet there remains a relative paucity of economic studies utilizing administrative data in America because most federal micro-level administrative data is very difficult for researchers to obtain.

Chapter 4: How Expert Leadership Works

1. E. Salas, M. A. Rosen, and D. DiazGranados, 'Expertise-Based Intuition and Decision Making in Organizations', *Journal of Management* 36(4), 2010, pp. 941–73, https://www.researchgate.net/profile/Michael-Rosen-8/publication/247570269_Expertise-Based_Intuition_and_Decision_Making_in_Organizations/links/53e2e3300cf2b9d-od832co9f/Expertise-Based-Intuition-and-Decision-Making-in-Organizations.pdf
2. W. G. Chase and H. A. Simon, 'Perception in Chess', *Cognitive Psychology*, 4, January 1973, pp. 55–81, https://andymatuschak.org/prompts/Chase1973.pdf
3. K. A. Ericsson, R. T. Krampe, and C. Tesch-Romer, 'The Role of Deliberate Practice in the Acquisition of Expert Performance', *Psychological Review*, 100, July 1993, pp. 363–406, https://www.research-gate.net/profile/Ralf-Krampe/publication/224827585_The_Role_of_Deliberate_Practice_in_the_Acquisition_of_Expert_Performance/links/0912f5118d15a691d2000000/The-Role-of-Deliberate-Practice-in-the-Acquisition-of-Expert-Performance.pdf?origin=searchReact&_iepl%5BgeneralViewId%5D=otm9MBOfdAJ70MNyMf7gxVN50q EgHUZ7CouA&_iepl%5Bcontexts%5D%5Bo%5D=searchReact&_iepl%5BviewId%5D=VyXavNCVcdR5eU6GookPE1vtVay1zVmH1 8qS&_iepl%5BsearchType%5D=publication&_iepl%5Bdata%5D%5BcountLessEqual20%5D=1&_iepl%5Bdata%5D%5BinteractedWit hPosition2%5D=1&_iepl%5Bdata%5D%5BwithEnrichment

%5D=1&_iepl%5Bposition%5D=2&_
iepl%5BrgKey%5D=PB%3A224827585&_iepl%5BinteractionType
%5D=publicationDownload

4. J. H. Bradley, R. Paul, and E. Seeman, 'Analyzing the Structure of Expert Knowledge', *Information & Management*, 43(1), 2006, pp. 77–91, https://doi.org/10.1016/j.im.2004.11.009

5. Interview with the author.

6. Rakesh Khurana, *Searching for a Corporate Savior*, Princeton University Press, 2011, Kindle edition, p. 57.

7. Challenger, Gray & Christmas, Inc., 'Annual CEO Turnover Report', 10 March 2022, https://www.challengergray.com/blog/feb-22-ceo-report-exits-jump-42-151-ceos-left-their-posts/, in Rakesh Khurana, *Searching for a Corporate Savior*, Princeton University Press, 2011, Kindle edition.

8. Jill Hamburg Coplan, '12 Signs America Is on the Decline', *Fortune*, 20 July 2015, https://fortune.com/2015/07/20/united-states-decline-statistics-economic/

9. Moira Ritter, 'CEOs Made 299 Times More Than Their Average Workers Last Year', CNN Business, 15 July 2021, https://edition.cnn.com/2021/07/14/investing/ceo-employee-pay-afl-cio-report/index.html

10. Rakesh Khurana, *Searching for a Corporate Savior*, Princeton University Press, 2011, Kindle edition, p. 97.

11. Booz & Company, CEO Succession Report: 12th Annual Global CEO Succession Study, 2011.

12. Tom Rees is now Executive Director for School Leadership at the UK's Ambition Institute, where Jennifer Barker also works.

13. Jennifer Barker and Tom Rees, 'School Leader Expertise: What is it and How Do We Develop It?', chrome-extension://efaidnbmnnnibp-cajpcglclefindmkaj/https://s3.eu-west-2.amazonaws.com/ambition-institute/documents/Ambition_Leadership_report_v2PW.pdf

14. Nick Grey, 'What I Learnt ... About Overheads', *The Times*, 10 June 2021, https://www.thetimes.co.uk/article/what-i-learnt-about-over-heads-wksb7nofb

15. The theory of expert leadership was developed in full with my main co-author Agnes Bäker. A. H. Goodall and A. Bäker, 'A Theory Exploring How Expert Leaders Influence Performance in Knowledge-Intensive Organizations', in *Incentives and Performance: Governance of Knowledge-*

Intensive Organizations, ed. I. M. Welpe, J. Wollersheim, S. Ringelhan, and M. Osterloh, Springer International, 2015, pp. 49–68, https://amandagoodall.com/wp-content/uploads/2022/01/Goodall_Baker_KIO-Chapter-June13FINAL.pdf; A. H. Goodall, 'A Theory of Expert Leadership (TEL) in Psychiatry', *Australasian Psychiatry*, 24(3), 2016, pp. 1–4, https://amandagoodall.com/wp-content/uploads/2022/01/Theory-of-Expert-Leadership-in-Psychiatry.pdf

16. Louise Pocock, 'Curbing Excessive Short-Termism: A Guide for Boards of Public Companies, Thought Leadership Paper, Australian Institute of Company Directors', April 2013, https://www.aicd.com.au/content/dam/aicd/pdf/news-media/glc/2015/Curbing-Shorttermism-Louise-Pocock.pdf

17. Those interviewed in the EY Report Poland (2014) included members of the Institute of Directors, leaders of trade unions, and business leaders, https://www.scribd.com/document/474236863/Short-termism-raport-EY

18. Geoffrey James, 'Why Unilever Stopped Issuing Quarterly Reports', Inc.com, https://www.inc.com/geoffrey-james/why-unilever-stopped-issuing-quarterly-reports.html

19. Ibid.

20. Ibid.

21. W. R. Persons (1954–73, President), Charles Knight (1973–2000, CEO), and David Farr (2000–2021, CEO).

22. 'About Us: Lal Karsanbhai, Chief Executive Officer and President', Emerson, https://www.emerson.com/en-gb/about-us/leadership/lal-karsanbhai

23. Oliver Staley, 'Jack Welch Was the Best and Worst Thing that Happened to GE', Quartz, 2 March 2020, updated 20 July 2022, https://qz.com/1811291/jack-welch-was-the-best-and-worst-thing-that-happened-to-ge/

24. Steve Forbes, 'Jack Welch: Managerial Genius Who Made One Disastrous Mistake', *Forbes*, 3 May 2020, https://www.forbes.com/sites/steveforbes/2020/03/03/jack-welch-managerial-genius-who-made-one-disastrous-mistake/

25. Kenneth Hopper and William Hopper, *The Puritan Gift: Reclaiming the American Dream Amidst Global Financial Chaos*, Bloomsbury, 2009, Kindle edition, p. 146.

26. Jerry Useem, 'Another Boss, Another Revolution', *Fortune*, 5 April 2004, https://fortune.com/2004/04/05/another-boss-another-revolution-jeff-

immelt-ge/; Kenneth Hopper and William Hopper, *The Puritan Gift: Reclaiming the American Dream Amidst Global Financial Chaos*, Bloomsbury, 2009, Kindle edition, p. 146.

27. Michael Schein, 'Jack Welch Was Wrong: Change Isn't Always Good', Inc.com, https://www.inc.com/michael-schein/jack-welch-was-wrong -change-isn-t-always-good.html

28. Ibid.

29. A. Hill, L. Mellon, and J. Goddard, 'How Winning Organizations Last 100 Years', *Harvard Business Review*, p. 13, https://hbr.org/2018/09/ how-winning-organizations-last-100-years

30. Ibid.

31. In a BBC interview, Kim Gittleson, 'Can a Company Live Forever?', BBC News, 19 January 2012, https://www.bbc.co.uk/news/business-16611040

32. Robert R. Locke and J.-C. Spender, *Confronting Managerialism (Economic Controversies)*, Zed Books, 2011, Kindle edition, p. 146.

33. V. L. Barker III and G. C. Mueller, 'CEO Characteristics and Firm R&D Spending', *Management Science*, 48(6), 2002, pp. 782–801, https:/ /www.researchgate.net/profile/Vincent-Barker-2/publication/ 227447520_CEO_characteristics_and_firm_RD_spending/links/ 5a2738b04585155dd42416b7/CEO-characteristics-and-firm-R-D-spending.pdf?origin=searchReact&_iepl%5BgeneralViewId%5D=6 MhMiUtjcZBPXYiB7soFybHAf45lko640JkM&_iepl%5Bcontexts% 5D%5B0%5D=searchReact&_iepl%5BviewId%5D=0y50JM7kcxLr Vi2NCLljqgiR1Lug4YTC3QAE&_iepl%5BsearchType%5D=publi cation&_iepl%5Bdata%5D%5BcountLessEqual20%5D=1&_iepl%5 Bdata%5D%5BinteractedWithPosition1%5D=1&_iepl%5Bdata%5 D%5BwithoutEnrichment%5D=1&_iepl%5Bposition%5D=1&_ iepl%5BrgKey%5D=PB%3A227447520&_iepl%5BinteractionType %5D=publicationDownload

34. Ibid.

35. Robert R. Locke and J.-C. Spender, *Confronting Managerialism (Economic Controversies)*, Zed Books, 2011, Kindle edition, p. 146.

36. J. Murray and M. Schwartz, *Wrecked: How the American Automobile Industry Destroyed Its Capacity to Compete*, Russell Sage Foundation, 2019.

37. Ibid.

38. 'The Largest Car Companies in the World (New)', carlogos.com, 21 February 2022, https://www.carlogos.org/reviews/largest-car-com panies.html

39. B. A. Hennessey and T. M. Amabile, 'The Conditions of Creativity', in *The Nature of Creativity*, ed. R. J. Sternberg, Cambridge University Press, 1988, pp. 11–38, p. 581.

40. M. Rother, *Toyota Kata: Managing People for Improvement, Adaptiveness and Superior Results*, McGraw-Hill, 2010.

41. Peter Cheney, 'The Rise of Japan: How the Car Industry Was Won', *Globe and Mail*, 5 November 2015, https://www.theglobeandmail.com /globe-drive/adventure/red-line/the-rise-of-japan-how-the-car-industry-was-won/article27100187/

42. J. Murray and M. Schwartz, *Wrecked: How the American Automobile Industry Destroyed Its Capacity to Compete*, Russell Sage Foundation, 2019, p. 8.

43. Robert R. Locke and J.-C. Spender, *Confronting Managerialism (Economic Controversies)*, Bloomsbury, 2011, Kindle edition, p. 114.

44. Kenneth Hopper and William Hopper, *The Puritan Gift: Reclaiming the American Dream Amidst Global Financial Chaos*, Bloomsbury, 2009, Kindle edition, p. 167.

45. Ibid.

46. Robert R. Locke and J.-C. Spender, *Confronting Managerialism (Economic Controversies)*, Bloomsbury, 2011, Kindle edition, p. 114.

47. Kenneth Hopper and William Hopper, *The Puritan Gift: Reclaiming the American Dream Amidst Global Financial Chaos*, Bloomsbury, 2009, Kindle edition, p. 108.

48. J. Murray and M. Schwartz, *Wrecked: How the American Automobile Industry Destroyed Its Capacity to Compete*, Russell Sage Foundation, 2019, p. 8.

49. This quote is taken from a direct communication with Josh Murray.

50. E. P. Lazear, K. L. Shaw, and C. T. Stanton, 'The Value of Bosses', *Journal of Labor Economics*, 33(4), 2015, pp. 823–61, https://www.nber. org/system/files/working_papers/w18317/w18317.pdf

51. CEO pay is different and has arguably exploded beyond all rationale.

52. Kenneth Hopper and William Hopper, *The Puritan Gift: Reclaiming the American Dream Amidst Global Financial Chaos*, Bloomsbury, 2009, Kindle edition, p. 130.

53. Ibid., p. 213.

54. Ibid.

55. Ibid.

56. Ibid., p. 216.

57. K. Owen, T. Hopkins, T. Shortland, and J. Dale, 'GP Retention in the UK: A Worsening Crisis. Findings from a Cross-Sectional Survey', BMJ open, 9(2), 2019, chrome-extension://efaidnbmnnnibpcajpcgl-clefindmkaj/https://bmjopen.bmj.com/content/bmjopen/9/2/e026048.full.pdf

58. We used statistical tests that made it possible to control for several factors to help us get closer to like-for-like analyses, and tried to cluster doctors who were reporting on the same manager. A. Bäker and A. H. Goodall, 'Do Expert Clinicians Make the Best Managers? Evidence from Hospitals in Denmark, Australia and Switzerland', *BMJ Leader*, 5(3), 2021, https://amandagoodall.com/wp-content/uploads/2022/03/BMJleader-2021-BestManagers.pdf

59. C. Handy, *The Future of Work*, Oxford University Press, 1984.

60. Think of the UK government's Downing Street parties during Covid lockdowns.

61. Atul Gawande, 'Why Doctors Hate Their Computers', *New Yorker*, 5 November 2018, https://www.newyorker.com/magazine/2018/11/12/why-doctors-hate-their-computers

62. Joe Cantlupe, 'Expert Forum: The Rise (and Rise) of the Healthcare Administrator', Athena Health, 7 November 2017, https://www.athenahealth.com/knowledge-hub/practice-management/expert-forum-rise-and-rise-healthcare-administrator

63. Marjolein Hurkmans, 'Jeanet geeft al 60 jaar les: "Dit vak is de vernieling in geholpen"', *Vrouw Magazine*, 14 August 2021, https://www.telegraaf.nl/vrouw/1253065988/jeanet-geeft-al-60-jaar-les-dit-vak-is-de-vernieling-in-geholpen

64. This term was introduced by S. Gjerde and M. Alvesson; see their 'Sandwiched: Exploring Role and Identity of Middle Managers in the Genuine Middle', *Human Relations*, 73(1), 2020, pp. 124–51, https://journals.sagepub.com/doi/epub/10.1177/0018726718823243

65. A. Bäker and A. H. Goodall, 'Feline Followers and "Umbrella Carriers": Department Chairs' Influence on Faculty Job Satisfaction and Quit Intentions', *Research Policy*, 49 (4), 2020, e103955, https://amanda-goodall.com/wp-content/uploads/2022/01/RPMasteMarcho2.pdf

66. Robert Cuffe, 'Does the UK Have Highest Covid Death Toll in Europe?', BBC News, 27 May 2021, https://www.bbc.co.uk/news/57268471

67. M. Lewis, *The Premonition: A Pandemic Story*, Allen Lane, 2021.

68. 'Fact Check: Claims on Trump Nepotism, Family Profiting from Presidency Is Partly False', *USA Today*, 16 September 2020, https://eu.usatoday.com/story/news/factcheck/2020/09/16/fact-check-claim-trump-white-house-nepotism-partly-false/3447695001/

69. Rachel Reeves, 'Forget Due Process: "Chumocracy" is Far More Valuable to the Conservative Government', *Independent*, 22 November 2020, https://www.independent.co.uk/voices/boris-johnson-cronyism-ppe-contracts-nao-b1759702.html; '"Chumocracy": How Covid Revealed the New Shape of the Tory Establishment', *Guardian*, 15 November 2020, https://www.theguardian.com/world/2020/nov/15/chumocracy-covid-revealed-shape-tory-establishment

70. Grant Robertson, '"We Are Not Prepared": The Flaws Inside Public Health That Hurt Canada's Readiness for COVID-19', *Globe and Mail*, 26 December 2020, updated 3 February 2021, https://www.theglobeandmail.com/canada/article-we-are-not-prepared-the-flaws-inside-public-health-that-hurt-canadas/

71. James Surowiecki, 'The Turnaround Trap', *New Yorker*, 25 March 2013, https://www.newyorker.com/magazine//2013/03/25/the-turnaround-trap

72. B. D. Baker and B. S. Cooper, 'Do Principals With Stronger Academic Backgrounds Hire Better Teachers? Policy Implications for Improving High-Poverty Schools', *Educational Administration Quarterly*, 41(3), 2015, pp. 449–79, https://doi.org/10.1177/0013161X04269609

73. Not his real name or his subject area.

74. Interview with a consultant in the NHS who wished to remain anonymous.

75. The American writer Leo Rosten is also cited as having said something similar: 'First-rate people hire first-rate people; second-rate people hire third-rate people.' In interviews with university presidents (A. H. Goodall, *Socrates in the Boardroom: Why Research Universities Should Be Led by Top Scholars*, Princeton University Press, 2009), a number of heads commented on the need to put the most outstanding scholars on hiring panels to ensure that the best academics are hired.

76. L. Festinger, 'A Theory of Social Comparison Processes', *Human Relations*, 7(2), 1954, pp. 117–40, https://www2.psych.ubc.ca/~schaller/528Readings/Festinger1954.pdf

77. Thanks to Patty Fahy for this comment.

Chapter 5: Expert Leaders Create Productive Workplaces

1. A. Edmans, 'The Link between Job Satisfaction and Firm Value, with Implications for Corporate Social Responsibility', *Academy of Management Perspectives*, 26(4), 2012, pp. 1–19, https://deliverypdf. ssrn.com/delivery.php?ID=027115021017124105016030022015069108008059093080069017118115075010116122078098120117120055019124104125055005125077082100102095009073089037037071125089071086108087085039081082021070093120115112019069104126009107114086090068027010108074124068005013003&EXT=pdf&INDEX=TRUE

2. We analysed survey data from 35,000 randomly selected employees and workplaces in the US and UK doing almost every kind of job and going back several decades. In our study we documented seven forms of evidence. We tracked large numbers of workers and workplaces over many years in longitudinal data. We controlled for the effect of self-selection, in other words, for those workers who change jobs when they are unhappy with their boss. And we adjusted for employees' personalities by checking whether it was merely that cheerful workers are more inclined to give higher job satisfaction or supervisor competence ratings, which could thus skew the data.

3. Job satisfaction, on the vertical axis, is measured on a 1 to 4 scale. The consequence of having a good supervisor is just under one-half of a job satisfaction point.

4. By the way, I am not denigrating MBAs per se. I teach on them myself and they are crucially important courses. But alone, they are not enough.

5. Every year the British Household Panel Survey interviews the same representative sample of individuals so that researchers can understand populations over time. For example, how people's personal and family situations and attitudes change, and how different life factors affect their health, wealth, employment, relationships, and so on, so you can look at changes within people instead of changes between people.

6. It took another decade before regular economists became interested. There is also a vast modern literature in the subject area of psychology.

7. Predictably, and sadly, this early paper questioning the panacea of the GDP target never made it into an economics journal. If the world had recognized, in the early 1970s, that happiness declines once growth passes a particular point, we might not have taken the planet so deeply into the climate crisis that we have.

8. The two 1993 conference papers appeared in the *Journal of Public Economics*. One was published three years after the conference and the other took an amazing eleven years. The second of these now famous papers, 'Wellbeing over Time in Britain and the USA', by David Blanchflower and Andrew Oswald, appeared in print in 2004, and is now the second most-cited paper in the journal's history, http://andrewoswald.com/docs/finaljpubecwellbeingjune2002.pdf

9. World Happiness Report, https://worldhappiness.report/

10. L. Winkelmann and R. Winkelmann, 'Why Are the Unemployed So Unhappy? Evidence from Panel Data', *Economica*, 65(257), 1998, pp. 1–15, https://www.jstor.org/stable/2555127

11. A. E. Clark and A. J. Oswald, 'Satisfaction and Comparison Income', *Journal of Public Economics*, 61(3), 1996, pp. 359–81; https://www.andrewoswald.com/docs/jpub.pdf; R. H. Frank, *Choosing the Right Pond: Human Behavior and the Quest for Status*, Oxford University Press, 1985.

12. The number of journal articles since 1994 that mention 'job satisfaction' alone is 29,000, according to the Web of Science.

13. B. Artz, A. H. Goodall, and A. J. Oswald, 'Boss Competence and Worker Well-Being', *Industrial and Labor Relations Review*, 70 (2), 2017, pp. 419–50, https://www.researchgate.net/publication/268491675_Boss_Competence_and_Worker_Well-Being; D. G. Blanchflower and A. J. Oswald, 'International Happiness: A New View on the Measure of Performance', *Academy of Management Perspectives*, 25(1), 2011, pp. 6–22, https://www.researchgate.net/profile/Andrew-Oswald/publication/277681942_International_Happiness_A_New_View_on_the_Measure_of_Performance/links/573aebbf08ae298602e41679/International-Happiness-A-New-View-on-the-Measure-of-Performance.pdf?origin=searchReact&_iepl%5BgeneralViewId%5D=YyCYligIyLhlXow2XGnJ4Hj7Je32vroHYDoA&_iepl%5Bcontexts%5D%5Bo%5D=searchReact&_iepl%5BviewId%5D=gfN1ZHooPURxzJ7V4B6obT9ifx2G8YGTEoko&_iepl%5BsearchType%5D=publication&_iepl%5Bdata%5D%5BcountLessEqual20%5D=1&_iepl

%5Bdata%5D%5BinteractedWithPosition2%5D=1&_iepl%5Bdata %5D%5BwithoutEnrichment%5D=1&_iepl%5Bposition%5D=2&_ iepl%5BrgKey%5D=PB%3A277681942&_iepl%5BinteractionType %5D=publicationDownload; A. E. Clark and A. J. Oswald, 'Satisfaction and Comparison Income', *Journal of Public Economics*, 61(3), 1996, pp. 359–81, https://www.andrewoswald.com/docs/jpub.pdf; S. C. Clark, 'Work Cultures and Work/Family Balance', *Journal of Vocational Behavior*, *58*(3), 2001, pp. 348–65, https://doi.org/10.1006/ jvbe.2000.1759; J. E. De Neve and J. D. Sachs, 'The SDGs and Human Well-Being: A Global Analysis of Synergies, Trade-Offs, and Regional Differences', *Scientific Reports*, 10(1), 2020, pp. 1–12, https://www. nature.com/articles/s41598-020-71916-9; J. E. De Neve and G. Ward, 'Happiness at Work', Saïd Business School WP, 7, 2017, http://eprints. lse.ac.uk/83604/1/dp1474.pdf; L. Winkelmann and R. Winkelmann, 'Why Are the Unemployed So Unhappy? Evidence from Panel Data', *Economica*, 65(257), 1998, pp. 1–15, https://www.zora.uzh.ch/id/eprint /1194/8/WinkelmannWhy2006V.pdf

14. B. Artz, A. H. Goodall, and A. J. Oswald, 'Boss Competence and Worker Well-being', *Industrial and Labor Relations Review*, 70(2), 2017, pp. 419–50, https://amandagoodall.com/wp-content/uploads/2022/01/ BossCompetenceILLRPub.pdf

15. B. Artz, A. H. Goodall, and A. J. Oswald, 'How Common Are Bad Bosses?', *Industrial Relations: A Journal of Economy and Society*, 59(1), 2020, https://amandagoodall.com/wp-content/uploads/2022/01/ BadBosses-Artz-Goodall-Oswald-forthcoming-IR-2019.pdf

16. A. Bryson, A. E. Clark, R. B. Freeman et al., 'Share Capitalism and Worker Wellbeing', *Labour Economics*, 42, 2016, pp. 151–8, https:// reader.elsevier.com/reader/sd/pii/S0927537116301051?token=BF797 06848FE76B74E807D376ECFD89D273257D5E91CF2CE9E4CD8 176CBC36CC6DE1E88584E30085AC6A37C71B991261&originRe gion=eu-west-1&originCreation=20221021153920

17. Robert Dur and Max van Lent, 'Socially Useless Jobs', *Industrial Relations: A Journal of Economy and Society*, 58(5), December 2018, https: //scholarlypublications.universiteitleiden.nl/access/item%3A2909855 /view

18. Starting with A. E. Clark and A. J. Oswald, 'Satisfaction and Comparison Income', *Journal of Public Economics*, 61(3), 1996, pp. 359–81, https:// www.andrewoswald.com/docs/jpub.pdf

19. E. R. Burris, J. R. Detert, and D. S. Chiaburu, 'Quitting before Leaving: The Mediating Effects of Psychological Attachment and Detachment on Voice', *Journal of Applied Psychology*, 93(4), 2008, p. 912, https://www.researchgate.net/profile/James-Detert/publication/51417022_Quitting_Before_Leaving_The_Mediating_Effects_of_Psychological_Attachment_and_Detachment_on_Voice/links/5474a54e0cf29afed-60f8ccc/Quitting-Before-Leaving-The-Mediating-Effects-of-Psychological-Attachment-and-Detachment-on-Voice.pdf?origin=searchReact&_iepl%5BgeneralViewId%5D=KkS9AZWaPChDm1uo4BxI6ZTD4PYv2H4bOgen&_iepl%5Bcontexts%5D%5B0%5D=searchReact&_iepl%5BviewId%5D=1feMVqDwdDxbMMZkV2c7octKdCop2cZu7CGm&_iepl%5BsearchType%5D=publication&_iepl%5Bdata%5D%5BcountLessEqual20%5D=1&_iepl%5Bdata%5D%5BinteractedWithPosition1%5D=1&_iepl%5Bdata%5D%5BwithEnrichment%5D=1&_iepl%5Bposition%5D=1&_iepl%5BrgKey%5D=PB%3A51417022&_iepl%5BinteractionType%5D=publicationDownload

20. A. Sagie, 'Employee Absenteeism, Organizational Commitment, and Job Satisfaction: Another Look', *Journal of Vocational Behavior*, 52(2), 1998, pp. 156–71, https://doi.org/10.1006/jvbe.1997.1581

21. E.g. A. Brayfield and W. Crockett, 'Employee Performance, Employee Attitudes and Psychological Bulletin', 52, 1984, pp. 396–424. A. M. Isen and R. A. Baron, 'Positive Affect as a Factor in Organizational-Behavior', *Research in Organizational Behavior*, 13, 1991, pp. 1–53. T. A. Wright and B. M. Staw, 'Affect and Favorable Work Outcomes: Two Longitudinal Tests of the Happy–Productive Worker Thesis', *Journal of Organizational Behavior: The International Journal of Industrial, Occupational and Organizational Psychology and Behavior*, 20(1), 1999, pp. 1–23, https://doi.org/10.1002/(SICI)1099-1379(199901)20:1<1::AID-JOB885>3.0.CO;2-W

22. One major source of evidence comes from simple experiments on small numbers of laboratory subjects who are made happier. See Alice Isen's long line of research, including in A. M. Isen and R. A. Baron, 'Positive Affect as a Factor in Organizational-Behavior', *Research in Organizational Behavior*, 13, 1991, pp. 1–53; and C. A. Estrada, A. M. Isen, and M. J. Young, 'Positive Affect Facilitates Integration of Information and Decreases Anchoring in Reasoning Among Physicians', *Organizational Behavior and Human Decision Processes*,

72(1), 1997, pp. 117–35, https://www.sciencedirect.com/science/article/abs/pii/S0749597897927345. A second involves large numbers of 'observational' studies, using sometimes complicated statistical methods, to see whether firms with happier employees do better or go on to do better, or whether happier people go on to have higher incomes from larger experiments in the lab or in the field, such as A. J. Oswald, E. Proto, and D. Sgroi, 'Happiness and Productivity', *Journal of Labor Economics*, 33(4), 2015, pp. 789–822, https://www.andrewoswald.com/docs/actualJOLEpublished2015WRAP_Oswald_681096.pdf; and C. Bellet, J. E. De Neve, and G. Ward, 'Does Employee Happiness Have an Impact on Productivity?', Saïd Business School WP, 13, 2019, https://papers.ssrn.com/sol3/Delivery.cfm/SSRN_ID4168015_code3123636.pdf?abstractid=3470734&mirid=1

23. Including e.g. A. Edmans, 'Does the Stock Market Fully Value Intangibles? Employee Satisfaction and Equity Prices', *Journal of Financial Economics*, 101(3), 2011, pp. 621–40, https://repository.upenn.edu/cgi/viewcontent.cgi?article=1046&context=fnce_papers; A. Edmans, 'The Link Between Job Satisfaction and Firm Value, With Implications for Corporate Social Responsibility', *Academy of Management Perspectives*, 26(4), 2012, pp. 1–19, https://d1wqtxts1xzle7.cloudfront.net/31053099/RoweAMP-with-cover-page-v2.pdf?Expires=1666376381&Signature=NkTAN4DqJf26K6WFPnAtXCk6CBu45FVmC7DdKtAjkGDdGv2nVKfB97MwE3PGdKvChaQOZX2d3i1rkTtN8HrcDRVA7kWHoUVodsGj7rfZvMsNVCBsf8vWa-lYXB5oP-yI1TmiTV-Tl7VDDsUvAbmarrx6AlSrmlxUtei-N5X8Ult5mST2DP7498q3OMt~qaQey9M2f-tixiwZkelG61ozwa2Pn8I-a767AHpx1BzD-ZG-kHN~xgZjyrMCFty6oQIuRm5ju58V35vsiennb8B-1arDEKUJc59OAAhj5iHEgMcoIKL1a7pUHYGhpG4WGXA8Lj6h~vJ5YWj5C1rb6yiuWCWg__&Key-Pair-Id=APKAJLOHF5GGSLRBV4ZA; J. E. De Neve and A. J. Oswald, 'Estimating the Influence of Life Satisfaction and Positive Affect on Later Income Using Sibling Fixed Effects', *Proceedings of the National Academy of Sciences*, 109(49), 2012, pp. 19953–19958, https://www.pnas.org/doi/epdf/10.1073/pnas.1211437109; A. Bryson, J. Forth, and L. Stokes, 'Does Employees' Subjective Well-Being Affect Workplace Performance?', *Human Relations*, 70(8), 2017, pp. 1017–37, https://www.researchgate.net/profile/Alex-Bryson-2/publication/316815858_Does_employees%27_subjective_well-being_affect_workplace_

performance/links/597902feof7e9b27772a247f/Does-employees-subjective - well - being - affect - workplace - performance. pdf?origin=searchReact&_iepl%5BgeneralViewId%5D=VYHy89Vn v45dYIeNJJ1IdfuozWCBp2pc1wyV&_iepl%5Bcontexts%5D%5B0 %5D=searchReact&_iepl%5BviewId%5D=v88EyFeY93CLD1CkyA 3ZkyNkYsRsrSp6nZE4&_iepl%5BsearchType%5D=publication&_ iepl%5Bdata%5D%5BcountLessEqual20%5D=1&_iepl%5Bdata%5 D%5BinteractedWithPosition1%5D=1&_iepl%5Bdata%5D%5Bwit houtEnrichment%5D=1& _iepl%5Bposition%5D=1&_ iepl%5BrgKey%5D=PB%3A316815858&_iepl%5BinteractionType %5D=publicationDownload

24. A. J. Oswald, E. Proto, and D. Sgroi, 'Happiness and Productivity', *Journal of Labor Economics*, 33(4), 2015, pp. 789–822, https://www. andrewoswald.com/docs/actualJOLEpublished2015WRAP_Oswald_ 681096.pdf

25. A. Mani, S. Mullainathan, E. Shafir et al., 'Poverty Impedes Cognitive Function', *Science*, 341(6149), 2013, pp. 976–80, https://doi.org/ 10.1126/science.1238041

26. M. A. Killingsworth and D. T. Gilbert, 'A Wandering Mind Is an Unhappy Mind', *Science*, 330(6006), 2010, p. 932, https://doi.org/ 10.1126/science.1192439

27. A. Bäker and A. H. Goodall, 'Do Expert Clinicians Make the Best Managers? Evidence from Hospitals in Denmark, Australia and Switzerland', *BMJ Leader*, 5(3), 2021, https://amandagoodall.com/wp -content/uploads/2022/03/BMJleader-2021-BestManagers.pdf

28. In a 2021 interview with the author.

29. J. R. Halbesleben and C. Rathert, 'Linking Physician Burnout and Patient Outcomes: Exploring the Dyadic Relationship between Physicians and Patients', *Health Care Management Review*, 33(1), 2008, pp. 29–39, https://doi.org/10.1097/01.hmr.0000304493.87898.72; K. B. Nørøxe, A. F. Pedersen, F. Bro et al., 'Mental Well-being and Job Satisfaction among General Practitioners: A Nationwide Cross-Sectional Survey in Denmark', *BMC Family Practice*, 19(1), 2018, pp. 1–11, https://www.researchgate.net/journal/BMC-Family-Practice-1471-2296/publication/326673841_Mental_well-being_and_job_ satisfaction_among_general_practitioners_A_nationwide_cross-sectional_survey_in_Denmark/links/5fc24bb0458515b7977d5292/ Mental-well-being-and-job-satisfaction-among-general-practitioners

-A-nationwide-cross-sectional-survey-in-Denmark.
pdf?origin=searchReact&_iepl%5BgeneralViewId%5D=WNoe8FYw
6qbytLrCxNiTGSKMZCypCQX4kkZl&_iepl%5Bcontexts%5D%5
Bo%5D=searchReact&_iepl%5BviewId%5D=uS6ueGoopDC6cFnw
1pwkkTdvS1iCgeOeroWz&_iepl%5BsearchType%5D=publicatio
n&_iepl%5Bdata%5D%5BcountLessEqual20%5D=1&_iepl%5Bdat
a%5D%5BinteractedWithPosition1%5D=1&_iepl%5Bdata%5D%5
BwithEnrichment%5D=1&_iepl%5Bposition%5D=1&_
iepl%5BrgKey%5D=PB%3A326673841&_iepl%5BinteractionType
%5D=publicationDownload

30. E.g. C. Duffield, G. Gardner, A. Doubrovsky et al., 'Manager, Clinician
or Both? Nurse Managers' Engagement in Clinical Care Activities',
Journal of Nurse Management, 2019(27): pp. 1538–45, https://doi.org/
10.1111/jonm.12841; BY-J Lin, C-PC Hsu, and C-W Juan, 'The Role
of Leader Behaviors in Hospital-Based Emergency Departments' Unit
Performance and Employee Work Satisfaction', *Social Science &
Medicine* 2011(72), pp. 238–46, https://doi.org/10.1016/
j.socscimed.2010.10.030; A. Robson and F. Robson, 'Investigation of
Nurses' Intention to Leave: A Study of a Sample of UK Nurses',
Journal of Health Organization and Management, 30, 2016, pp. 154–73,
https://doi.org/10.1108/JHOM-05-2013-0100

31. E.g. D. E. Guest, 'Human Resource Management and Employee Well-
Being: Towards a New Analytic Framework', *Human Resource
Management Journal*, 27, 2017, pp. 22–38, https://doi.org/10.1111/
1748-8583.12139; P. Böckerman and P. Ilmakunnas, The Job
Satisfaction-Productivity Nexus: A Study Using Matched Survey and
Register Data', *ILR Review*, 65, 2012, pp. 244–62, https://doi.org/
10.1177/001979391206500203; A. Bryson, J. Forth, and L. Stokes,
'Does Employees' Subjective Well-Being Affect Workplace
Performance?', *Human Relations*, 70(8), 2017, pp. 1017–37, https://
www.researchgate.net/profile/Alex-Bryson-2/publication/316815858
_Does_employees%27_subjective_well-being_affect_workplace_
performance/links/597902feof7e9b27772a247f/Does-employees-
subjective-well-being-affect-workplace-performance.
pdf?origin=searchReact&_iepl%5BgeneralViewId%5D=VYHy89Vn
v45dYIeNJJ1IdfuozWCBp2pc1wyV&_iepl%5Bcontexts%5D%5Bo
%5D=searchReact&_iepl%5BviewId%5D=v88EyFeY93CLD1CkyA
3ZkyNkYsRsrSp6nZE4&_iepl%5BsearchType%5D=publication&_

iepl%5Bdata%5D%5BcountLessEqual20%5D=1&_iepl%5Bdata%5
D%5BinteractedWithPosition1%5D=1&_iepl%5Bdata%5D%5Bwit
houtEnrichment%5D=1&_iepl%5Bposition%5D=1&_
iepl%5BrgKey%5D=PB%3A316815858&_iepl%5BinteractionType
%5D=publicationDownload; J. Oswald, E. Proto, and D. Sgroi,
'Happiness and Productivity', *Journal of Labor Economics*, 33(4), 2015,
pp. 789–822, https://www.andrewoswald.com/docs/actualJOLEpub-
lished2015WRAP_Oswald_681096.pdf

32. A. Bäker and A. H. Goodall, 'Do Expert Clinicians Make the Best
Managers? Evidence from Hospitals in Denmark, Australia and
Switzerland', *BMJ Leader*, 5(3), 2021, https://amandagoodall.com/wp-
content/uploads/2022/03/BMJleader-2021-BestManagers.pdf

33. From a personal interview.

34. A. E. Clark, 'Your Money or Your Life: Changing Job Quality in
OECD Countries', *British Journal of Industrial Relations*, 43(3), 2005,
pp. 377–400, https://doi.org/10.1111/j.1467-8543.2005.00361.x; A.
Bryson, J. Forth, and L. Stokes, 'Does Employees' Subjective Well-
being Affect Workplace Performance?', *Human Relations*, 70(8), 2017,
pp. 1017–37, https://www.researchgate.net/profile/Alex-Bryson-2/
publication/316815858_Does_employees%27_subjective_well-being
_affect_workplace_performance/links/597902feof7e9b27772a247f/
Does-employees-subjective-well-being-affect-workplace-perfor-
mance.pdf?origin=searchReact&_iepl%5BgeneralViewId%5D=24sN
A2A2M8uPoEWvaq1DJnpFff7016sG1doY&_iepl%5Bcontexts%5D
%5B0%5D=searchReact&_iepl%5BviewId%5D=Vc6loto1hXHAz1j
zjtg2fG56zToTnsuFCjLI&_iepl%5BsearchType%5D=publication&_
iepl%5Bdata%5D%5BcountLessEqual20%5D=1&_iepl%5Bdata%5
D%5BinteractedWithPosition1%5D=1&_iepl%5Bdata%5D%5Bwit
houtEnrichment%5D=1&_iepl%5Bposition%5D=1&_
iepl%5BrgKey%5D=PB%3A316815858&_iepl%5BinteractionType
%5D=publicationDownload

35. In a further study with Ben Artz and Andrew Oswald, we examined bad
bosses in a dataset of 28,000 randomly selected European employees
from the European Working Conditions Survey in 2015.

Chapter 6: Spotting Expert Leaders

1. Many of the examples used in this and the next chapter to illustrate our point are from personal communication and come from medical settings. This is because I do a lot of research in health management, and I created and ran a master's degree in leadership and management for physicians.
2. Kenneth Hopper and William Hopper, *The Puritan Gift: Reclaiming the American Dream amidst Global Financial Chaos*, Bloomsbury, 2007. Rakesh Khurana, 'Searching for a Corporate Savior', in *Searching for a Corporate Savior*, Princeton University Press, 2011.
3. Claudio Fernández-Aráoz, '21st-Century Talent Spotting', *Harvard Business Review*, June 2014, https://hbr.org/2014/06/21st-century-talent-spotting
4. B. Groysberg, N. Nohria, and C. Fernández-Aráoz, 'The Definitive Guide to Recruiting in Good Times and Bad', *Harvard Business Review*, May 2009, https://hbr.org/2009/05/the-definitive-guide-to-recruiting-in-good-times-and-bad
5. Ibid.
6. Ibid.
7. A. Bäker, M. Bech, J. M. Geerts et al., 'Motivating Doctors into Leadership and Management: A Cross-sectional Survey', *BMJ Leader*, 4(4), 2019, https://amandagoodall.com/wp-content/uploads/2021/12/MotivatingDoctorsBMJLeaderPublishedJuly2020.pdf
8. Patricia Fahy, 'How to Avoid Hiring a Narcissist', *Medical Practice Management*, November/December 2017, https://fahyconsulting.com/wp-content/uploads/2020/03/How-to-Avoid-Hiring-a-Narcissist-by-Patty-Fahy-MD.pdf
9. Interview with Jaason Geerts.
10. 'Physicians Are Licensed to Lead', Patty Fahy podcast, https://mailchi.mp/fahyconsulting/provocative-questions-and-leadership-challenges-14155286?e=92a8be4fc9
11. Interview with a former employee who wished to remain anonymous.
12. Interview with a doctor who wished to remain anonymous.
13. M. Osterloh, A. H. Goodall, and M. Fong, 'Women Have to Enter the Race to Win: A Novel Approach to Leadership Selection', working paper, https://www.econstor.eu/bitstream/10419/120984/1/dp9331.pdf

14. Some of this material first appeared in Amanda Goodall, 'Random Selection for Top Jobs Is Not a Crazy Idea', *Financial Times*, 7 September 2020, https://www.ft.com/content/bfd389c6-7a68-4c51-ad1b-3634149742e6 and Amanda Goodall, 'If You Want to Know Why People Are Reluctant to Be Leaders, Ask Them', *Financial Times*, 6 September 2021, https://www.ft.com/content/4e4f467a-5bef-44a6-bf19-7442f4b78abb

15. B. Artz, A. H. Goodall, and A. J. Oswald, 'Do Women Ask?', *Industrial Relations: A Journal of Economy and Society*, 57(4), 2018, pp. 611–36, https://amandagoodall.com/wp-content/uploads/2022/01/DowomenaskPub.pdf

16. S. Page, 'The Diversity Bonus', in *The Diversity Bonus*, Princeton University Press, 2017.

17. N. Theodoropoulos, J. Forth, and A. Bryson, 'Are Women Doing It for Themselves? Gender Segregation and the Gender Wage Gap', IZA Discussion Paper No. 12657, IZA Institute of Labor Economics, https://docs.iza.org/dp12657.pdf

18. David Olusoga, MacTaggart Lecture, Edinburgh TV Festival 2020, https://www.thetvfestival.com/whats-on/speakers/2020-speakers/david-olusoga-obe/

19. BBC Diversity and Inclusion Plan 2021–3, https://www.bbc.co.uk/diversity/plan

20. Interview with Natasha Maw.

21. Not her real name.

22. Much has been written about this: see Mats Alvesson, https://www.lunduniversity.lu.se/lucat/user/091f4799ef44464bd39adb572fc5c3a3 and Laura Empson, https://www.lauraempson.com/

23. A. Bäker, M. Bech, J. M. Geerts et al., 'Motivating Doctors into Leadership and Management: A Cross-sectional Survey', *BMJ Leader*, 4(4), 2019, https://amandagoodall.com/wp-content/uploads/2021/12/MotivatingDoctorsBMJLeaderPublishedJuly2020.pdf (study done with the Organization of Danish Medical Societies (LVS)).

24. A. Bäker, M. Bech, A. H. Goodall et al., 'Leader Identity, Professional Expertise, and Middle Manager Effectiveness?', working paper, October 2022.

25. B. Kumar, M. L. Swee, and M. Suneja, 'Leadership Training Programs in Graduate Medical Education: A Systematic Review', *BMC Medical Education*, 20(175), 2020, https://bmcmededuc.biomedcentral.com/articles/10.1186/s12909-020-02089-2

26. T. A. Kolditz, *In Extremis Leadership*, Jossey-Bass, 2007.
27. Rakesh Khurana, *From Higher Aims to Hired Hands*, Princeton University Press, 2007, Kindle edition.
28. Ibid.
29. Of the Mid and South Essex Health and Care Partnership.
30. Ben S. Kuipers and Laura M. Giurge, 'Does Alignment Matter? The Performance Implications of HR Roles Connected to Organizational Strategy', *International Journal of Human Resource Management*, 28(22), 2017, pp. 3179–201, https://www.tandfonline.com/doi/pdf/10.1080/09585192.2016.1155162?needAccess=true

Chapter 7: Developing Experts into Leaders

1. See K. A. Ericsson and J. Smith, eds, *Toward a General Theory of Expertise: Prospects and Limits*, Cambridge University Press, 1991, or K. A. Ericsson, *The Road to Excellence: The Acquisition of Expert Performance in the Arts and Sciences, Sports, and Games*, Psychology Press, 2014.
2. K. A. Ericsson, R. T. Krampe, and C. Tesch-Römer, 'The Role of Deliberate Practice in the Acquisition of Expert Performance', *Psychological Review*, 100(3), 1993, p. 363, https://www.researchgate.net/profile/Ralf-Krampe/publication/224827585_The_Role_of_Deliberate_Practice_in_the_Acquisition_of_Expert_Performance/links/0912f5118d15a691d2000000/The-Role-of-Deliberate-Practice-in-the-Acquisition-of-Expert-Performance.pdf?origin=searchReact&_iepl%5BgeneralViewId%5D=ooUGe1nh6bWT1miROnXpvxgozU7w5ftjAcX6&_iepl%5Bcontexts%5D%5Bo%5D=searchReact&_iepl%5BviewId%5D=Ict1NE3Y1HgZMLqM3uYXwhplIYkqr2F1EoJz&_iepl%5BsearchType%5D=publication&_iepl%5Bdata%5D%5BcountLessEqual20%5D=1&_iepl%5Bdata%5D%5BinteractedWithPosition2%5D=1&_iepl%5Bdata%5D%5BwithEnrichment%5D=1&_iepl%5Bposition%5D=2&_iepl%5BrgKey%5D=PB%3A224827585&_iepl%5BinteractionType%5D=publicationDownload
3. As Steven Kurutz pointed out in his *New York Times* obituary of Ericsson, 1 July 2020, https://www.nytimes.com/2020/07/01/science/anders-ericsson-dead.html
4. F. Ullén, D. Z. Hambrick, and M. A. Mosing, 'Rethinking Expertise: A Multifactorial Gene–Environment Interaction Model of Expert

Performance', *Psychological Bulletin*, 142(4), 2016, p. 427, https://doi.org/10.1037/bul0000033

5. Interview with Natasha Maw.

6. P. Salovey and J. D. Mayer, 'Emotional Intelligence', *Imagination, Cognition and Personality*, 9(3), 1990, pp. 185–211, https://doi.org/10.2190/DUGG-P24E-52WK-6CDG

7. D. Goleman, *Emotional Intelligence: Why It Can Matter More than IQ*, Bloomsbury,1996.

8. D. Goleman, *What Makes a Leader?*, Harvard Business Review, 2004.

9. Elizabeth McLaughlin, 'Air Force Leader's Impassioned Tweets Spark Candid Conversation about Racism in America: "I Am George Floyd"', ABC News, 3 June 2020, https://abcnews.go.com/Politics/air-force-leaders-impassioned-tweets-spark-candid-conversation/story?id=71047498#:~:text=The%20most%20senior%20enlisted%20member,I%20am%20George%20Floyd%E2%80%A6

10. A. L. Hinen, 'Toxic Leadership in the Military', *Muma Business Review*, 4, 2020, pp. 65–79, http://pubs.mumabusinessreview.org/2020/MBR-04-05-065-079-Hinen-ToxicLeadership.pdf

11. Daniel Zwerdling, 'Army Takes on Its Own Toxic Leaders', NPR, 6 January 2014, https://www.npr.org/2014/01/06/259422776/army-takes-on-its-own-toxic-leaders

12. US Army Doctrine Publication, https://capl.army.mil/Resource-Library/Doctrine/adp6-22.php

13. WO2 Sheridan Lucas, 'Toxic Leadership: A Call for Change', Centre for Army Leadership, Leadership Insight, 25, May 2021, https://www.army.mod.uk/media/12690/leadership-insight-no25-toxic-leadership.pdf

14. G. Reed, *Tarnished: Toxic Leadership in the U.S. Military*, University of Nebraska Press, 2015.

15. This quote and subsequent ones not otherwise cited are taken from interviews with the author.

16. Ibid.

17. J. Geerts, A. H. Goodall, and S. Agius, 'Evidence-Based Leadership Development for Physicians: A Systematic Literature Review', *Social Science & Medicine*, 246(112709), 2020, https://amandagoodall.com/wp-content/uploads/2022/03/LeadershipDevSSandM2019Pub.pdf

18. Matthew Evans, *Leaders with Substance: An Antidote to Leadership Genericism in Schools*, John Catt, 2019, p. 37.

19. Ibid. pp. 111–12.

20. J. Geerts, A. H. Goodall, and S. Agius, 'Evidence-Based Leadership Development for Physicians: A Systematic Literature Review', *Social Science & Medicine*, 246(112709), 30 November 2020, https://amanda-goodall.com/wp-content/uploads/2022/03/LeadershipDevSSandM2019Pub.pdf

21. Michael A. West, *Compassionate Leadership*, Swirling Leaf Press, 2021, p. 5.

22. Serena Evans, Fearless Speaking, https://serenaevans.co.uk/

23. A. C. Edmondson and Z. Lei, 'Psychological Safety: The History, Renaissance, and Future of an Interpersonal Construct', *Annual Review of Organisational Psychology and Organizational Behvavior*, 1(1), 2014, pp. 23–43, https://www.ixistenz.ch/objectcomponent774.pdf

24. Timothy R. Clarke, *The 4 Stages of Psychological Safety: Defining the Path to Inclusion and Innovation*, Berrett-Koehler, 2020, p. xi.

25. Michael A. West, *Compassionate Leadership*, Swirling Leaf Press, 2021, p. 87.

Chapter 8: The Expert-Friendly Organization

1. J. Z. Muller, 'Capitalism and Inequality: What the Right and the Left Got Wrong', *Foreign Affairs*, 92(2), 2013, https://www.researchgate.net/profile/Jerry-Muller/publication/296918516_Capitalism_and_Inequality_What_the_Right_and_the_Left_Get_Wrong/links/5d31141b92851cf44909013b7/Capitalism-and-Inequality-What-the-Right-and-the-Left-Get-Wrong.pdf?origin=searchReact&_iepl%5BgeneralViewId%5D=U7j3qc2Z2TwEdVvRCVLZzEGrFgyEx9PUrZUS&_iepl%5Bcontexts%5D%5B0%5D=searchReact&_iepl%5BviewId%5D=dNS0TuYfTOfm4Bkg8fbPjNQsHSoL1651US9d&_iepl%5BsearchType%5D=publication&_iepl%5Bdata%5D%5BcountLessEqual20%5D=1&_iepl%5Bdata%5D%5BinteractedWithPosition1%5D=1&_iepl%5Bdata%5D%5BwithoutEnrichment%5D=1&_iepl%5Bposition%5D=1&_iepl%5BrgKey%5D=PB%3A296918516&_iepl%5BinteractionType%5D=publicationDownload; Rakesh Khurana, *Searching for a Corporate Savior*, Princeton University Press, 2011, Kindle edition.

2. J. Z. Muller, 'Capitalism and Inequality: What the Right and the Left

Got Wrong', *Foreign Affairs*, 92(2), 2013, https://www.researchgate.net/profile/Jerry-Muller/publication/296918516_Capitalism_and_Inequality_What_the_Right_and_the_Left_Get_Wrong/links/5d31141b92851cf4409013b7/Capitalism-and-Inequality-What-the-Right-and-the-Left-Get-Wrong.pdf?origin=searchReact&_iepl%5Bgeneral ViewId%5D=U7j3qc2Z2TwEdVvRCVLZzEGrFgyEx9PUrZUS&_iepl%5Bcontexts%5D%5B0%5D=searchReact&_iepl%5Bviewid%5D=dNS0TuYfTOfm4Bkg8fbPjNQsHSoL1651US9d&_iepl%5BsearchType%5D=publication&_iepl%5Bdata%5D%5BcountLessEqual20%5D=1&_iepl%5Bdata%5D%5BinteractedWithPosition1%5D=1&_iepl%5Bdata%5D%5BwithoutEnrichment%5D=1&_iepl%5Bposition%5D=1&_iepl%5BrgKey%5D=PB%3A296918516&_iepl%5BinteractionType%5D=publicationDownload

3. Jerry Z. Muller, *The Tyranny of Metrics*, Princeton University Press, 2019, Kindle edition, p. 148.

4. Ibid.

5. This is not to ignore or agree with all of their corporate practices.

6. J. R. Hollingsworth, 'Research Organizations and Major Discoveries in Twentieth-Century Science: A Case Study of Excellence in Biomedical Research', working paper, 2002, p. 14, https://www.ssoar.info/ssoar/bitstream/handle/document/11297/ssoar-2002-hollingsworth-research_organizations_and_major_discoveries.pdf?sequence=1&isAllowed=y&lnkname=ssoar-2002-hollingsworth-research_organizations_and_major_discoveries.pdf

7. Ron Chernow, *Titan: The Life of John D. Rockefeller, Sr*, Random House, 1998.

8. 'John D. Rockefeller Net Worth', Celebrity Net Worth, https://www.celebritynetworth.com/richest-businessmen/richest-billionaires/john-rockefeller-net-worth/

9. 'Our History', Rockefeller University, https://www.rockefeller.edu/about/history/

10. 'Why Rockefeller is Unique', Rockefeller University, https://www.rockefeller.edu/support-our-science/why-rockefeller/

11. J. R. Hollingsworth, 'Research Organizations and Major Discoveries in Twentieth-Century Science: A Case Study of Excellence in Biomedical Research', working paper, 2002, https://www.ssoar.info/ssoar/bitstream/handle/document/11297/ssoar-2002-hollingsworth-research_organizations_and_major_discoveries.pdf?sequence=1&isAll

owed=y&lnkname=ssoar-2002-hollingsworth-research_organizations
_and_major_discoveries.pdf

12. A. Hill, L. Mellon, and J. Goddard, 'How Winning Organizations Last
    100 Years', *Harvard Business Review*, September 2018, p. 13, https://hbr.
    org/2018/09/how-winning-organizations-last-100-years

13. Originally called the Shakespeare Memorial Theatre, https://www.rsc.
    org.uk/about-us/history

14. J. R. Hollingsworth, 'Research Organizations and Major Discoveries
    in Twentieth-Century Science: A Case Study of Excellence in
    Biomedical Research', working paper, 2002, p. 63, https://www.ssoar.
    info/ssoar/bitstream/handle/document/11297/ssoar-2002-hollings-
    worth-research_organizations_and_major_discoveries.pdf?sequence=
    1&isAllowed=y&lnkname=ssoar-2002-hollingsworth-research_
    organizations_and_major_discoveries.pdf

15. Ibid.

16. Ibid.

17. Interview with Natasha Maw.

18. Netflix Investors, https://ir.netflix.net/ir-overview/profile/default.aspx

19. Reputation Institute, https://www.reptrak.com/

20. Reed Hastings and Erin Meyer, *No Rules Rules: Netflix and the Culture
    of Reinvention*, Ebury, Kindle edition, p. xix.

21. Ibid.

22. Ibid.

23. Ibid

24. Ibid.

25. Ibid. All subsequent quotes are from ibid.

26. Ibid.

27. N. Kroner, *A Blueprint for Better Banking*, Harriman House, 2010.

28. Richard Milne, 'Handelsbanken to Close Almost Half of Swedish
    Branches', *Financial Times*, 16 September 2020, https://www.ft.com/
    content/7b1dccc7-2e7d-4d8e-9ac3-0c666b14d998

29. Ibid.

30. Martin Arnold, 'UK Account Holders Flock to Swedish Bank's "Church
    Spire"', *Financial Times*, 25 August 2014, https://www.ft.com/content/
    ff114ac0-2a2e-11e4-a068-00144feabdc0

31. Ibid.

32. A. Bryson, A. E. Clark, R. B. Freeman et al., 'Share Capitalism and
    Worker Wellbeing', *Labour Economics*, 42, 2016, pp. 151–8, https://doi.

org/10.1016/j.labeco.2016.09.002; J. Blasi, D. Kruse, and R. Freeman, 'Having a Stake: Evidence and Implications for Broad-Based Employee Stock Ownership and Profit Sharing', Third Way's NEXT, 2017, pp. 1–51, https://cleo.rutgers.edu/articles/having-a-stake-evidence-and-implications-for-broad-based-employee-stock-ownership-and-profit-sharing/; NBER study: A. Bryson and R. Freeman, 'How Does Shared Capitalism Affect Economic Performance in the UK?', (https://www.nber.org/system/files/chapters/c8091/c8091.pdf) in *Shared Capitalism at Work: Employee Ownership, Profit and Gain Sharing, and Broad-Based Stock Options*, ed. D. Kruse, R. Freeman, and J. Blasi, University of Chicago Press, 2010, pp. 201–24. A. Bryson, A. E. Clark, R. B. Freeman et al., 'Share Capitalism and Worker Wellbeing', *Labour Economics*, 42, 2016, pp. 151–8, https://doi.org/10.1016/j.labeco.2016.09.002

33. A. Case and A. Deaton, *Deaths of Despair and the Future of Capitalism*, Princeton University Press, 2020; A. J. Oswald and D. G. Blanchflower, 'Trends in Extreme Distress in the USA, 1993–2019', *American Journal of Public Health*, September 2020, https://www.ncbi.nlm.nih.gov/pmc/articles/PMC7483105/pdf/AJPH.2020.305811.pdf

34. J. Blasi, D. Kruse, and R. Freeman, 'Having a Stake: Evidence and Implications for Broad-Based Employee Stock Ownership and Profit Sharing', Third Way's NEXT, 2017, pp. 1–51, https://cleo.rutgers.edu/articles/having-a-stake-evidence-and-implications-for-broad-based-employee-stock-ownership-and-profit-sharing/; A. Bryson and R. Freeman, 'How Does Shared Capitalism Affect Economic Performance in the UK?' (https://www.nber.org/system/files/chapters/c8091/c8091.pdf), in *Shared Capitalism at Work: Employee Ownership, Profit and Gain Sharing, and Broad-Based Stock Options*, ed. D. Kruse, R. Freeman, and J. Blasi, University of Chicago Press, 2010, pp. 201–24. A. Bryson, A. E. Clark, R. B. Freeman et al., 'Share Capitalism and Worker Wellbeing', *Labour Economics*, 42, 2016, pp. 151–8, https://doi.org/10.1016/j.labeco.2016.09.002

35. Richard Milne, 'Handelsbanken to Close Almost Half of Swedish Branches', *Financial Times*, 16 September 2020, https://www.ft.com/content/7b1dccc7-2e7d-4d8e-9ac3-0c666b14d998

36. Ibid.

37. Gary Hamel and Michele Zanini, 'The End of Bureaucracy', *Harvard Business Review*, November/December 2018, https://hbr.org/2018/11/the-end-of-bureaucracy

38. Ibid.

39. Ibid.
40. Ibid.
41. Ibid.
42. Ibid.
43. Ibid.
44. Ibid.
45. Benjamin F. Jones, 'The Knowledge Trap: Human Capital and Development Reconsidered', 2014, Northwestern University Working Paper, https://www.kellogg.northwestern.edu/faculty/jones-ben/htm/ResearchframeKnowledgeTrap.htm
46. M. Ahmadpoor and B. F. Jones, 'Decoding Team and Individual Impact in Science and Invention', *Proceedings of the National Academy of Sciences*, 116(28), 2019, pp. 13885–90, https://www.pnas.org/doi/epdf/10.1073/pnas.1812341116
47. I. L. Janis, 'Groupthink', *Psychology Today*, 5(6), 1971, pp. 43–6.
48. Anonymous interview taken for a study on the medical mindset.
49. Charlan Nemeth, *In Defense of Troublemakers: The Power of Dissent in Life and Business*, New York: Basic Books, retitled in the UK as *No!: The Power of Disagreement in a World that Wants to Get Along*, Atlantic, 2018, Kindle edition, p. 3.
50. Ibid.
51. Henry Mance, 'Britain Has Had Enough of Experts', *Financial Times*, 3 June 2016, https://www.ft.com/content/3be49734-29cb-11e6-83e4-abc22d5d108c
52. Jonah Lehrer, 'Groupthink: The Brainstorming Myth', *New Yorker*, 30 January 2012, https://www.newyorker.com/magazine/2012/01/30/groupthink
53. Ibid.
54. Reed Hastings and Erin Meyer, *No Rules Rules: Netflix and the Culture of Reinvention*, Ebury, 2019, Kindle edition.
55. Bill Taylor, 'How Coca-Cola, Netflix, and Amazon Learn from Failure', *Harvard Business Review*, November 2017, https://hbr.org/2017/11/how-coca-cola-netflix-and-amazon-learn-from-failure
56. Ibid.
57. 'Pixar Headquarters and the Legacy of Steve Jobs', Office Snapshots, https://officesnapshots.com/2012/07/16/pixar-headquarters-and-the-legacy-of-steve-jobs/ (taken from Y. S. Rudall, *Steve Jobs: The Exclusive Biography*, Kybernetes, 2012).

58. J. Hobsbawm, *The Nowhere Office: Reinventing Work and the Workplace of the Future*, Basic Books UK, 2022.

59. E. L. Glaeser, H. D. Kallal, J. A. Scheinkman et al., 'Growth in Cities', *Journal of Political Economy*, 100(6), 1992, pp. 1126–52, https://www.nber.org/system/files/working_papers/w3787/w3787.pdf

60. Dan Robinson, 'Story Behind the Tel Aviv Tech Hub That's Now One of the Best in the World', NS Business, 22 January 2019, https://www.ns-businesshub.com/technology/tel-aviv-tech-hub/

61. 'A Profile of Reg Revans', http://www.gullonline.org/affiliate/getting-started/resources/3-Briefing-resources-forms/2-Foundation-levels-1-2-resources/A-profile-of-Reg-Revans.pdf

62. Simon Caulkin, 'Reg Revans', *Guardian*, 8 March 2003, https://www.theguardian.com/news/2003/mar/08/guardianobituaries.simoncaulkin

63. Reginald Revans, obituary, *The Times*, 21 February 2003, https://www.thetimes.co.uk/article/reginald-revans-w2fkbjrq7gq

64. Simon Caulkin, 'Reg Revans', *Guardian*, 8 March 2003, https://www.theguardian.com/news/2003/mar/08/guardianobituaries.simoncaulkin

65. Ibid.

66. Revans wrote three books: *Developing Effective Managers* (Praeger, 1971), *The Origins and Growth of Action Learning* (Chartwell-Bratt, 1982), and *ABC of Action Learning* (R. W. Revans, 1983).

67. Ibid.

68. J. R. Hollingsworth, 'Research Organizations and Major Discoveries in Twentieth-Century Science: A Case Study of Excellence in Biomedical Research', working paper, 2002, p. 33, https://www.ssoar.info/ssoar/handle/document/11297

Index

Amanda Goodall is professor of leadership at Bayes Business School (formerly Cass), City, University of London, where she specialises in how leaders and managers influence performance. She began her career as a fashion model at the age of sixteen. At twenty-two she lived on a small development project in Andhra Pradesh, India, and spent the next few years working with international NGOs.

In 1997, she completed a degree at the London School of Economics and subsequently a PhD, at Warwick Business School, focused on leaders' characteristics. After two years at IZA Institute for the Study of Labor in Bonn, Germany, in 2012 she joined Bayes Business School's Faculty of Management. She has been a visiting scholar at Cornell University, the University of Zurich, and Yale University.

Dr Goodall is widely published in academic journals, practitioner publications and the media. Her PhD, *Socrates in the Boardroom: Why Research Universities Should be Led by Top Scholars*, was published by Princeton University Press in 2009. Her publications are available at www.amandagoodall.com. Dr. Goodall examines leadership, workplace happiness, and the gender pay gap. She is a committed environmentalist, an ambassador for Save Wild Tigers, and a founder member of Pembrokeshire Seal Research Trust.

PublicAffairs is a publishing house founded in 1997. It is a tribute to the standards, values, and flair of three persons who have served as mentors to countless reporters, writers, editors, and book people of all kinds, including me.

I. F. Stone, proprietor of *I. F. Stone's Weekly*, combined a commitment to the First Amendment with entrepreneurial zeal and reporting skill and became one of the great independent journalists in American history. At the age of eighty, Izzy published *The Trial of Socrates*, which was a national bestseller. He wrote the book after he taught himself ancient Greek.

Benjamin C. Bradlee was for nearly thirty years the charismatic editorial leader of *The Washington Post*. It was Ben who gave the *Post* the range and courage to pursue such historic issues as Watergate. He supported his reporters with a tenacity that made them fearless and it is no accident that so many became authors of influential, best-selling books.

Robert L. Bernstein, the chief executive of Random House for more than a quarter century, guided one of the nation's premier publishing houses. Bob was personally responsible for many books of political dissent and argument that challenged tyranny around the globe. He is also the founder and longtime chair of Human Rights Watch, one of the most respected human rights organizations in the world.

·　　·　　·

For fifty years, the banner of Public Affairs Press was carried by its owner Morris B. Schnapper, who published Gandhi, Nasser, Toynbee, Truman, and about 1,500 other authors. In 1983, Schnapper was described by *The Washington Post* as "a redoubtable gadfly." His legacy will endure in the books to come.

Peter Osnos, *Founder*